UNDERSTANDING
OCTAVIA E. BUTLER

UNDERSTANDING CONTEMPORARY AMERICAN LITERATURE
Matthew J. Bruccoli, Founding Editor
Linda Wagner-Martin, Series Editor

Also of Interest

Understanding Alice Walker, Thadious M. Davis
Understanding Barbara Kingsolver, Ian Tan
Understanding Colson Whitehead, Derek C. Maus
Understanding James Baldwin, Marc Dudley
Understanding John Edgar Wideman, D. Quentin Miller
Understanding John Rechy, María DeGuzmán
Understanding Margaret Atwood, Donna M. Bickford
Understanding Marge Piercy, Donna M. Bickford
Understanding Philip K. Dick, Eric Carl Link
Understanding Randall Kenan, James A. Crank

UNDERSTANDING
OCTAVIA E. BUTLER

Kendra R. Parker

© 2025 University of South Carolina

Published by the University of South Carolina Press
Columbia, South Carolina 29208

uscpress.com

Printed in the United States of America

Library of Congress Cataloging-in-Publication Data
can be found at https://lccn.loc.gov/2024049623

ISBN: 978-1-64336-576-3 (hardcover)
ISBN: 978-1-64336-577-0 (paperback)
ISBN: 978-1-64336-578-7 (ebook)

Quotations from "The Octavia E. Butler Papers" at the Huntington Library.
Copyright © by Octavia E. Butler. Reprinted by permission of the
Octavia E. Butler Estate.

*For Maria, Safi, and Hodari in loving memory of
Gregory J. Hampton (1968–2019)*

*For Marissa, Shane, Aalia, and Zara in honor of
Alexander Noah Pinto (2020–2021)*

All that they touched, they changed.

CONTENTS

Series Editor's Preface ix
Acknowledgments xi

Chapter 1
An Introduction to Octavia E. Butler 1

Part I
Writing through the Decades: Butler's Evolving Craft

Chapter 2
The 1970s: A Breakthrough Decade 21

Chapter 3
The 1980s: Perfecting Her "Adapt or Die" Refrain 43

Chapter 4
1990–2006: A (Bitter)Sweet 16 66

Part II
Writing across Genres: Butler's Literary Range

Chapter 5
"Where I actually say so": Lessons from Her Freedom Narratives 91

Chapter 6
"This time, I want a love story": Her Early Romance Novels 109

Chapter 7
Word Weaver, World Maker:
The Art of Her Nonfiction   128

Afterword: Living Forever, Leaving Legacies   144

Notes   153
Works Cited   169
Index   179

SERIES EDITOR'S PREFACE

The Understanding Contemporary American Literature series was founded by the estimable Matthew J. Bruccoli (1931–2008), who envisioned these volumes as guides or companions for students as well as good nonacademic readers, a legacy that will continue as new volumes are developed to fill in gaps among the nearly one hundred series volumes published to date and to embrace a host of new writers only now making their marks on our literature.

As Professor Bruccoli explained in his preface to the volumes he edited, because much influential contemporary literature makes special demands, "the word *understanding* in the titles was chosen deliberately. Many willing readers lack an adequate understanding of how contemporary literature works; that is, of what the author is attempting to express and the means by which it is conveyed." Aimed at fostering this understanding of good literature and good writers, the criticism and analysis in the series provide instruction in how to read certain contemporary writers—explicating their material, language, structures, themes, and perspectives—and facilitate a more profitable experience of the works under discussion.

In the twenty-first century Professor Bruccoli's prescience gives us an avenue to publish expert critiques of significant contemporary American writing. The series continues to map the literary landscape and to provide both instruction and enjoyment. Future volumes will seek to introduce new voices alongside canonized favorites, to chronicle the changing literature of our times, and to remain, as Professor Bruccoli conceived, contemporary in the best sense of the word.

Linda Wagner-Martin, Series Editor

ACKNOWLEDGMENTS

Understanding Octavia E. Butler led me to archival research for the first time. This experience allowed me to truly meet Octavia Estelle Butler. I met her as I gazed up at the San Gabriel mountains every morning as I looked out of my window. "My mountains," she called them. I met her as I walked the Rose Bowl stadium on Saturday mornings, taking in the July morning air, or as I hiked Eaton Canyon on Sundays, taking in the sounds of the waterfall, the sights of the ravines, marveling at my sheer insignificance when faced with the San Gabes. I met her as I rode Bus 10 on Pasadena Transit on my way to the Huntington Library, greeting the driver, Maria, with a big smile each morning. I met her as I rode the Metro Bus 660 North on Fair Oaks to Altadena, stopping to pay my respects at her final resting place at Mountain View Cemetery. As I walked the corridors and stacks of the Los Angeles Central Library. As I walked from Octavia E. Butler Magnet to La Pintoresca Branch Library. As I spoke with Nikki High, owner of Octavia's Bookshelf. As I participated in a Book Club discussion at La Pintoresca. As I spent twenty-eight days in her Pasadena. I met her. She was a walker, a rider, an observer. I knew her through her novels, short stories, essays, and interviews. I knew her through shared conversations with other Butler devotees. And that knowledge grew as I mined the archives of her life at the Huntington. But I met Octavia E. Butler, truly met her, walking miles in her shoes, through her Pasadena.

The financial support I received for my research trip to the Huntington Library, Art Museum, and Botanical Gardens in San Marino, California, where Octavia E. Butler's journals, unpublished manuscripts, and ephemera reside, made this experience possible. I am grateful to Georgia Southern University for awarding me a Scholarly Pursuit Grant and the Huntington's Fellowship Committee for the Andrew W. Mellon Fellowship. I cannot sufficiently convey my gratitude to Dana A. Williams and Tarshia L. Stanley for their unhesitant "Of course!" when I requested letters of recommendation for several grant applications. Thank you both for your continued investments in me. I can't say enough about Beauty Bragg, whose NEH seminar on grant applications helped me craft two successful applications. I sincerely appreciate Georgia Southern's J.T. Hughes, Rachel Martin, and Laura Regassa, who offered guidance on budgeting and logistical aspects of grants, and Beth Howells, David Owen, and David C. Weindorf, who tag-teamed to help me secure funding for this book's index. Special thanks to the grant and fellowship coordinators, reviewers, and selection committees, whose time commitment and expertise make work like mine possible.

There's so much support I received, and though I may miss some names, I'd be remiss if I didn't try to thank everyone. I'm grateful for the library and archival experts who supported me: the Georgia Southern librarians, Kailee Faber from the Schomburg Center for Research in Black Culture, Nathaniel De Gala and Karla Nielsen from the Huntington's Munger Research Center, the gracious Ann Marie Kolakowski, and Emily Ravenscraft. Shout out to my research assistants, D'Yanna Coffey, Te'Ara Marshall, Makay Walsh, and Destinee Walker for being, among other things, my beta readers, and big-ups to the enrollees in my undergraduate and graduate Octavia E. Butler classes, with a special head nod to My'Kayle Pugh, C'Drick Henderson, and Megan L. Bowen. Thanks to Roger Smith, Debbie Hornsby, and the attentive and curious attendees at the SCI Learning Center in Savannah whose interest in my presentation, "Octavia E. Butler's Brave New Worlds," led to a three-week lecture series at SCI. What I could not have known was that the three-week session helped shape what turned out to be my favorite chapters in this book. Roger, thank you for the invitation, and Debbie, thank you for handling the technical logistics!

The successful creation of any book hinges on the collaborative efforts of a behind-the-scenes team. Shout out to my editor, Aurora X. Bell; series editor, Linda Wagner-Martin; production editor, Kerri Tolan; the copyeditor; editorial review board; external readers; and the entire team at the University of South Carolina Press. Mary Ann Lieser, thank you so much for your indexing services. And, of course, I am immensely grateful for the Octavia E. Butler Estate because this book would be far less interesting without their permission to reproduce quotes from her archived material.

Thank you to my family, who have long supported my book-writing endeavors. And to Mojito: thanks for being my purr-fect line-editing companion. To my sister-friends, Brittany, Marissa, Nici, Shayla, and Tiffany, thank you for listening to me endlessly share about this book. Your companionship means more than I can express. And Britt, I expect your full review of the romance chapter since you've consistently said, "I'm reading that one first!" Shout out to David for a random text message about hush harbors that helped get me out of writer's block with chapter 5. And high fives and hugs to Andre,

ACKNOWLEDGMENTS

Barbra, Cydney, Gerald, Orrie, Trevon, and Wallis for work sessions, video chats, text messages, phone calls, and all-around good vibes. To Dr. Sandra Y. Govan: thank you for your kindness, friendship, and photos of Ms. Goldie.

And finally, to my dear readers: thank you for embracing *Understanding Octavia E. Butler.*

CHAPTER 1

An Introduction to Octavia E. Butler

At forty, Octavia Estelle Butler imagined she was halfway through her career, envisioning herself writing well into her eighties. However, her stellar career was ultimately cut short by her unexpected passing at fifty-eight years old. At forty, she had already completed *Kindred* (1979), the five-book Patternist Series (1976–84), and the first book of her Xenogenesis Trilogy (1987–89). Five more novels and two editions of *Bloodchild and Other Stories* (1995, 2005) would follow along with the posthumous publication of *Unexpected Stories* (2014). Her short stories were honored with several Hugo and Nebula awards, and perhaps most importantly, Butler became the first science fiction author to receive the MacArthur Fellowship (which we refer to as the "Genius Grant") in 1995. Additionally, Butler received PEN's Lifetime Achievement Award in 2000, six years before her death.

Despite her critical success during her lifetime, many publishers struggled with how to market Butler's novels, which often featured sexually ambiguous women protagonists and focused on complex social issues, including religious fundamentalism, racial, sexual and gender identity, and the frailties of human nature. For example, the first edition cover of *Dawn* (1987) featured two white women. Yet the novel's protagonist is a Black woman awakened from sleep by aliens. As a Black science fiction writer who began publishing in the early 1970s, Butler knew she was "a dancing bear, a novelty, a black woman who writes successfully." However, she was keenly aware that "Being a dancing bear may get me through the door, but for me, only being a fine storyteller will stave off the hook."[1] And what a storyteller she was.

Butler was not the first author of Black science fiction. Still, she is considered the foundational figure in the development of Black women's speculative fiction, which is an umbrella term for science fiction, fantasy, and horror. She is often referred to as the Grand Dame of Afrofuturism—though she loathed the term because "Well, it's another word for grandmother! I'm certainly old enough to be someone's grandmother, but I'm not."[2] Afrofuturism is both a literary and a cultural aesthetic, and its definition varies. In its simplest form, Afrofuturism is a way to explore possible futures for Black people from Black cultural perspectives. The term emerged in 1994 with the publication of Mark Dery's essay "Black to the Future," Alondra Nelson's *Social Text* special issue, and Nelson's Afrofuturism Listserv. Dery writes about common features in African American art, literature, music, and science fiction and calls the phenomenon Afrofuturism. According to Dery, Afrofuturism is first "speculative fiction that treats African-American themes and addresses African-American concerns in the context of 20th-century technoculture"—like the work of Butler—and second "African-American signification that appropriates images of technology and a prosthetically enhanced future"—like the music of Sun Ra, George Clinton, the OutKast, and Janelle Monáe, or the art of Laolu Senbanjo, Krista Franklin, and Joshua Mays.[3]

As a literary aesthetic, Afrofuturism combines speculative fiction, historical fiction, and Afrocentrism to critique contemporary dilemmas of Black people and to (re)examine historical events with the hope of shaping a more just future for Black people. Butler's fiction explores varying themes of race, gender, sexuality, class, slavery, colonization, and difference through time travel, new technologies, scientifically advanced non-human communities, and future dystopian societies. Her fiction, though cynical, offers the "expectation for transformative change"—something that "undergirds" Afrofuturism literature.[4] Often presenting new, complex visions of difference and otherness, complicating standardized belief systems concerning race, gender, and sexuality, and weaving the speculative or the fantastic with her social commentary, Butler's work is indeed an exemplar of Afrofuturism. Excluding *Kindred* and *Wild Seed*, Butler's published novels are set in futuristic societies where her Black heroines endure—and sometimes transcend—their marginalization, enslavement, or oppression.

Kindred, Butler's first stand-alone and most famous novel, spans at least three genres: historical fiction, science fiction, and neo-slave narrative. The heroine, Dana, is pulled back in time to the antebellum South to save her white slave-owning ancestor to ensure her own survival in the present. *Kindred* emerged during what scholars now refer to as the renaissance of Black women writers—during the 1970s and 1980s when Black women writers were making their voices and perspectives heard. *Kindred* is specifically important in the context of other Black women's writing about enslaved Black women's experiences, including Margaret Walker's *Jubilee* (1966), Toni Morrison's *Beloved* (1987), and Sherley Anne Williams's *Dessa Rose* (1986). *Kindred* may not appear to have any apparent Afrofuturism traits as a work of historical fiction with a time-traveling character. However, Dana's quest to save her slave-owning ancestor to ensure her future existence offers a re-examination of the past so that Dana can reconstruct her present and influence her future.

Butler's first and second book series, the Patternist series and the Xenogenesis Trilogy, were published before an institutionalized scholarly interest in Afrofuturism emerged in the early 1990s. Though a series, the Patternist books were not originally published in sequential order; Butler published the last book of the series, *Patternmaster* (1976), first, followed by *Mind of My Mind* (1977), *Survivor* (1978), *Wild Seed* (1980), and *Clay's Ark* (1984). In 2007, the Patternist series—except for *Survivor*, which is out of print at Butler's request but would have preceded *Patternmaster*—was published as Seed to Harvest in sequential plot order: *Wild Seed*, *Mind of My Mind*, *Clay's Ark*, and *Patternmaster*. The Patternist series is a litany of interconnected stories concerning the use of genetic breeding, the development of mental powers, and enslavement to construct a superior race and class of humans, as well as various protagonists' attempts to remove themselves from—but not dismantle—the social and mental systems that enslave certain groups of people.

The Xenogenesis Trilogy, composed of *Dawn*, *Adulthood Rites* (1988), and *Imago* (1989), was republished as Lilith's Brood in 2000 and tells the story of humans preserved by the Oankali—a nonhuman species—after a human-led nuclear war destroys Earth. The trilogy follows Lilith Iyapo, a human held in a state of suspended animation, during which the Oankali alter her body; they improve her memories, strength, and life span; they remove her cancer; and they also sterilize her to ensure that any children born will be a product of human-alien/human-Oankali breeding. The Oankali choose Lilith to convince human survivor-captives to accept interdependence, coexistence, and advanced technologies, but also to accept interspecies intercourse as the only way to experience sexual pleasure and to conceive. While the Oankali recognize their relationship with humans as the beginning of a utopian existence, most humans perceive it traumatically as a form of colonization. For humans, their forced existence with the Oankali represents a loss of humanity. Butler presents the Oankali as a metaphor for difference that humans are invited to embrace—or risk extinction by defying. With concerns raised about the ethics of experimenting on humans calling to mind experiments on enslaved Blacks in the United States, Butler's Xenogenesis Trilogy forces readers to ask, "What else is at stake in a possible future?"

In creating future worlds with both the Patternist series and the Xenogenesis

Trilogy, Butler was influenced by the social turmoil of the 1960s, '70s, and early '80s. Her prominent themes were related to the concerns raised by the varied liberation movements and shifts in the political atmosphere, including the Moral Majority, the Family Values campaign, and Reaganomics. Such context influences her futuristic vision of the United States, one that presents oppression, exploitation, and eugenics in terms of alien benefactors and telepathic and telekinetic humans, and the hierarchies among these technologically advanced groups. With Afrofuturism, there is a perceived distance from the "real world" that allows for a nuanced exploration of a society, which then begins to translate to the existing society. Butler's Afrofuturist visions in the Patternist series and the Xenogenesis Trilogy enable readers to explore the time in which the novels were published to critique the past as well as the present and future, to learn from the past to grapple with concepts such as multiculturalism, colonization, slavery, consent, and reproductive justice to understand the present and thereby engender and shape change for the future.

Butler's *Parable of the Sower* (1993) and *Parable of the Talents* (1998)—referred to the Parable Series, Parable Duology, or Earthseed Series—are a hallmark of Afrofuturism. Just as the Patternist Series and the Xenogenesis Trilogy emerged in part out of sociopolitical issues of the 1960s to the early 1980s, the Parable Series is influenced by the predominant social problems in the late 1980s and throughout the 1990s, including social concerns over recreational drug usage, the proliferation of gated communities, global warming, and Christian fundamentalism. The series depicts the struggle and triumph of Lauren Olamina, from fifteen to eighty-one years old. We meet Lauren while she lives in a dilapidated gated community in California in 2020 with her father (a Baptist preacher), her stepmother, and her two brothers. Forced to leave her community after her home burns and her family is killed, Olamina endures the varied social, economic, and political collapses of twenty-first-century America by establishing kinship bonds with men, women, and children from various racial and ethnic groups. To survive outside her gated community, Olamina eschews the Baptist teachings of her father and forges a new philosophical religion—Earthseed—and a new community—Acorn.

Olamina's imagination of a new future and new possibilities for herself and those who join her community is a feature of Afrofuturism fiction. More than imagining change, however, Olamina's Earthseed philosophy shapes change, so much so that the sequel, *Talents*, reveals the hostile takeover of Acorn by Christian zealots. The zealots are inspired by the novel's presidential candidate, who urges his constituency to help "Make America Great Again." *Talents* is an epistolary novel—told through Olamina's journal—with the entries framed by the perspectives of Olamina's daughter. Olamina is portrayed as African American freedom fighter Harriet Tubman, a woman in search of freedom for her brother, daughter, and other enslaved peoples, and one who champions change and becomes a palpable threat to the existing status quo in America. The last of Olamina's journal entries is a maiden voyage away from Earth on a spaceship called Christopher Columbus. While Afrofuturism aims to envision a more just future for Black people, the ending of *Talents* may signal that a future without a dismantling of an oppressive system will remain bleak. The exodus of Earthseed followers aiming to go to Mars on the Christopher Columbus to discover a new world is rife with colonizing impulses, suggesting that those "Earthseeders aren't escaping the nightmare of history at all, but bringing it with them instead."[5]

Her last novel, *Fledgling*, is also considered Afrofuturist, but not just because it rescues the vampire genre from the typical white male bloodsucker and offers readers a Black girl vampire heroine. *Fledgling* is an exemplar of Afrofuturism because of the "mutualism" between vampire and host that, as scholar Susana M. Morris writes, "recalibrates the traditional power dynamics in vampire lore to illuminate a possible future where negotiations of power successfully function in ways that bear little resemblance to our own patriarchal power structures."[6] In other words, Afrofuturism concerns itself with reimaging systems of oppression, making new structures that center the most vulnerable, and making the world livable, caring, and equitable for the historically marginalized and dispossessed.

Although she is primarily known as a novelist, Butler's short stories have won coveted science-fiction awards. "Speech Sounds" (1983) received a Hugo Award in 1984, and "Bloodchild" (1984) earned a Hugo Award in 1984, a Nebula Award in 1985, and a Science Fiction Chronicle Award in 1985. Butler's collection of short stories, *Bloodchild and Other Stories*, takes its title from the critically acclaimed and Hugo Award-winning story, "Bloodchild." Originally published in 1995 with five stories and two essays, *Bloodchild and Other Stories* was updated in 2005 with two additional stories. Although Butler was loath to place labels on her work, her designation as the foremother of Afrofuturism is well-earned. Her work introduced African American women's perspectives into science fiction—a genre almost exclusively dominated by white men when she began writing. Like later Black authors of speculative fiction, Butler's fiction provided social commentary on a wide range of topics, including but not limited to race, gender, class, sexuality, religion, environment, slavery, and politics. However, two of Butler's main goals were to "tell a good story" and to "make people feel."

Who Is Octavia E. Butler?

Born on June 22, 1947, in Pasadena, California, Butler was an only child. Her father, Laurice, worked as a shoe shiner. He passed away during her childhood, as did her four brothers, who died before she was born. Her mother, Octavia Margaret Guy Butler, sent young Octavia to live with her grandmother and uncles in Victorville after her father passed away. After Mrs. Butler was back on her feet, young Octavia returned to Pasadena. Mrs. Butler worked as a maid, and sometimes she took in boarders.[7] Young Octavia was sometimes called "Junie" because she was born in June and shared her mother's first name. As an only child with a mother who worked long hours as a domestic, Butler was extremely shy and spent much of her time alone. As she moved from childhood to adolescence, her shyness was exacerbated by her self-consciousness about her dyslexia and height; she was nearly six feet tall as a teenager. At twelve, she was so tall that she could get a temporary job as a restroom attendant at the Rose Bowl on New Year's Day.[8] Butler turned to writing at age ten to combat her self-consciousness, drawing on her Baptist upbringing to shape her stories. She admits to loving the Old Testament stories of incest, murder, and betrayal, which later influenced *Survivor*, *Wild Seed*, the Xenogenesis Trilogy, and "The Book of Martha." Butler attended James A. Garfield Elementary School, reciting a poem when she matriculated in 1959. She attended William McKinley Junior High for seventh grade and George Washington Junior High for eighth and ninth grade, graduated from John Muir High School in 1965, and earned her associate degree in history from Pasadena City College in 1968. She enrolled in the Screen Writers Guild of America's Open Door Workshop one year later. It was an outreach program for historically underrepresented writers. She continued taking classes, often at California State University, Los Angeles but did not earn a bachelor's degree.

Much of what shaped Butler's life and career was getting swindled by a publisher and a fear of poverty, loneliness, and an initial fear of writing. To pay her bills early on in her writing career, Butler worked a series of jobs, like factory work, secretarial work, or other temporary employment. To pay her bills in between publications, Butler worked "slave market jobs," jobs that she gives some of her characters, notably Dana in *Kindred* and Jane in "Crossover." She was 23 years old when she went to her first Clarion Science Fiction Writer's Workshop, and it was there that she learned her devotion to writing was not unrealistic in the way her family and friends seemed to think it was. Clarion was a transformative experience for her, not just because she was affirmed for wanting to be a writer but also because she readily admits there was no great enthusiasm for her novel fragments. But that was the feedback

AN INTRODUCTION TO OCTAVIA E. BUTLER

she needed—open, honest, and clear. To pay her bills and to give her time to write, Butler sometimes plotted how to get unemployment. In 1974, she hoped to get laid off to get unemployment at $64 a week. That amount would have been a dollar less than she would make while employed as a phone solicitor for the Heart Association. It was enough for her to pay her bills and do what she wanted: finish writing the first three books in her Patternist Series. A few days later, she got her wish: she and her coworkers were laid off. For Butler, nothing mattered except writing. To her, writing was like breathing. Admittedly, Butler never had a job that she liked. ". . . most of the jobs I had were pretty grubby," she admits in an unpublished interview.[9] "Unlike Dana," Butler jokes, "I found no interesting-looking young man to make things more pleasant."[10]

Amidst her money concerns, Butler was deeply invested in and affected by the world around her. In her twenties, she journaled about her depression, loneliness, suicidal ideation, and unrequited romantic interests alongside pop culture events, the assassination of Black political leaders, the growing women's liberation movement, rising food prices, and general social unease. In 1968, Butler witnessed Lt. Uhura (performed by Black actress Nichelle Nichols) kiss Captain Kirk (performed by white actor William Shatner) during season 3, episode 10 of *Star Trek: The Original Series*. She wrote about the 1968 assassinations of Rev. Dr. Martin Luther King Jr and Robert F. Kennedy Sr. when she was 21. Eighteen months later, she wrote about the assassination of Chicago activist and Black Panther Party leader Fred Hampton. As early as 1972, she considered joining the National Organization of Women and even conversed with a friend about the benefits of the women's liberation movement for Black women. At 27, amidst rising costs and food insecurity, she recalls the Los Angeles Bus Strike in 1974 and the 10-week strike that impacted her mobility since she relied on public transportation, walking, or people to give her rides.

At 29, she published *Patternmaster*, and four novels followed in rapid succession for the next five years. Writer's block slowed her publications in the early years of the 1980s, but with "Speech Sounds," "Bloodchild," and *Clay's Ark* published in 1983 and 1984, the writing seemed to flow with "The Evening and the Morning and the Night" (1987) and the Xenogenesis Trilogy. The nineties were her leanest decade, with only two novels, *Sower* and *Talents*, but her work at the turn of the twenty-first century, "Amnesty" (2003), "The Book of Martha" (2003), and *Fledgling* was promising. Although her publications slowed some, she continued writing and encouraged others to write. She returned to the Clarion Writer's Workshop as an instructor, and in 1997, while teaching at Clarion, she received a surprise: her first-ever surprise birthday party. She was 50 years old.

Like many women, Butler had a complex relationship with her appearance and self-perception, and she was not immune to the beauty industrial complex. In a cover letter to Cheryll Greene, the executive editor of *Essence* magazine, Butler wrote, "If you should want a different photo of me, you might be interested in those taken by Miriam Berkeley . . . I warn you, though, I wear no makeup at all in her photos and some of them look just like me!"[11] The self-deprecating remark attempts to mask how she felt unattractive. Her feelings of ugliness, combined with a negative body image, led to a complicated relationship with food. She details instances of restrictive eating, making contracts with herself to limit food intake and sugar consumption. "Two days of beverage and shredded wheat only," she wrote in an October 28, 1982, journal entry. "No whole fruit. No ANYTHING except beverage and shredded wheat."[12] A character in an unpublished story draft, named Kyna, expresses fears of being fat and ugly, seeming to reflect Butler's own concerns and experiences. By the turn of the twenty-first century, Butler began keeping a food diary, not necessarily for calorie counting or restrictive eating as she did when she was younger, but for monitoring her health amidst high blood pressure.

Though not immune to the ravages of anti-fatness, restrictive eating, and self-loathing, she did ruminate on how she could cultivate a public self who takes up space in the world. She wanted her public persona to take up space, undiscipline her body, and free herself from the shackles that told her to make herself smaller, less noticeable, less like a brightly shining star. For her public self, she wanted to wear bright colors, jewelry, clothing, and dresses at all times, and she wanted to wear shoes that would make her taller.[13] Long dangly silver earrings seemed to be her only self-concession to any luxury—aside from books. A friend remembers how she adored them and how they complemented her short hair despite not spending much on them.[14] She shopped at Lane Bryant, searching for clothing that made her feel attractive and confident; she used Noxzema for skincare and occasionally bought Zest bar soap. She was also a faithful user of Lady Clairol's black hair dye. Once a year, she would buy two pairs of black Reeboks, one for walking around the San Gabriel Valley. The other pair were her indoor shoes that did not set foot outside of her house.[15] Though Butler often considered herself unattractive, writer Sherley Anne Williams describes her as "a tall, striking woman . . . with skin the dark, lustrous brown of espresso beans and a rich, mellifluous voice."[16]

Regardless of her feelings about herself, most of what occupied Butler's mind was her writing and her loneliness. She chides herself for moving on from a novel to writing short stories when she claims she does not like writing (or reading) short stories and because she writes too slowly to make any sort of profit (she says) from her stories. In her twenties, she often described herself as lazy and undisciplined, but she would try to trick herself into writing. If suffering from writer's block, she would write a contract to herself giving herself a deadline or a task to write. She would even sign them. But she often broke the contracts to herself. Other times, she would give herself a task, a library assignment, or a reading assignment, something to trick her into writing something. For Butler, writing was her ticket to freedom, to live the way she wanted. She wanted to be free. Free to practice on a piano or take a self-defense or physical fitness class. Free for lunch, writing, and leisure reading. On weekends? Free to meet with writers and photographers and go to the movies. Paradoxically, her writing was palliative for her loneliness, but it also exacerbated her isolation. She was desperate for human connections, but her social anxiety often prevented her from forming the relationships she so desperately wanted. Part of that social anxiety stemmed from people continuing to make assumptions about her sexuality and her appearance because she was tall and appeared to others to be masculine. People could be cruel, she knew, and she explored cruelties in her work. Despite the loneliness, fear of poverty, writer's block, and self-loathing, Butler had a stubborn desire to write. And write she did.

If there was one thing that Butler wanted to convince people of, it was her merits as a storyteller. Butler was clear—if not singular—in her aim: "I am not out to proselytize anyone on my worthiness as a black person, as a woman, as anything beyond a hell of a good storyteller."[17] Butler had three main goals as a storyteller: to create herself, tell a good story, and make people feel. This creation of self appears in some of her characters from their professions or passions as writers, but also in specific details about her characters, like their left-handedness, which mirrors her own, and their height. Butler was six feet tall, had often been misgendered as a man, and met with homophobic insults by her peers in school and by strangers as an adult. Unsurprisingly, she re-creates some of her Black women protagonists, like Lauren from the *Parable* duology, Alanna from *Survivor*, and Dana from *Kindred*, to look like her: androgynous looking, tall, built like so-called men, and "not pretty." "I used to be mistaken for a man a lot," she once shared, "and, occasionally, somebody would try to chase me out of the ladies' room, which used to upset the hell out of me."[18] Butler also created some of her characters to be things she did not see herself to be or envision herself as. In an interview, Butler once shared that she "tried to experience being a small person in *Mind of My Mind* and in *Wild Seed*," which proved "interesting," because she "had to think of some of the problems that a small person might have to deal with, and to think as a small person."[19] Another reason Butler wrote to create herself was simply that she did not see herself in the things she was reading. "When I began writing science fiction, when I began reading, heck, I wasn't in any of this stuff I read," she shares.

"The only black people you found were occasional characters or characters who were so feeble-witted that they couldn't manage anything, anyway. I wrote myself in since I'm me and I'm here and I'm writing."[20]

Butler's second goal, to tell a good story, was made possible because she lived as an ethnographer, a person who studies and describes the culture of a particular society or group.[21] Her interest in human and animal emotions and intentions and how peoples' actions left an indelible mark on her—even as a child. In an autobiographical essay, she writes about the mistreatment of a chimpanzee at the zoo that she witnessed at seven years old. "The chimp had somehow become the target of some of the kids' attention," she recalled. "They shouted at him, laughed, and threw peanuts—threw them at him rather than to him. The chimp had nowhere to hide [. . .] and if I could have left the zoo at that moment, I would have. I was still too young to understand the concept of being ashamed of my species. I just felt horrible. I wanted the other kids to shut up. I wanted the chimp to be free."[22]

At seven, she was witnessing something she would explore extensively in her own work: the hierarchical and violent behavior of humans. "Amnesty," where a group of shrubbery-like aliens arrive on Earth and settle across various deserts, is one such example. As part of that settlement, they capture human children and adults, conducting experiments on them to understand them. At some point, these aliens offer the captives the opportunity to leave. The protagonist, a Black woman named Noah, agrees to leave the aliens' clutches. When freed, she is captured by humans who torture her. "The only difference between the way they treated me and the way the aliens treated me during the early years of my captivity," Noah reveals to a group of humans, "was that the so-called human beings knew when they were hurting me. They questioned me . . . drugged me [. . .] kept me locked up, alone, isolated from everyone but them."[23] Here, Butler was less concerned about the pain that another species inflicted (because they did not know any better) and more concerned about the actions of other humans who *did* know that they were harming another human. What does it say, then, that we humans harm other humans—even though we *know* it is painful? One of the difficult things about reading Butler's work, especially those that have non-humans, is that readers can quickly vilify the aliens for the things they are doing yet we are slow to translate that same disgust to ourselves. Therein lies the allure of Butler's work. It causes you to think and resist easy conclusions and easy categorizations. Her work is designed to make readers uncomfortable.

Other personal eye-witness events, like cancer diagnoses in friends, impacted Butler's writing. She admits that a character from *Wild Seed* came from watching "one person die of cancer,"[24] and so she created Anyanwu, an

African woman shapeshifter who had total control of her body from external transformations such as different genders, races, and species to internal transformations that would allow her to prevent semen from inseminating her womb, or disconnecting her fallopian tubes, or even allowing herself to die by suicide. By watching friends and loved ones succumb to illness or disease, Butler wrote to make sense of these tragedies and probe science fiction's what-if premise. What if we could take our cancerous cells and make them into something useful? What would we give up or accept in exchange for having cancer eradicated and our lives prolonged? These questions are explored in *Dawn*, and other explorations of disease or illness can be found in *Clay's Ark*, "The Evening and the Morning and the Night," and "Bloodchild."

Another eye-witness event that influenced a scene in *Sower* comes from an early childhood memory. In *Sower*, the fire ravages the protagonist's home and neighborhood, destroys her gated community, displaces her, and forces her to embark on an on-foot-journey towards an uncertain future. *Sower* has its roots in an early childhood memory. In an interview with Jelani Cobb, Butler shares a memory of being carried out of her grandmother's burning house—a house that used either a "candle or kerosene lantern" because there was no electricity.[25] ". . . I was only about four years old," Butler recalls, "so I don't know how it happened. I know I was awakened out of a sound sleep by somebody snatching me up and running out of the house with me. This was a house that my uncles had built with their own had, so it was especially . . . it had everything in it that my grandmother owned as far as mementos, and records of her children's birth [. . .] A memory that imprints that early you can't help keeping."[26] These sorts of eye-witness experiences color Butler's work throughout her life, finding themselves interwoven throughout her work across time.

Even *Kindred*, her longest-running in-print novel, was written out of her desire to "get people to feel slavery . . . to get across the kind of emotional and psychological stones that slavery threw at people . . . to make real the emotional reality of slavery . . . to make people feel more about the data they had learned . . . to make the past real and [show] how it scars the present."[27] With these reflections, Butler's second goal marries her third goal: to make people feel. In *Kindred*, Dana witnesses an enslaved Black man being tied to a tree and beaten in front of his wife and young daughter:

> I could literally smell his sweat, hear every ragged breath, every cry, every cut of the whip. I could see his body jerking, convulsing, straining against the rope as his screaming went on and on. My stomach heaved, and I had to force myself to stay where I was and keep quiet. Why didn't they stop! [. . .]

> I shut my eyes and tensed my muscles against an urge to vomit. I had seen people beaten on television and in the movies. I had seen the too-red blood substitute streaked across their backs and heard their well-rehearsed screams. But I hadn't lain nearby and smelled their sweat or heard them pleading and praying, shamed before their families and themselves. I was probably less prepared for the reality than the child crying not far from me. In fact, she and I were reacting very much alike. My face too was wet with tears.[28]

The sensory overload—of smelling (and tasting) sweat, of hearing the breathing, the crying, the cracking of the whip, the sight of his body moving is magnified against the manufactured beatings Dana sees on television. Through Dana, Butler paints a very vivid picture, intended to elicit a visceral reaction from her readers.

A consequence of Butler's eyewitness experiences as shaping her career is a repetition of themes across her body of work. The Bible and Christianity are certain themes that appear in her work. Her work also reveals her interest in biblical stories, biblical allusions, Christian references, and her interest in revising, revisiting, and rethinking Christianity. "I've always loved the Bible for the quotable things I could borrow from it," she told interviewers in 1988.[29] As a self-described former Baptist, she admits that the biblical stories "stories of conflict, betrayal, torture, murder, exile, and incest" drew her in.[30] We see biblical elements, whether revisions, critique, or just allusions throughout her work. In *Mind of My Mind*, we meet Rachel, a "faith healer," who uses her telepathy to mentally feed on her parishioners and give them something in return. In *Survivor*, Alanna navigates the dogma of The Missionaries, a group of human refugees who have left Earth for a new planet and retained their misogynistic, sexist, and racist belief systems. *Wild Seed* is structured after the biblical book of Genesis, and the Parable duology critiques religious fundamentalism. Further, she names some of her characters—Isaac, Noah, Martha, Eli, and Mary—after biblical characters.

Her work reveals her ongoing interest and investment in exploring captivity, enslavement, imprisonment, and institutionalization. In *Dawn*, Lilith's condition is reminiscent of solitary confinement. In *Talents*, the captives at Camp Christian are enslaved in prison re-education camps that are reminiscent of nineteenth-century slave plantations. In *Wild Seed* and *Dawn*, both Anyanwu and Lilith are described as prisoners, one even describing her isolation as akin to solitary confinement. In "The Evening and the Morning and the Night," the DGD ward is compared to a prison, and in "Bloodchild," the humans are kept in pens, denied weapons, and parceled out to the Tlic, a scorpion-like alien species. Though Butler is hesitant to describe some of her works as akin to slavery, the prison industrial complexes are part of the complex legacies of the 13th Amendment and chattel enslavement. Related to this investment in captivity, enslavement, imprisonment, and institutionalization is her work positioning Black women as survivors, leaders, and heroes. Throughout Butler's fiction, Black women who survive captivity become liaisons for bridging the gap between humans and non-humans and become responsible for ushering in a new era of humanity or existence. Such examples appear in *Survivor*, *Kindred*, *Dawn*, *Wild Seed*, and "Amnesty." These women are also captives of or enslaved or imprisoned by others to make Black human women the scapegoat.

Connected to these themes of captivity, enslavement, imprisonment, and institutionalization is Butler's investment in dismantling hierarchies that are often predicated on patriarchal violence. Many men and patriarchal women—one "who has internalized the norms and values of patriarchy"[31]—in Butler's work bring patriarchal violence to already struggling environments to assert their masculinity or their investment in patriarchal masculinity and patriarchal bargains. We see it in "Speech Sounds" with Obsidian, in *Dawn* with Paul, Peter, and Curt, in The Parable Duology with Reverend Olamina, Keith, Marc, and the Faircloth sisters, in *Clay's Ark* with father-daughter duo Blake and Rane, in *Kindred* with Rufus, in *Survivor* with Jules, in "Bloodchild" with Qui, and in "Childfinder" with The Organization. Many of the men and patriarchal women in her works usually cannot adapt to new surroundings or circumstances in the ways Butler's female, androgynous, or adaptable male characters do. Being put in unfavorable circumstances seems to make them feel the need to assert their investment in the hierarchy of patriarchal masculinity, which usually results in violence or death (all of which are unnecessary). Such explorations expose Butler's fears about humanity's investments in hierarchies.

The loneliness these isolated characters experience, combined with Butler's own loneliness and social anxiety, informs another theme in her works: the necessity of community, interdependence, and coexistence—and the dangers of its absence. Although she was a celebrated public figure after her death, Butler was a recluse and suffered from depression. In interviews and her work, she writes about the importance of community and establishing a community with others. Fostering a safe community in "The Evening and the Morning and the Night" becomes central for those considered socially and medically undesirable. In *Fledgling*, for example, Shori Matthews learns the importance of physical touch. In *Imago*, Aaor exists in a catatonic state, nearly dying because they cannot connect with others. In an early story, "Crossover," readers witness the importance of community by seeing first-hand the dangers of isolation, and

Sower and *Talents* demonstrate the necessity of multigenerational, multiracial communities for the collective survival of all.

Sometimes, though, the need for community is inhibited by preconceived notions about difference, notably disability, disease, illness, and impairment, which appear as motifs across Butler's work. *Dawn*'s protagonist is grateful that her captors can spare her pain and disability when she sees she has a scar on her abdomen, and she later learns that they removed cancer from her. In *Kindred*, readers are introduced to a nonverbal enslaved Black woman, Carrie, and a newly enslaved Black woman, Alice, who experiences temporary amnesia and incontinence, both traumatic injuries that obscure the fact that her husband has been taken from her, and the novel's protagonist, Dana, is an amputee by the novel's end. In *Imago*, humans with physical impairments choose to live free from an alien species that thrive on skin growths, appearance impairments, and disease. These humans value their independence more than the promises of illness, disease, and deformity-free living. We meet a badly burned, physically scarred, and amnesiac in *Fledgling*, where readers learn that physical dismemberment—or disability as punishment—is often meted out for crimes and offenses. In *Mind of My Mind*, migraines plague the telepathic protagonist, and humans are derisively called "mutes." The award-winning "Speech Sounds" questions whose lives matter at the story's end when the protagonist affirms the value of two children once she learns that they can speak after a global pandemic strips humanity of its ability to communicate effectively with traditional speech patterns. Appearing in print four years after "Speech Sounds," the award-winning "The Evening and the Morning and the Night" depicts a society where disabled people wear emblems to mark their differences and are shuttled off to ward-like prisons to waste away behind closed doors. And the protagonist in *Sower* and *Talents* lives with hyperempathy syndrome, a disability that makes her and others like her good candidates for slavery and exploitation.

Blurred lines of consent, which are often paired with addiction and sedation, occur throughout Butler's fiction. In *Dawn*, humans are drugged without their consent to make them more docile when their alien captors first appear to them, and readers witness one human captive realize that she has been impregnated without her consent. In "Bloodchild," a political ruler drugs an "unwillingly obedient" former friend."[32] Closely connected to consent and sedation is addiction. In *Survivor*, addiction is present through the effects of a fruit that an extraterrestrial Indigenous community uses to manipulate new arrivals to their community and to prevent their enemies or prisoners of war from escaping. Substance abuse, alcohol abuse, and addiction find their way into Butler's fiction, ranging from her earliest published works to her final novel.

In one of her final interviews before her death, Butler asks, "Who would want to live in a world where there are fewer educated people?"[33] This question of education is perhaps the most significant as it impacts her life, writing, and beliefs. The importance and necessity of reading and writing through her emphasis on education may be her most enduring theme across her fiction and nonfiction. Butler was not your typical educator. She never worked as a schoolteacher, though she tutored at The Central Library in Los Angeles, and she often returned to the Clarion Writers Workshop as a workshop leader. But she certainly had a passion for education, literacy, and encouraging others—especially writers—to write. Butler's passion for education does not show up in advanced degrees, but it does show up in her persistence in always enrolling in classes—and encouraging others to do the same. Although she did not earn a degree beyond her history associate degree, she dreamed of getting a PhD with a keen interest in anthropology. The thought of becoming an academic "electrified her."[34] as did the thought of becoming a best-selling author. Although Butler did not pursue the PhD further, *Dawn*'s protagonist holds this advanced degree. And many of her Black women and girl protagonists, spanning from *Kindred* to "The Book of Martha" to the Parables to *Dawn* to *Fledgling*, are either writers by profession or have a passion for reading, writing, and learning.

Her passion for education and literacy extended beyond her fiction work; it appears in her essays, speeches, and interviews. One of her most consistent pieces of advice for burgeoning writers was for them to take classes. In "Furor Scribendi," which is Latin for "mania for writing," she offered nine pieces of advice for writers. Her second piece of writing advice encouraged writers to take classes and solicit feedback on their work. "Writing is communication," she writes in "Furor Scribendi." "You need other people to let you know whether you're communicating what you think you are and whether you're doing it in ways that are not only accessible and entertaining, but as compelling as you can make them."[35]

In her 1998 speech at MIT, "Devil Girl from Mars: Why I Write Science Fiction," she laments the apparent loss of literacy. "Several years ago, when I was publicizing *Parable of the Sower*, I heard on National Public Radio that the population of America could be considered about 46% semi-literate. Now that's scary," she remarked. Butler herself was dyslexic; she was not suggesting that folks had to read books in print. She was fond of listening to them on tape (though we now can listen to them on our cell phones or tablets). But what she gets at in this portion of her speech is this: education is key for creating informed citizens who do not parrot the rhetoric of others, a sentiment echoed in lines from *Talents*: "Beware: / All too often, / We say / What we hear others say."[36] Butler was quite fearful that we would become citizens so uninformed, so attuned to not reading for comprehension that we would also "see what we're told to see."[37]

Her passion for reading and publicly available education is also evident in her lament. In a journal entry, we learn that Butler was devastated by the loss of The Central Library in Los Angeles, which burned to the ground on April 29, 1986. Butler did not drive, so she was on the city bus when she found out. She told the bus driver where she was going. And he told her she wouldn't be going there because the library was on fire. "He could have announced the death of one of my friends and not hit me as hard," Butler wrote, "This was the death of so many friends. Books. Burning."[38] In later portions of the journal, she wrote, "I don't know how I will write this. It isn't the first time I've seen a friend—a loved friend—die. But it is the first time I've seen one killed."[39] That Butler personifies the library as a beloved friend speaks to the depths of how much she treasured reading and the library and all that it provided—an education. Butler may not have been an educator in the traditional sense, but she was a proponent of education and non-traditional forms of education, and these forms of education are rooted in African American Literary and Literacy Traditions.

Butler's emphasis on education is part of a longstanding tradition in African American Literature and Culture, but she consistently emphasized the importance of writing. Butler's emphasis on writing is evident in her life and work. Throughout her body of work, the theme of writing functions in five ways: as freedom, as a catalyst for change, as currency, as comfort, as lamentation or honoring the dead, and as an archive. Although all five of these appear in both *Sower* and *Talents*, which I discuss at length in chapter 4, they crop up sporadically across her body of work. In *Kindred*, Dana's shorthand writing style provides her with the freedom to express her thoughts without being understood by prying eyes. Writing as scriptotherapy—or therapeutic writing—emerges from an unlikely source in *Wild Seed*: Doro, an ancient being who writes in a now-defunct language, which is both a source of comfort and one way that writing becomes an expression to lament and honor the dead.[40] If her essays "Positive Obsession" and "Furor Scribendi" best characterize the theme of writing as a compulsion, then her own journal writing reinforces the need for writing as an archive, which appears in her Parable Series. Truly, as a writer and educator, it is unsurprising that the *ars scribendi*, the act of writing, becomes an undercurrent for many of her characters.

The following chapters are divided into two sections: Writing through the Decades: Butler's Evolving Craft (part I) and Writing across Genres: Butler's Literary Range (part II). Part I explores Butler's fiction chronologically through chapters 2, 3, and 4, which respectively cover the years 1970–79,

1980–89, and 1990–2006. Part II explores Butler as a writer of specific genres—neo-slave narrative (chapter 5), romance (chapter 6), and nonfiction (chapter 7)—and takes great care not to repeat the plot summary from part I. This structure gives us two ways of understanding Butler: a temporal perspective that highlights her evolution as a writer and a thematic perspective that examines her contributions to different genres. I end with an Afterword, focusing on Butler's legacies.

So Much to So Many

On June 24, 2018, I was invited to speak at the University of Maryland at Baltimore County (UMBC) as part of their First Year Experience series. The text? *Kindred*. I accepted the invitation, and I began reflecting on Immigration and Customs Enforcement's (ICE) separation of families that summer and their placement of immigrant children in what amounts to concentration camps. I reflected on the continued assaults of women, persons of color, queer, transgender, gender expansive, and nonbinary people. I reflected on the confirmation hearings of newly appointed Supreme Court Justice Brett Kavanaugh, the testimony of Dr. Christine Blasey-Ford, and the eerily similar parallels to Anita Hill's testimony before the Senate Judiciary Committee in 1991. On June 24, 2020, precisely two years later, I was invited to co-edit and contribute to a special issue of the *College Language Association Journal* titled *For Us, To Us, About Us: Racial Unrest and Cultural Transformation*. Again, I found myself in a deep state of reflection and sorrow. George Floyd. Breonna Taylor. Tony McDade. Rayshard Brooks. Riah Milton. Dominique Fells. Atatiana Jefferson. Ahmaud Arbery. COVID-19. And again, I found myself returning to Butler's work. Days after a white supremacist murdered nine Black people at a grocery store in Buffalo, New York, days after a domestic terrorist murdered nineteen children and two teachers in Uvalde, Texas, I found myself, once again, leaning into Butler, her life, her legacy, and her wisdom, but this time for a presentation at the Learning Center at Senior Citizens Inc., in Savannah, GA, on May 25, 2022. Whether for leisure, the classroom, or public speaking, I return to Butler. I am grateful for the opportunity to return to Butler once again and share insights into her.

On February 24, 2006, Octavia Estelle Butler died after a fall outside of her home where her head struck the cobblestone walkway. She was fifty-eight. This is the same writer who, eleven years before her death, said, "Who am I? I am a forty-seven-year-old writer who can remember being a ten-year-old writer and who expects someday to be an eighty-year-old writer."[41] She was a major force in American prose during the later twentieth century, and she used science fiction to make profound observations about the human experience.

A volume about Octavia E. Butler as part of the University of South Carolina Press's Understanding Contemporary American Literature series is overdue, but like Butler's work, it is perfectly timed. Butler was writing until her tragic, untimely death, and her prolific work deserves special consideration. I hope that *Understanding Octavia E. Butler* serves as a worthy eulogy to one bright star who meant so much to so many.

Part I

Writing through the Decades

Butler's Evolving Craft

CHAPTER 2

The 1970s
A Breakthrough Decade

> Every day in Every way
> I write faster,
> Better
> And more!
>
> —Octavia E. Butler, OEB 990,
> The Butler Papers, Huntington Library

Written in verse format and in blue ink, these words open Octavia E. Butler's August 8, 1974, journal entry. Her affirmations come on the heels of years of not publishing. Her only publication at the time was "Crossover" (1971). Her journal entries from the 1960s and mid-1970s document her frequent self-loathing, where she lamented her writing speed and skill. But dawn broke. Below her August 8, 1974, affirmation is an entry that begins, "Some things continue. Every day in every way, I write faster, better, and more." These lines are written in black ink, dated August 14, 1979—five years and one week after her previous entry. "I have sold five books now."[1] She was referring to *Patternmaster* (1976), *Mind of My Mind* (1977), *Survivor* (1978), *Kindred* (1979), and *Wild Seed*, which would be published in 1980. A decade that begins as a dud for her writing ends with the publication of four novels, one on the way, and the hope of more. "I am a good writer getting better," she pens and draws the entry to a close repeating her affirmation: "Every day in every way, I am writing better, faster, and more."[2] Truly, it was a breakthrough decade.

"Childfinder" and "Crossover"

Although Butler was a prolific writer in the 1970s, she struggled with being torn between what was expected of her as a writer and what she wanted to do. In a 2002 interview, the award-winning writer shared that her early writing had been considered by some "almost a betrayal, a waste of time at best" because she "was supposed to, according to some people, be contributing to the struggle and not writing things that weren't real."[3] In an interview in 1994, she remarked, "My work isn't all that political really. Actually, I was pressured in the opposite direction. I was pressured to politicize it more like, 'Why are you writing science fiction? Why are you writing something so unreal? Why don't you write something that would be meaningful?' In the sixties, meaningful was the big word and I was supposed to be writing more about Black history or about the struggle. . . ."[4] Despite her comment that some saw what she was writing as a waste of time at best, "Childfinder" (1970, 2014) embraces The Black Aesthetic principles and the Black Power Movement's political aims and objectives. Butler usually does not come to mind when one thinks about the Black Arts Movement, Black Nationalism, or Black Power Movement. Indeed, she had mixed feelings about the Black Panthers' methods noting that many of them spent unproductive time in prison.[5] Yet there is merit in examining "Childfinder" within and against the Black Nationalist Discourse, which I am using as an umbrella term for the collective principles, rhetoric, aims, and objectives of the Black Arts Movement, the Black Power Movement, and the Black Panther Party.

The Black Arts Movement was a collective Black nationalist movement composed of Black artists and intellectuals who focused on creating politically engaged work exploring Black American cultural and historical experiences.[6] The Black Arts Movement is generally thought to begin in 1965 and end in 1975, but the Movement "cannot be comprehended as a time-bound event."[7] Eleanor W. Traylor reminds us that its "revolutionary spirit continues to ask ethical questions and to demand ethical answers."[8] Characterized as polyvocal and multifaceted, The Black Arts Movement bore a "wide range of ideological and aesthetic stances," but remained unified by beliefs in self-determination and social change.[9] These Black Arts Movement practitioners, including poets Amiri Baraka, Nikki Giovanni, Larry Neal, and Sonia Sanchez, rejected the pacifist nonviolence of the Civil Rights Movement and embraced the militancy of Malcolm X, the Nation of Islam, the Black Power Movement, and the Black Panther Party. The Black Power Movement was a revolutionary movement of the 1960s and '70s, and it has been described as the political sister of the

Black Arts Movement. It emphasized Black economic empowerment, Black pride, and Black political and cultural institutions. The Black Panther Party for Self-Defense emerged in tandem with the Black Power Movement. The Black Panther Party, founded in 1966 in Oakland, California, is often remembered for its militant stance; however, it should also be remembered for providing basic needs to Black citizens, including free breakfast for school children, medical care (e.g., sickle cell anemia screenings), legal aid, and adult education. The decline of the Black Arts Movement began in 1974 when the Black Power movement, the Black Panther Party, and Black political organizations were disrupted, harassed, and infiltrated by government surveillance measures, notably the Counterintelligence Program (Cointelpro).

Though the Black Power Movement, Black Panther Party, and the Black Arts Movement emphasized Black pride, Black empowerment, and Black institutions, they were plagued by sex and gender-based discrimination. Sexism, homophobia, and paternalism characterized the public-facing ideological beliefs that undergirded these movements. One repeating theme readers will notice about Butler's work published in the 1970s is that her writing seems to reject the gender-based oppression that was characteristic not only of Black liberation movements but also of American culture more broadly. However, Butler is not alone in this reaction. She exists in an African American women's literary tradition of questioning gender assumptions that undergirded Black nationalist discourse.[10] Of course, in the United States, Black women's writing post-civil rights were not ideologically uniform or monolithic. Whereas some writers like Mari Evans, Nikki Giovanni, and Sonia Sanchez embraced a Black nationalist ideology,[11] other writers like Toni Morrison, Gayl Jones, Alice Walker, and Butler stepped away from the founding assumptions of Black Nationalist Discourse.

Completed in 1970 at the Clarion Writer's Workshop, "Childfinder" was scheduled for publication in Harlan Ellison's anthology titled *Last Dangerous Visions*, but the anthology's publication never came to fruition. Instead, "Childfinder" was published posthumously in 2014, eight years after her death, in a two-story collection titled *Unexpected Stories*. "Childfinder" is the first-person story of Barbara, a Black woman who adopts Black pre-telepathic children, teaches them to use their telepathic ability, and creates a telepathic community, which I call "The Court." The Court is in a dilapidated section of town. The "rat and roach" description of Barbara's living conditions depicts the housing issues and poverty that plague Black communities and that civil rights advocates like Malcolm X called attention to.[12] The central conflict of the story is between The Organization and The Court. The Organization, a group of white telepaths who are referred to as "pigs," police Barbara and The Court because they are an independent, self-sufficient, all-Black group.[13] The Organization first attempts to bargain with Barbara and, after failing, resorts to threatening her adoptees. The conflict between Barbara and The Organization is the classic archetype of the renegade outsider fighting for moral good versus the pressure to conform to the status quo. Barbara, as a hero and freedom fighter, rebels. In the end, Barbara gives herself total amnesia to save her Black telepaths so that perhaps one day they can revolt against The Organization. The use of "pigs" to describe The Organization is classic rhetoric from the Black Power Movement. Passing the torch and letting the youth lead the movement links to the various leaders of Black Power and Civil Rights Movements of the 1960s and 1970s, with young leaders like Stokely Carmichael and Fred Hampton being two prominent figures and faces of these movements.

Although these are some of the obvious links, there are three ways that "Childfinder" thematically links to the Black Nationalist Discourse of the time. First, "Childfinder" opens with a scene of instruction. According to Charles T. Davis and Henry Louis Gates Jr., a scene of instruction is the scene in an emancipatory narrative where the formerly enslaved narrator learns to read and write or where enslaved Black people teach others to read and write.[14] But scenes of instruction are not limited to emancipatory narratives. Barbara teaches a young Black telepath named Valerie to read, but not in the traditional sense. Barbara does not teach Valeries to read words on the page; instead, she teaches her psionic communication by mentally "hit[ting] her with a scene from the book. Herself in Harriet's place . . ."[15] The "Harriet" here refers to Harriet Tubman. This scene of instruction is doubly important; it showcases the literacy instruction Valerie receives while simultaneously emphasizing the importance of educating Black children about their own heroes. This principle, rooted in the Black Power movement, is the fifth principle from the Black Panther Party's 10-Point Program. It is no accident that Butler chooses Harriet Tubman. Tubman is positioned as a (folk) hero for Valerie. Young Valerie is presented with an image of the revolutionary Harriet Tubman, who is faced with not only presenting enslaved Black people with an opportunity for freedom but also faced with shooting them if they decide to turn back because of their fear. It is important that Barbara chooses an enslaved Black person who was willing to use violence—even against those she was seeking to liberate—if it meant saving the group. The young girl's question in response, "They always got halfway up north and then somebody would get scared and want to go back. How come they were so scared to just go ahead and be free?" indicates some semblance of that disgust for Black people who were too scared to do anything.[16] Butler's decision to choose Harriet Tubman as the hero for young Valerie is best thought of as a nod to the role Black women played in Black people's liberation movements, though their contributions were often neglected in favor of Black male leaders.

Barbara's creation of a pocket universe is a second indicator that "Childfinder" can be read as a text conversant with Black Nationalist ideas. In science fiction, a pocket universe is described as "a universe or reality completely separate from ours which is much smaller, may have different natural laws, and may be artificially created."[17] Others describe the pocket universe as "a space within a space governed by its own rules [and where] the "larger world envelops this isolated space, this miniature universe."[18] Barbara creates this pocket universe for several reasons. First because The Organization was originally only for "exceptions"—meaning individuals who showed prominent psionic abilities rather than others—who were like Barbara herself—who only had latent abilities that needed to be cultivated. Second, she realized that The Organization was only using her for her special skill of being a childfinder. Third, her skills as a childfinder were used only to find the children The Organization deemed desirable. As readers we learn: "These are the same kids you wouldn't even consider before I left. You took one look into them and you couldn't get out fast enough."[19] That rejection turned into a need for Barbara to reach the people whom The Organization had ignored, rejected, and discarded. Barbara cultivates a trajectory of growth to establish a legacy that will ensure a future for the formerly rejected, ignored, and discarded Black telepaths where they could maintain their lives untouched and unfettered by The Organization, or a nod to white supremacist organizations. At the story's opening, Barbara's community consists of eight houses "all set in a straggly row and called a court."[20] Though The Court exists as a pocket universe, Barbara aims to create a Black-o-sphere, or "an area untouched by white supremacy."[21] She tries to create a free Black community, which The Organization describes as an "opposing organization," and she wants them to be able to remain "alive and together and hidden" until they are "too strong for the organization to touch."[22] The Court exists as a stand-alone nation within a nation, and it dovetails with the first major point of the Black Panther Party's ten-point program, "We Want Freedom. We Want Power to Determine the Destiny of Our Black Community." Barbara's provision of basic needs for her children through The Court mirrors the Black Panther Party's community care model with literacy classes, adult education, and free breakfast programs. The Organization rejected and ignored the Black pre-telepaths, and when Barabra recognized her own complicity, she left The Organization and began to prioritize and center Black telepaths. Barbara's desire for her and her adoptees to manage their own lives and create their own worlds, communities, and spaces, is rooted in this concept of self-determination.

Barbara's pocket universe, like many Black independent and revolutionary organizations or movements, is labeled as a threat by The Organization—a third indicator that it aligns with the Black Panthers in terms of how they were perceived by mainstream Americans. When Eve, a representative from The Organization arrives, she remarks, "So the others are right. You're forming an opposing organization . . . A segregated black-only group."[23] Eve then threatens Barbara and the children, "you can't watch *all* the kids you've collected *all* the time. Especially since you're still looking out for new ones. We would hate to do anything, but . . ."[24] Eve's threat to harm Barbara's progeny becomes more sinister if we recall Fred Hampton's assassination. Hampton, a prominent Black Panther leader, activist, and advocate for economic and social justice, was assassinated on December 4, 1969. He was twenty-one. Butler wrote about Hampton's assassination in her journal as she also lamented Rev. Dr. Martin Luther King Jr's assassination in 1968. When placed in the context of Butler's lived experiences, Eve's threat to Barbara becomes frighteningly realistic. The Organization attempts to reassert its power by harassing and policing Barbara because they recognize the power of self-determination and collective power—both of which are Black Nationalist principles—and they deem her skills as a childfinder a threat to their organization because she is no longer working for them, *and* their organization has not grown.

Importantly, the stunted growth The Organization experiences does not become a moment to appeal to The Organization's morality. In this way, "Childfinder" does not become protest literature. African American Protest literature is generally when Black authors use their writing to challenge injustices, inequalities, and the secondary status Black people face in America to provoke change. For Black Arts practitioners like Ethridge Knight and Larry Neal, protest literature was something to be avoided. ". . . implicit in the act of protest [literature]," Knight writes, "is the belief that a change will be forthcoming once the masters are aware of the protestor's 'grievance' . . . Only when that belief has faded and protestings end, will Black art begin."[25] "Childfinder" neither appeals to white morality nor attempts to defend the humanity of Black people. Instead, "Childfinder" functions as a call to arms—or at least a call to organize. Butler herself is ambivalent about this call to arms. She described the Black Panthers' five-hour shootout with police on Central Avenue as a "Stupid Scene!!!"[26] Despite her own ambivalence, she allows Barbara and her adoptees to embrace this call tenuously. Barbara admits to "crippling" white pre-telepaths to prevent The Organization from growing. She does not kill them but prevents them from being capable of harming others. And though she admonishes her adoptees for attacking three Organization members, she sacrifices herself so they may have "a chance" and so they can "settle some scores" for Barbara in the future.[27] She cares for them as a mother and a leader and wants them to live, carry the torch, and survive.

At first glance, Barbara's role as a mother figure appears in alignment with the more masculinist and sexist Black liberation principles. Barbara is a mother figure trying to reproduce for the future generation by finding, adopting, and teaching as many Black telepaths as possible. And by doing what is necessary: crippling white pre-telepaths so The Organization cannot advance. However, understanding Barbara's role as mother only (and thus in alignment with the misogynistic beliefs that the only thing that Black women were good for was reproducing for the next generation) ignores Barbara's role as a leader, organizer, protector, and defender. Barbara operates covertly and alone. Barbara's gender and leadership role echoes the women in the Black Power Movement who were alongside Black men and, in many cases, at the forefront of community organizing and Black political and artistic thought. Though Barbara's role as a mother may seem to reinforce certain gendered scripts of women as mother figures, Butler's choice to make the main character a Black woman is intentional and important. Butler offers a narrative on Black womanhood, caretaking, and organization: Barbara more than nurtures psi-kids; she teaches, organizes, and protects them with a clear intent: to help them grow as a free nation.

Butler did not consider herself part of the Black Arts Movement; however, as a Black writer, she embraced the principles of self-determination and advocated for Black peoples' creation of their own worlds, communities, and spaces. "When I began writing science fiction, when I began reading, heck, I wasn't in any of this stuff I read," Butler once shared. "The only black people you found were occasional characters or characters who were so feeble-witted that they couldn't manage anything, anyway. I wrote myself in, since I'm me and I'm here and I'm writing."[28] Part of self-determination is inspiring hope in Black people with positive images of themselves, including the artists inspiring themselves. Butler admittedly wrote the stories she needed and wanted to see when she was a young reader. She was neither trying to prove her humanity through protest literature nor was she imitating white aesthetics. Nor did she uncritically adhere to Black nationalist rhetoric, principles, or aesthetics. Thinking about this early story as conversant with Black nationalist discourse stresses her desire not to be easily categorized, to explore the things she was passionate about, and to see her writing craft develop.

Her development as a writer continues to take shape with "Crossover" published in 1971. "Crossover" is unique among her body of work being that it is one of two stories that is not characterized as science fiction. "Crossover" opens with alienation and isolation. Jane is alienated by her coworkers for working too hard and chastised by her supervisor if she does not work hard enough. When confronted by her co-workers, she is sitting at a "solitary corner table."[29] And more than once she has been written up by her boss for "bad attitude" and has yet to receive a raise in two years.[30] To add insult to injury, Jane is the subject of street harassment—a wino propositions her, and we get the sense that her face is either disfigured or is not conventionally attractive because some boys jeer, "Lady, you sure shouldn't have let that car run over you[r] face!"[31] No one attempts to intervene; she persists alone—until a headache alerts her to the presence of one she would rather forget: a scar-faced man. This unnamed scar-faced man appears to be an on-again/off-again boyfriend until readers learn he is visible only to her. The revelation that Jane is hallucinating a lover underscores one of several "crossovers" in the text: sanity/insanity, partnership/isolation, sobriety/inebriation, worthy/unworthy, wellness/illness, ability/disability, desirability/undesirability, and life/death. At its core, the story is about Jane's encounter with *something*. The something Jane encounters results from her fear of moving forward. Jane is immobilized. She lacks the courage to quit her job, "afraid" that she will have to "start all over again at a new place where the people might even be worse."[32] It is not the only thing she fears. Speaking her mind, even to a hallucination is "just another of the things she didn't have the courage to do. Like accepting the loneliness or dying."[33] Her immobilization, her fear of movement, or her fear of crossing over into new territory prompts the headache she initially feels, which is a sign that her scar-faced hallucination will appear.

Jane's hallucination invites us to explore the gothic elements in "Crossover." After all, gothic stories often toggle between the question, "Is it madness, or is it a ghost?" The community around her—liquor stores, pool halls, and cheap hotels—is described as a place that "made it a gathering place for certain kinds of people."[34] These establishments that have "the usual drunks and prostitutes" are signals that the world around Jane is crumbling and is in moral decline.[35] The story's setting, combined with Jane's work environment, isolation, and stress, contribute to the mania she experiences and highlights the story's gothic undertones. Jane's anger (characterized by her violent outburst of throwing items in her apartment) and her depressive low (where she takes a wino to a hotel room to numb the pain of her unwanted mental intrusion) are evidence of the intense emotions characteristic of gothic literature.

"Crossover" also conforms to the three-part structure of nineteenth-century gothic texts. Christopher Craft shares that the gothic story "first invites or admits a monster, then entertains and is entertained by monstrosity for some extended duration, until in its closing pages it expels or repudiates the monster and all the disruptions that he/she/it brings."[36] Jane welcomes the scar-faced man whose facial disfigurement casts him as monstrous. She is entertained by the scar-faced man; they share a meal, have sex, and argue. Finally, she repudiates the scar-faced man, "slamm[ing] the door in his face."[37] The story ends with Jane, the "mad woman," numbing her pain with alcohol and temporary sexual relief with a wino she ignored earlier.

The story's end is enriched further if we consider the varied interpretations of Jane's name. First, Jane's name could be seen as a reference to anonymity, akin to "Jane Doe," a term commonly used for unidentified individuals, suggesting a lack of identity or individuality. Such an interpretation has merit, considering the theme of dehumanization prevalent in her work experience. Charles Dickens described factory workers as "hands" in *Hard Times* (1854), pointing to their function in the production process and underscoring their lack of full embodiment, which isolates and dehumanizes them. Though Jane is not referred to as a "hand," our introduction to her echoes her function as a "hand." In the story's opening paragraph, we learn Jane is expected to perform tasks at an accelerated pace, leading to resentment from her coworkers and neglect from her superiors. Despite her efforts, she faces a cycle of mistreatment and disregard; when she excels, her superiors ignore her, and her coworkers resent her. When her work suffers, her coworkers ignore her, and her superiors label her as having a "bad attitude."[38] The absence of a raise for two years further emphasizes her dehumanizing and isolating experiences. In this context, her name, potentially symbolizing anonymity, is reinforced by her reduced status and lack of individual recognition as a factory worker. Second, Jane may represent an Everywoman figure, symbolizing the struggles of ordinary people facing unsatisfactory working conditions or other life challenges. In the story's afterword, Butler describes how the story grew out of her own fear of remaining stuck working in factory jobs, though she clarifies that she did not begin hallucinating or turn to alcohol like Jane. Third, there's the possibility that Jane's name subtly nods to drug use, especially considering "Mary Jane" as a euphemism for marijuana, which can induce hallucinations in some cases. Whether we read "Crossover" as a nod to gothic literature or as Butler's outlet for her own frustrations at the time she was writing, Jane's hallucination prompts readers to consider whether our sanity is a sacrifice we are prepared to make or if we have the courage to face our fears and cross over into something new.

Patternmaster, Mind of My Mind, **and** Survivor

After several years of not publishing, working grubby jobs, and berating herself for not writing, Butler's writing frustration gave way to a breakthrough, and her big three—*Patternmaster*, *Mind of My Mind*, and *Survivor*—emerged. *Patternmaster* introduces readers to the fictional universe of the Patternists, a community of telepaths governed by a near-death monarch, Rayal. The hierarchical community structure of *Patternmaster* is divided broadly into three groups: the Patternists, those with telepathic abilities; Mutes, humans with non-telepathic abilities; and Clayarks, who are described in this novel only as "savages" and are the Patternists' enemies. In *Patternmaster*, Butler examines two central figures, Teray and Coransee, their mutual love interest, Amber, and challenges readers to think about what it means to be a good, effective leader.

Teray's journey in *Patternmaster* resembles the Hero's Journey. Readers meet Teray in the ordinary world. He leaves school, and a Housemaster named Joachim accepts him as an apprentice. But Teray is called to adventure when he is intercepted by Coransee, a powerful Housemaster, a son of Rayal, a viable successor for the title of Patternmaster, and, to Teray's surprise, Teray's biological brother. In some hero's journey stories, the hero initially resists or refuses the call to adventure. Initially, Teray refuses the two options Coransee provides him: be a mentally controlled apprentice or become a slave. Teray chooses slavery, forfeiting his freedom, his wife, and his wife's freedom as well. During this call to adventure, Teray meets Amber, his mentor. She is a Black woman, a healer, and an Independent who encourages him to find community, flee Coransee, and seek sanctuary in Forsyth. When Teray decides to escape, he crosses the threshold. He invites Amber to accompany him, and she acts as his healer, teacher, and advisor. Together, Teray and Amber encounter Clayarks and Patternists allied with Coransee. From Amber, Teray learns how to kill Clayarks expeditiously and effectively. Amber's tutelage proves vital when Coransee captures Amber and Teray and proves effective for Teray's final battle with Coransee. Teray baits Coransee into a fight and kills him, and as his reward, Teray inherits the role and title of Patternmaster.

Patternmaster is a classic story of two feuding siblings who vie for power to take the ultimate reward: the role of Patternmaster. Yet, the novel explores the danger of the corrupting influence of power. "I began writing about power because I felt I had so little,"[39] Butler once shared. *Patternmaster* is not only an exploration of that power, but it also provides readers with a blueprint for what makes a good leader. As the heir apparent to Rayal's proverbial throne, Coransee is queerphobic, paranoid, and individualistic, and he lacks compassion, restraint, and strategy. *Patternmaster* is emphatic that these are not desirable traits for a leader. Teray is the foil to Coransee, highlighting Teray's positive leadership skills and Coransee's undesirable ones. Where Coransee is queerphobic and seeks to use compulsory heterosexuality to punish and control Amber, Teray remarks, "after all, you're not that unusual,"[40] when she reveals her bisexuality. Where Coransee is paranoid and individualistic, Teray understands the value of trust and community. Through Joachim and Amber, Teray learns that community and an ethic of caring are essential to his emotional well-being and to establishing and maintaining power. Teray observes that Joachim's house is strong because he has intentionally created a house with people who are compatible and close in proximity in the pattern. That closeness, Teray notes, explains the power in Joachim's household. Conversely, Coransee refuses to mentally connect with the telepaths in his House, which angers Teray. "What good did it do Coransee to have ten people with him if he didn't use them sensibly?" he thinks.[41] Teray even tells Coransee, "But you know as well as I do that you should link up with at least some of your people. You could stand it with a couple of them even though they're not close to you. Hell, you're the one who wants the Pattern. That will link you with everyone."[42]

Coransee's rejection of closeness exemplifies his individualism and distrust of others and points to his less-than-noble desire for the Pattern. When Teray learns from Amber that a woman named Suliana is constantly subjected to abuse at the hands of a man named Jason, Teray also learns that Coransee does not concern himself with the ordeal. Instead, he allows physical abuse to go unchecked so long as it does not interfere with his daily affairs or his goal: obtaining the role of Patternmaster. When Teray asks why this is the case, Amber shares, "Coransee wants the Pattern the way you and I want to go on breathing,"[43] uncaring about anything else. Teray learns about mutes, Clayarks, and other Patternists and begins to see the value of people he once thought himself superior to. He becomes a man among the people, familiarizing himself with their concerns or, at the very least, learning about them as potential people who need his leadership. Teray is also a foil against Rayal, whose lack of leadership has allowed the Clayarks to run rampant throughout the Patternist sectors. In one of his first acts as the yet-to-be-crowned Patternmaster, Teray kills thousands of Clayarks. Ultimately, Teray does not want to be the Patternmaster, but he witnesses his father's apathy and his brother's tunnel vision and wonders who will care for the people. Teray emerges as the reluctant leader who rises for the good of the people. Through Teray, *Patternmaster* offers an aspirational leadership model where leaders value the importance of creating compatible communities and fulfilling working conditions, where leaders center compassion, queer-inclusivity, and strategic organization, and where leaders value an ethic of caring and community.

Teray's reluctant leadership reappears in *Mind of My Mind* with Mary, who is not so much a reluctant leader but one who cannot control her leadership. With *Mind of My Mind* acting as *Patternmaster*'s prequel, Butler continues in the fictional universe of the Patternists, this time inviting readers to learn how the Pattern was created. At the novel's beginning, Mary is an eighteen-year-old pretransition telepath who is forced by Doro, her father, to marry and survive her transition—a telepathic form of what we know as puberty—that moves her from a latent telepath to a telepath with fully realized potential. When Mary awakens from her transition, her telepathic powers blossom, and she discovers that she is mentally linked with her husband and five telepaths from across the United States. She mentally calls these five people—Clay, Seth, Rachel, Jesse, and Ada—and they are compelled to travel to her home in Forsyth. They form the "First Family" of what becomes the Patternist community.

The "First Family" formation is only the beginning, and Mary realizes that she has a talent for sensing latent telepaths and pushing them through the transition. She unintentionally creates The Pattern that readers first encounter in *Patternmaster*. The telepaths Mary senses have varying degrees of control over their power and often unexplained side effects like fatigue and migraines. Many of them live in squalor. But once she links with them, their side effects disappear completely, and she helps elevate them from their sordid living conditions. When her Patternist community experiences rapid growth in two years, Doro is threatened by her power and offers her an ultimatum: stop growing your community or die. Mary refuses because her philanthropy uplifts women and children from the squalid living conditions that Doro is content to let them live in. Doro's inaction echoes Rayal and Coransee's inaction in *Patternmaster*. These three are positioned as apathetic and power-hungry leaders who ignore those who need them and limit, harm, or prevent those, like Mary, who are willing to help those who have been forgotten, neglected, or discarded by the men in power.[44] Mary rejects Doro's ultimatum, resulting in a battle to the death. His death. Like Teray, Mary battles for her community. She challenges Doro, kills him, saves her community, and becomes the first Patternmaster.

As much as the story revolves around Mary, her ascendance to power, and her role as the first Patternmaster, *Mind of My Mind* also demonstrates Butler's fascination with Christian evangelists and faith healers. In the novel, Rachel is a "faith healer" who craves energy, attention, and adoration from humans, and she becomes weak and sick without them.[45] Her solution? She holds church services, successfully markets herself as a vessel for the Christian God's healing powers, and after penetrating the minds of a crowd, she draws energy from them. "They fed her, strengthened her, drove out her sickness, which was, after all, no more than a need for them, their adoration."[46] In return, she heals them. Rachel is likely modeled on Kathryn Kuhlman, an American evangelist and faith healer. Kuhlman was known for her healing ministry and ability to attract large crowds to her services to her "healing crusades" held in the 1940s until her death in 1976. Kuhlman, like Rachel, was popular, though her success rates were questioned.[47] Whether Rachel's similarities to Kuhlman are evidence of Butler's critique of Christian healers is less important than the opportunity Butler takes to explore the *what if?* question that drives so many of her works. What if we could heal people with a single touch? Regrow limbs? Cure cancer?

If *Mind of My Mind* appears ambivalent about Christian Evangelism and healing services, *Survivor*, her third novel of the decade, is her first sustained critique of Christian fundamentalism. Structurally, the novel uses both first-person and third-person narration. The use of the third-person narration signals readers that we are in the "present," and first-person narration indicates to readers that we are witnessing the protagonist's past from one of two perspectives: hers or her husband's. *Survivor* tells the story of Alanna Verrick, an Afro-Asian girl who is adopted by Jules Verrick and his wife, Neila, when she is fifteen years old. Jules is the leader of The Missionaries, a Christian religious sect that worships the Sacred Image of God. After living with the Verricks for two years on Earth, Alanna joins them on their journey to a new planet. Jules and all inhabitants of the Verrick Missionary Colony leave the disease-addled Earth because of their loyalty and good behavior as slaves to the Patternists. They arrive in space, land on a planet they name Canaan, and begin a new life. On Canaan, they find themselves confronted with the Kohn, an indigenous humanoid species divided into two enemy factions: the Garkohn and the Tehkohn. The Missionaries ally themselves with the Garkohn whose leader, Natahk, offers them protection and an endless supply of meklah fruit. In exchange? The Missionaries would teach the Garkohn their language. After one year on Canaan, Alanna and several other Missionaries are kidnapped by the Tehkohn. She remains in captivity for two years where she marries Diut, her captor, bears his child, Tien, and learns that the Garkohn have been poisoning and addicting the Missionaries to the meklah fruit. When she returns to the Missionary settlement, Alanna tries to save her Missionaries from the disingenuous Garkohn alliance. When Alanna learns that the Missionaries' so-called allies are capturing and impregnating Missionary women, she splits herself in three directions, playing the role of leader, slave, and ally to expose the faux allies, save the Missionaries, and return to Diut.

Regarding genre, *Survivor* is a captivity narrative. Traditionally, captivity narratives are first-person accounts written by people who report on their experiences as abductees of Indigenous individuals. In the captivity narrative, the author relates their trials of captivity, escape, rescue, and/or assimilation into the Indigenous community. Captivity narratives are usually stories of people captured by enemies whom the captive considers uncivilized or whose beliefs and customs they oppose, and the captivity takes a narrator away from the social support structures of family, home, language, law, and culture, and often replaces these with a new family, social order, and authority figures.[48] However, what we tend to understand as the captivity narrative gets repackaged as the captivity myth. The captivity myth becomes bound within the ideology of the frontier myth, which is "central to a specifically American ideology and identity, configured as white and Christian in opposition to Indian and savage, and it figures in a large number of different cultural and political contexts throughout American history."[49] Yet, Christopher Castiglia differentiates between the captivity myth and the captivity narrative. "In the majority of captivity narratives," Castiglia writes, "editors obscure and revise the captive's story in order to strengthen flagging religious devotion, to justify westward expansion and the extermination of Indians, and to create the illusion of a stable and paternal nation."[50] In editing these captivity narratives to "create the illusion of a stable and paternal nation," the editors offer a captivity myth rooted in the "frontier myth," that positions the Indigenous captors as savages and the captive women as helpless.[51] But white women's captivity narratives present the captive women "as cunning, physically fit . . . and willing to revise their racial, gender, and national identifications"[52]

An initial reading of *Survivor* positions Alanna as a captive of the Tehkohn. After fleeing from Earth with her adoptive parents and becoming allies with the Garkohn community, Alanna is captured by the Tehkohn and kept in captivity for two years. After enduring a five-day detox from her meklah addiction, Alanna assimilates into Tehkohn culture. She works alongside them, trains as a fighter, learns their language, marries their leader, and bears his child. Alanna legally adopts the Tehkohn's values and customs. Though they do capture her, they also expose the Garkohn for their dishonesty and their meklah addiction. Jules and the other Missionaries interpret Alanna's captivity through the lens of the captivity myth. They express surprise that the Tehkohn can read, write, and practice medicine. Yet, Alanna's own recollections of her captivity among the Tehkohn are in alignment with Castiglia's findings: Alanna's time with the Tehkohn proves to be valuable; she is indeed cunning, physically fit, and more than willing to adopt the customs and culture of the Tehkohn. She is made a

Hunter, and she is considered an equal among the Tehkohn, and in doing so, she is—like many writers of historical captivity narratives—afforded the opportunity to "challenge white American patriarchy" and "[escape] the gender constraints" of Missionary culture.[53] But Alanna was challenging Missionary patriarchy long before she was first taken by the Tehkohn. When adopted on Earth, Alanna was required to accept the Missionaries' belief system in exchange for food, protection, and shelter. But her acceptance was tenuous. She undermined patriarchal Missionary laws by having sexual relations with Missionary boys. As one scholar notes, Alanna's sexuality is "predicated on internal referents" or "terms she defines and controls for herself."[54] Refusing to allow the Missionaries' "prohibition on premarital sex inhibit her expression of her sexuality," Alanna adopts a "healthy view of herself and her body," and decides on her own terms to explore sexually.[55] Part of this exploration lies in her refusal to continue sexual interactions with Missionary men who feigned indifference and contempt for Alanna because she was, by Missionary custom, no longer "pure": "I had shared pleasure with some of them. I was guilty of sin, but somehow, they were all still innocent."[56] Although Alanna's captivity among the Tehkohn grants her a place of prestige as a Hunter and as Diut's wife, the captivity itself is *not* responsible for her being free to challenge white patriarchal norms. She was already challenging and undermining these norms through her sexual politics long before her capture by the Tehkohn.

Survivor takes a surprising tone if we understand the Missionaries as Alanna's captors because the captivity myth becomes a captivity nightmare for Alanna. On Earth, Alanna survives outside of an established community with her parents, and the Missionaries separate Alanna from that life, one where she is described as a "wild human."[57] Readers witness Alanna being taken away from the social support structures of family, home, language, law, and culture and watch that be replaced with a new family, social order, and authority figures. Jules cares for Alanna after she is shot by one of his guards, marking the initial point of separation from the family and home she has known. Jules and Neila envision Alanna as a replacement child for their deceased children. They put her through a re-education or civilizing conversion. In exchange for food, shelter, protection, and security, she must accommodate their beliefs, effectively replacing her "wild human" ways with their law and culture. Alanna's captivity among the Missionaries ends abruptly. After she has helped the Missionaries free themselves from the Garkohn, Alanna reveals to her adoptive father that she has borne a Tehkohn child and married a Tehkohn male. He punches her in response. When Jules strikes Alanna, he releases her from her captivity. His response dissolves the bond because Alanna is no longer a person Jules recognizes. She can no longer take their mission and spread it to the world because, in Jules's eyes, she has defiled the Sacred Image and is no longer worthy of the mission, his love, or his parental protection.

In allowing Alanna to tell her own story without editorial remarks or framers, Butler rejects the paternalism inherent in the captivity myth and offers a critique of Christian fundamentalism. Alanna's story does more than share her growth and development in the Tehkohn community; it exposes The Missionaries' deeply ingrained stereotypes and prejudices, including that the Kohn species is unintelligent, morally inferior, and prone to violence. The Missionaries describe them as "animals without spiritual beliefs" and as "higher than apes, but lower than true humans who had been made in the image of God."[58] When a Missionary doctor learns that Tehkohn can read, his disbelief is apparent: "Now you're saying they read and write as well as practice medicine . . . It's impossible. They couldn't . . ."[59] The Missionary men held onto the belief that Missionary women were vulnerable and susceptible to rape by the Garkohn. However, when Jules is presented with the possibility that Missionary men and boys are sexually attracted to Garkohn women, he chalks it up to it only being a select few, the "same ones we would have seen looking at goats and female guard dogs back on Earth."[60] When presented with the possibility that Missionary men may rape Garkohn women, Jules matter-of-factly responds, "They won't. At least not without a lot of co-operation from those bull women. And if a Garkohn woman does co-operate, what's she got to complain about."[61] The sexual politics held by the Missionaries—those that vilify the Garkohn and absolve Missionary men of any wrongdoing—are products of their human prejudices and Missionary background that they transported from Earth to a new planet in space. The Missionaries' prejudiced and facile thinking causes them to underestimate the Garkohn who offer the Missionaries a meklah fruit. The Missionaries accept it, making it part of their daily diet, not knowing that the fruit is addictive and withdrawal from it is often deadly. The Missionaries' refusal to believe that the Garkohn are intelligent is to their detriment. Despite the Garkohn's apparent intentions to treat the Missionaries as equals, The Missionaries' Christian-cloaked bigotry causes them to underestimate them. As one scholar puts it, "the Missionaries' prejudiced assumptions about the Kohn as well as their ignorance about their environment prove to be detrimental to the Missionary settlement and mission."[62]

Butler's decision to use the meklah fruit becomes "an ironic allusion to the biblical Garden of Eden."[63] Meklah symbolizes the forbidden fruit, and according to one scholar, "The act of eating meklah marks the beginning of the Missionaries' 'Fall' from Edenic innocence."[64] If the Missionaries represent the fallen Adam and Eve (and the fall of humanity), the Garkohn leader

Natahk represents the deceiving serpent, and the Tehkohn (Alanna included) are the salvific figures. Alanna and Diut's salvific role after exposing and saving the Missionaries from the Garkohn is predicated on Alanna and Diut's positioning as the new Adam and Eve. Diut is a Hao, a leader of his tribe, and their reproductive numbers have dwindled. After Diut and Alanna discover that she is pregnant with his child, their discovery opens the possibility of survival for both their species. Alanna and Diut seem to be destined to create a new world. Of course, when Diut reveals that Natahk has already begun his own breeding program with the captured Missionaries, he proposes an offer to Jules: we will help you escape addiction and forced breeding, but in exchange, they must choose to mate with the Garkohn.

Survivor is thematically conversant with its sister novels of the 1970s and the remainder of Butler's work, but Butler disavowed this novel. At the time of this writing, it remains out of print. "When I was young, a lot of people wrote about going to another world and finding either little green men or little brown men, and they were always less in some way," Butler begins. "People ask me why I don't like *Survivor*, my third novel. And it's because it feels a little bit like that. Some humans go up to another world, and immediately begin mating with the aliens and having children with them."[65] Butler sold *Survivor* because she needed the money; it funded her trip to Maryland, which became the backdrop for *Kindred*, one of her most widely read novels. Though Butler was unconvinced of *Survivor*'s merit, the novel's implicit questions, *What does it mean to survive?* and *What does it cost to survive?* are undercurrents that ripple from "Childfinder," *Patternmaster*, and *Mind of My Mind* and ripple throughout *Kindred*.

Kindred

Kindred is Butler's longest-running in-print novel. A blend of historical fiction, neo-slave narrative, fantasy, and romance, this novel is arguably her most popular. Taking place in antebellum Maryland and 1976 California, *Kindred* is written from the perspective of Dana Franklin, a twenty-six-year-old Black woman. Dana time travels from California in the mid-1970s back to antebellum Maryland six times. The goal? Saving her white slave-owning ancestor, Rufus Weylin, from several near-death experiences until her several times removed grandmother, named Hagar, is born to Alice Greenwood, Dana's nineteenth-century doppelganger and ancestor. The novel is divided into several sections: "Prologue," "The River," "The Fire," "The Fall," "The Fight," "The Storm," "The Rope," and "Epilogue." Each time Dana is drawn back to the past, her stay gets longer and grows more dangerous. The reader and Dana wonder if she will ever return home to California permanently. Yet the prologue's ominous opening line, "I lost an arm on my last trip home," positions Dana as a woman who survives something, but the how is the mystery readers turn the pages to discover.[66]

Explaining that she wrote *Kindred* in response to the contempt she witnessed for enslaved Black people by other Black people, Butler shared in 1988 that the novel "grew out of something I heard when I was in college, during the mid-1960s."[67]

> I was a member of a black student union, along with this guy who had been interested in black history before it became fashionable. He was considered quite knowledgeable, but his attitude about slavery was very much like the attitude I had when I was thirteen—that is, he felt that the older generation should have rebelled. He once commented, 'I wish I could kill off all these old people who have been holding us back for so long, but I can't because I would have to start with my own parents.' [. . .] In *Kindred*, I wanted to take somebody with this guy's upbringing . . . and put him in the antebellum South to see how well he stood up.[68]

Butler recalls this incident in at least six interviews spanning from 1988 to 2004.[69] Butler's repeated return to it shows how the incident had a profound impact on her; it left an indelible mark on her. She had to write about it. The disdain this person expressed for older Black people was what Butler perceived as part of a larger set of belief systems that were rooted in the liberation movements of the 1960s and 1970s. Scholar Sarah Wood notes that *Kindred* should be read as Butler's "response to the ideological disparities" of this time.[70] In fact, the novel's contemporary setting in California is likely no accident. While it is true that Butler sets much of her work on the West Coast, typically California, as she does with *Mind of My Mind*, *Kindred*'s contemporary setting in California is arguably a signpost to it as the birth state of the Black Panther Party.

Perhaps considering this signposting, scholars have begun discussing *Kindred* as conversant with Black Nationalist Discourse. Philip Miletic observes that one key aspect of the discourse that *Kindred* rejects is Afrocentric Ahistory. Afrocentric ahistory is defined as the centering of African traditions while removing, rejecting, or abandoning any connection with the slavery past and white people.[71] James Smethhurst writes that Black Arts practitioners viewed Africa as an "alternative to history" and a means of "return[ing] to a cultural wholeness."[72] Larry Neal's 1968 essay "The Black Arts Movement," described the past "with all of its painful memories" as the "enemy of the revolutionary."[73] Conversely, Butler views the past as necessary for progress and rejects ideas of cultural wholeness. Butler's choice to allow Dana to return as an amputee speaks to this rejection of Afrocentric ahistory: "I couldn't really let her come all the way back," she tells writer Randall Keenan. "I couldn't let her return to what she was, I couldn't let her come back whole and that, I think, really symbolizes her not coming back whole. Antebellum slavery didn't leave people quite whole."[74] Butler also does not allow Dana to embrace this Afrocentric ahistory. Dana embraces her white ancestor, Rufus; she continues to research her family history even in the novel's epilogue, which positions her as an archeologist or anthropologist. Instead of viewing her knowledge of the past as an enemy and instead of seeking to divest herself from the past, Dana keeps searching to unearth the mysteries of the past so she can understand and reconcile that past with her present and future. Through Butler's skillful writing, she positions *Kindred* as a text that celebrates and necessitates communion with the past instead of destruction and escape from the past.

A common characteristic of Black liberation movements in the 1960s and 1970s was that Black women should take on a maternal role. "The role of the black woman in the black liberation struggle is an important one and cannot be forgotten," begins Robert Staples. He continues, "From her womb have come the revolutionary warriors of our time."[75] Dana's characterization in *Kindred* functions to dismantle these sexist belief systems through her mode of dress, her education, and her propensity for being a fighter. Dana's pants-wearing gets her mistaken for a man. As one scholar observes, "Although the pants are a subtle detail, the multiple mistaken references to Dana's gender that occur *repeatedly*" in *Kindred* are indicative of Butler's subversion of gender roles by questioning the "1960s' and '70s' constructions of black womanhood" as silent, submissive, weak birthers of Black revolutionaries.[76] One character makes Dana a dress remarking, "I'm sick of seeing you in them pants [. . .] Least you look like a woman when your man comes for you."[77] In addition to her androgynous appearance, Dana is educated; she teaches Nigel, an enslaved child to read, and she even teaches Rufus, the white enslaver's son, to read. While education may position Dana in a traditionally maternal role, it's the fact that she is *not* supposed to be teaching Nigel to read and that she hopes to instill certain values in Rufus. She teaches, yes, but she does so subversively. This resistance positions her as a covert operative who seeks to chip away at the institution of enslavement bit by bit. Additionally, Dana engages in several forms of active resistance. She disarms a patroller, runs away from the Weylin plantation, attempts suicide, and murders Rufus instead of letting him rape her. All of these reject the belief that Black women are passive, weak, and submissive; in fact, Dana embodies a warrior, "challenging the literary constructions of women as mothers and procreators of the black revolution and men as warriors and protectors of black women."[78]

Compared to "Childfinder," *Kindred* seems more hesitant to embrace Black Nationalist principles, and Butler's shift away from trying to write in a particular mold from the "Childfinder" to *Kindred* results from maturity and confidence. Though she wrote "Childfinder" in 1970, she had yet to publish her work, but by the time *Kindred* was published, she was well on her way to becoming a powerhouse in science fiction. The confidence boost her early publications gave her, coupled with her determination to rebut a college classmate's disdain for enslaved Black people, seem to solidify her resolve to write on her own terms, infusion her science fiction with a range of narrative practices, genres, and foci.[79]

"Near of Kin"

If "Crossover" straddles the lines between realism and gothic fiction, the decade's final story, "Near of Kin," seems firmly rooted in a possible (if frowned upon) reality. After finding out a shocking secret, an abandoned and resentful daughter relearns what kin means to her. "Near of Kin" tells the story of an unnamed college-aged girl and her uncle, Stephen, as they go through the belongings of their late mother and sister. The story opens *in media res* with Stephen's emphatic "She wanted you," reassuring his niece that her now-deceased mother did want her as a child.[80] Readers enter in the middle of a conversation, one where the daughter confides in her uncle, expressing her doubt, resentment, and anger at her mother's abandonment and their estranged relationship. Her mother, Barbara, sent her to be raised by her grandmother. As the daughter goes through her mother's belongings, Stephen tries to assure her that her mother did what was best for her, and he tries to get her to accept the money left to her in the will.

As the dialogue fades into the background, the daughter's internal monologue reveals that though she never connected with her mother, she often felt a kinship with her uncle. "He had always been a friend as well as a relative," she thinks, "my mother's five-years-older brother, and the only relative other than my grandmother who'd ever paid more than passing attention to me."[81] This line, coupled with the daughter's suggestion to her mother that she was adopted, is at the heart of the daughter's resentment toward her mother. She felt abandoned and isolated from her mother, yet she felt a belonging with her uncle. "He treated me like a little adult," she reminds herself.[82] But her fear of abandonment returns: "What would he do now? Leave? Would I lose him, too?"[83] The emphasis on "too" reminds us that this story is as much about a complex mother-daughter relationship as it is about a girl finding her way to belonging, family, acceptance, and kin.

In the story's afterword, Butler calls "Near of Kin" a "sympathetic story of incest,"[84] yet the story's surprising reveal—that siblings Barbara and Stephen created a love child—is second to the story's central conflict: their daughter's navigation of the resentment and abandonment created by her mother and her fear of being abandoned by her uncle-father once she shatters the illusion that she is unaware of her biological feather. This fear of abandonment is palpable, and her desire for validation is connected to that. Her uncle-father twice insists, "She wanted you,"[85] and questions how long she will remain invested in the resentment, but the daughter simply wants her feelings validated. Part of that validation comes from Stephen acknowledging himself as her father because the daughter's patriarchal affiliation is a secret that lurks between the lines of the story, in a grandmother–mother–daughter photograph, and stretches over twenty-two years. The abandonment, however, is not limited to the daughter. Barbara is abandoned by her husband, who "had found someone else—someone who had borne him a live child instead of having a miscarriage."[86] Barbara's abandonment and grief seek solace with her brother. "She came to me," Stephen tells his daughter-niece, "when he left—came to talk, to cry, to work out some of her feelings . . . We loved each other . . . As it was, we were afraid when she realized she was pregnant, but she wanted you."[87]

The daughter's abandonment is further symbolized by her namelessness. The absence of a name, especially when both of her parents are named, indicates that the daughter does not have a fully formed identity. It is no accident that the daughter's search for rootedness—for kin—happens as she is looking through boxes of her mother's paperwork. The daughter is connected to her mother's paperwork four times in the story. "At my feet were papers stuffed into a large cardboard lettuce box," she first observes, "papers loose and dog-eared, flat and enveloped, important and trivial, all jumbled together."[88] Second, she recalls that she "stared at the box on the floor. The bottom of it had broken with the weight of the papers when I took it from my mother's closet."[89] As the story progresses, she "fingered a few of the dog-eared papers in the box" and "pressed [her] fingers nervously into the jumble of paper."[90] The papers move from being "at her feet" and "on the floor," lying passive and uninvolved, to being actively engaged as they are "fingered" and "pressed." These papers are a repository of information about her mother's life. The daughter's move from passive to active engagement with the remnants of her mother's life coincides with her active intention to confirm what she suspects to be true: that her uncle is also her father. As papers and documentation are archival materials, the paperwork is linked to the daughter's lack of name. The daughter initially only passively engages in that history, that archived material, but once she actively engages it, rifles through papers, and confirms what she suspects to be true, she is validated and in the process of forming and shaping her own identity. She remains nameless, but she is no longer a nameless void. The story ends on a hopeful note: The daughter will return to school, and with the knowledge of who her father is, she will accept the money in her mother's will and live her life.

Breaking Through . . .

By the end of the decade, Butler is poised to become a powerhouse in science fiction. Despite the seemingly different storylines and purpose, the thread of survival undergirds much of this decade's fiction. In 1978, she reflected on the moral compass of twelve-year-olds—a crucial developmental stage before we learn to think critically for ourselves. She wondered if the inner twelve-year-old must adapt or die or if they will be replaced by an inner adult equipped to navigate the world as it is, not as in its idealized form. This wondering becomes central to her fiction in the 1980s. While the theme of adapt or die is apparent in her work from this decade, it becomes even more pronounced—almost dire—in her writings of the 1980s and beyond. Moving from her 1970s fiction toward a new decade, she anticipates her most successful phase. Despite the challenges, she adapts and crafts scenarios for characters who, like our childhood moral understandings, must either adapt—or face consequences.

CHAPTER 3

The 1980s
Perfecting Her "Adapt or Die" Refrain

By all accounts, the 1980s was a successful decade for Butler. She published five novels and three short stories, several of which were award-winners. She received the James Tiptree Award for *Clay's Ark* (1984), the Hugo Award for "Speech Sounds" (1983), and the Nebula Award for "Bloodchild" (1984). Anyone would consider such literary output and recognition a success. Butler did not. The failed publication of *Blindsight*, a novel, and *Black Futures*, which was to be her debut as an editor of an anthology of Black Science Fiction stories, weighed heavily on her. So did the poverty she thought she was escaping. The 1980s finds her back in the habit of calculating how much money she can possibly make from novels and stories she has completed, though the preoccupation does not appear as desperate as it did in her journals a decade or more prior. Perhaps this is because this time she has money makers in hand, that she has written salable work. The uncertainty of when she is getting paid—rather than having no content to sell—is what drives her concern.

It is not just publication politics and poverty that cloud the decade. It is death. Death shrouds her. She described 1982 as a long year, and in a December 31, 1982, journal entry, she recalled the deaths of a friend, an uncle, a friend's father, another friend's mother, and platonic friendships. And the near-death by suicide of another friend. As she watched her close friend Phyllis die from cancer, she was writing *Clay's Ark*, and she "shared chapters with the friend with the bleak sense that she might not live to see the book completed."[1] Unsurprisingly, these deaths impacted her writing. By 1986, Butler is writing in her journals that she has not "done anything worth doing for quite a while,"[2] which is perplexing because, by 1986, *Wild Seed*, "Speech Sounds,"

Clay's Ark, and "Bloodchild" are published, and the very next year both "The Evening and the Morning and the Night" and *Dawn* will be released. Despite the external validation of her work, she did not consider this decade a success. She even considered writing under a pen name towards the end of the decade in hopes that a pseudonym would free her from her "own notions of who OEB is and what OEB does."[3]

And who exactly was she? A woman deeply concerned with humanity's propensity for survival, or, more accurately, for its potential for destruction. "How can we make ourselves a more survivable species?"[4] is the question driving much of her work throughout this decade, where she explores and perfects what I call her "adapt or die" refrain. In this era, her characters, humans, enhanced humans, and aliens alike face life-changing—and in some cases life-ending—scenarios. In this decade, she challenges readers to confront their discomfort, biases, and entrenched ways of thinking and holds a mirror up for us. Do we recognize elements of our stubbornness in certain characters who are unwilling to embrace change? Do we see echoes of our own hubris in those who meet their downfall? Or are we among those who welcome transformation?

Wild Seed

Wild Seed was Butler's reward for writing *Kindred*, which she described as depressing to research and write. Perhaps that is why *Wild Seed* explores a torrid, centuries-long affair between two immortal Africans, Doro and Anyanwu. Doro, a spirit who takes over other people's bodies like a parasite, kills anyone who interferes with his plan to genetically engineer telepaths through selective breeding. Anyanwu, a shape-shifting woman able to heal herself and others, appears to be the key ingredient to making Doro's breeding project a success. The central conflict? Anyanwu learns she must adapt to Doro's reprehensible lifestyle not just to save herself and her children but also to save Doro from himself. But he resists. By the novel's end, Doro has a choice to make. Will he recognize his humanity and need for Anyanwu and save her, himself, and the future he desires in the process? Or will he refuse to adapt and watch someone he loves die?

To understand *Wild Seed*, careful consideration of it as revisionist biblical text is necessary. *Wild Seed* is divided into three sections—"Covenant 1690," "Lot's Children 1741," and "Canaan 1840"—making it a model of the key points in the Genesis narrative of the Old Testament. Two schools of thought emerge regarding which Genesis narrative *Wild Seed* is modeled on. For John R. Pfeiffer and Ingrid Thaler, "Covenant" refers to the relationship established between God and Abram, found in Genesis 12.[5] I maintain that the

Covenant section refers to the covenant God establishes with Hagar beginning in Genesis chapter 16, verse 9—an important verse to note since the "Covenant" section begins in the year 1690. Scholars agree that "Lot's Children" refers to the destruction of Sodom and Gomorrah in Genesis 19 and the need for the survival of God's people, and "Canaan" refers to the land promised to Abram by God which extends to his son, Isaac, his grandson, Jacob, and their descendants.[6]

Whether we interpret the covenant established between Doro and Anyanwu as representative of the covenant between God and Abram or between God and Hagar, one fact remains: both covenants rely on sexual exploitation, and much of *Wild Seed* follows Anyanwu's attempts to negotiate, resist, and finally adapt to Doro's sexual exploitation of her. Doro's goal is to create an immortal family and to extend himself into the future but for Anyanwu, his ethics and methods of ensuring that future are questionable and reprehensible. "Let me give you children who will live!"[7] is Doro's promise to Anyanwu when they first meet in 1690, but Anyanwu soon learns his promise is tainted with deception and trickery that ends in Anyanwu's sexual exploitation and enslavement. Anyanwu agrees to leave her homeland, taking Doro on as her husband. Together, they board a ship from Africa to the Americas (a nod to the Middle Passage), where Doro introduces Anyanwu to Isaac, his son. Upon their arrival at Doro's Wheatley settlement in New York, he reveals his plan: Anyanwu will marry Isaac, bear the children Doro demands, or she will die. "You have left your village . . . You are here where I rule . . . You will obey," he tells her.[8] She initially resists, reshaping herself internally to "avoid giving any children at all, to avoid being used."[9] Anyanwu, like so many enslaved Black women, including Harriet Jacobs, took measures to resist sexual exploitation.[10] Such resistance did not occur by happenstance. Angela Davis, Dorothy Roberts, and Deborah Gray White[11] note that as a mode of resistance, enslaved Black women would use other methods of birth control or abortion. Some committed infanticide to "[spare] their children the yoke of slavery,"[12] and others harmed themselves to prevent them from bearing children for their enslavers.

For the sake of her own life and the lives of her children, Anyanwu resigns herself to the situation with the one-day hope of escape. She reverses her self-sterilization and takes Isaac as her mate. She chooses to adapt rather than die or be responsible for her children's deaths. Yet the same-day deaths of her daughter, Nweke, and her husband, Isaac, prompt her to flee and escape Doro for ninety-nine years. Anyanwu's ability to adapt to her new circumstances and her various forms of resistance echo the experiences of enslaved Black women in the Americas. Anyanwu's concessions are part of a lineage of Black feminist resistance strategies where Black women "made a way out of no way" and navigated circumstances, negotiated situations, and made choices that were best for them and their livelihoods. Some enslaved Black women filed lawsuits to emancipate themselves, and others "chose to cause harm and stress to their enslavers," like one woman who killed the master's daughter in her sleep.[13] Some bided their time and ran away; others bided their time and participated in uprisings. Enslaved Black women, like Anyanwu, made choices that may seem illusory to us twenty-first-century readers, but their choices shed light on Black women's consistent ability to adapt to new circumstances and survive them.

After ninety-nine years in hiding, Doro finds Anyanwu living on a New Orleans plantation under an assumed name, and their reunion becomes Doro's moment of truth: he must decide whether he will adapt or die. To Doro's surprise, Anyanwu has begun her own breeding project. Unlike Doro's forced couplings, Anyanwu allows couples to pair together of their own volition, and they birth children with special abilities. Doro's arrival disrupts Anyanwu's tranquil, ethical lifestyle. He arrives to gather her human descendants and begins forcing them to mate with people of his own. One of Doro's people, Joseph, attempts to rape Anyanwu's daughter and successfully kills her son. Anyanwu kills him. After more than a century of Doro's countless abuses, conceding to his demands, and adapting to his way of living, killing, and existing, Anyanwu shifts the dynamic and forces Doro into the position he has placed her in during their time together: adapt or die. "Don't say no to me anymore" is her response when he denies her request that he fulfill the covenant he established with her 150 years prior.[14] Here, the narrative shifts. Throughout the novel's first two sections, Anyanwu begged for her freedom; she verbally defied Doro and sought to act contrary to his will. Now, Anyanwu decides to die by suicide. She maintains an eloquent silence, which is "an active means chosen by the speaker to communicate [their] message."[15] In other words, sometimes it is "those who [are in] control who remain silent."[16] Doro's cries, "Anyanwu, you must not leave me!" and the desperate "Anyanwu!" are met with silence.[17] She remains hushed and "pull[s] back the blanket and sheet and [lies] down." Doro continues, "'Please,' he said, not hearing himself any longer. 'Please, Anyanwu. Listen.'"[18] The narrative shift in voice and voicelessness, speaking and silence, signifies a pivotal power transferal. Throughout their time together, Anyanwu exhausted her voice asking Doro for things—to spare his breeders from death, not to force her to have intercourse with relatives. Her voice rendered her powerless. However, this time, her eloquent silence speaks volumes and convicts Doro. He was "like a palsied old man" whose "face [was] wet with perspiration" as he watched her prepare to die.[19] In a reversal of the power dynamics between the two, Anyanwu speaks through her silence; she silently demands and receives what she longed for: freedom for herself and her children. Through her silent actions—or "weapons of the weak"[20]—Anyanwu's resistance is an exercise of power; she forces Doro to fulfill the covenant he first established and forces Doro to make a choice: adapt and live with Anyanwu or refuse and live a life analogous to death without Anyanwu.

The silent standoff ends with new life. Doro awakens and finds himself in the "comfort of her arms, [with] the warmth of her body next to him."[21] The image of Doro awakening into the embrace of Anyanwu is strikingly maternal. Like a motherly figure, she protects Doro from the eternal pain her suicide surely would have caused him. Anyanwu's embrace is an allusion to Michelangelo's Pieta—a marble statue in the Roman Basilica depicting Mary cradling a dead Jesus. Anyanwu's cradling of a reborn, resurrected Doro signals his recognition of his humanity and his commitment to adapting, changing, and growing—for his sake and hers. Doro's tears and perspiration function as his baptism, metaphorical death, and ultimate resurrection, an image that is the epitome of adaptation and transformation and ends in a tacit negotiation of peace and partnership. No longer is Anyanwu his broodmare. She secures his promise that he will not discard and murder those who have done nothing but serve him, and because of his concession, she will not leave him.

That the novel ends with Doro's adaptation is significant given the period in which Butler was writing it. Historians note that relationships between Black men and Black women were strained, largely because of the heterocentric, patriarchal ideals that permeated the Black Liberation Movements of the 1960s and 1970s. Doro's paternalism and desire for an empire that exploits Anyanwu and countless others become renegotiated at the novel's end. Such an ending seems to suggest that for positive progress forward, the necessity for concession and adaptation is not the responsibility of women to bear alone. If the visual image of Anyanwu and Doro embracing each other is not evidence enough, the novel's epilogue confirms that their mutual adaptation to each other, new surroundings, and new circumstances is a necessary and life-long project. "When it became clear that within a few years that there would be a war between the Northern and Southern states," the epilogue reveals, "she chose to move her people to California."[22] Doro follows. Though Anyanwu's decision to expand westward to California is done with the safety and longevity of her people in mind, it also functions as a nod to westward expansion and manifest destiny. Such an end is fitting because *Wild Seed* is the first chronological book of the Patternist Series and Butler's remaining works of the decade echo this kind of forward movement, this expansion through adaptation.

"Speech Sounds"

The adapt-or-die refrain that subtly emerges in *Wild Seed* becomes more prominent in "Speech Sounds," and the refrain emerges in the context of disability. Is it because Butler herself had a disability? Perhaps. "I'm a bit dyslexic." Butler shares this in several interviews over the course of her career. She explains how she reads slowly, loves audiotapes, and fears driving because of her dyslexia. However, "Not at all," is Butler's response when asked if her story "Speech Sounds" has anything to do with her dyslexia. Why not? "[B]ecause dyslexia hasn't really prevented me from doing anything I've wanted to do, except drive," she continues. "I can read, for example, but I can't read fast. I never had a problem reading because I was lucky enough to be taught before I got into school by my mother and grandmother."[23] Although Butler's dyslexia seems not to be a factor in her decision to write "Speech Sounds," she did adapt her lifestyle to persist through her dyslexia. Disability Studies scholar Sami Schalk convincingly argues that "Butler's lived experiences of disability throughout her life influenced her research on and representation of disability throughout her career."[24] Theri Pickens, another Disability Studies scholar, identifies the importance of "Situating disability at or near the center of Butler's work (alongside race and gender)" noting that to do so "lays bare how attention to these categories of analysis shifts the conversation about the content of Butler's work."[25] "Speech Sounds" explores disability as more than a convenient plot device; it becomes another way Butler explores her adapt-or-die refrain.

"Speech Sounds" is a dystopian short story, complete with fuel shortages, unreliable public transportation, the absence of traditional currency, and the absence of a social structuring authority like a government. In fact, "Law and order were nothing—not even words any longer."[26] Written in the third person, the story opens in media res, with the protagonist, Valerie Rye, riding a bus and witnessing a fight because the two men cannot communicate meaningfully. "Speech Sounds" is set during the aftermath of a pandemic, where an unexplained "stroke-like" illness led to a mass disabling event, including language loss, paralysis, intellectual impairment, and death. The story investigates communication and language as technologies and meditates on what happens if and when communication—speech, writing, reading—ceases to exist. Readers witness the characters becoming less human, with the narrator noting that the illness "had cut even the living off from one another."[27] By the story's end, readers learn that Rye and the two orphaned children can speak, her short-term sexual partner, Obsidian, can read and write, and most people can read symbols, like the "pasted old magazine pictures"[28] that show items that are accepted as bus fare, and hand gestures. Early on, the story reveals humanity's willingness to adapt. The use of symbols, pictographs, and hand gestures as replacements for their traditional forms of communication indicates that attempts to adapt and move forward—even without a centralized government—are happening.

Despite these minor attempts at adapting to new circumstances, these attempts at forward progress are buttressed by humans' propensity toward violence. The words, "There was trouble aboard the Washington Boulevard bus," open the story.[29] Rye witnesses a fight between two men on the bus. Significantly, the violence Rye witnesses is part of Butler's lived experience. She once witnessed a fight on the Washington Boulevard bus, describing it as "short and bloody" and one that left her "more depressed than ever" and "hating the whole hopeless, stupid business and wondering whether the human species would ever grow up enough to learn to communicate without using fists of one kind or another."[30] That fight and that hopelessness became the basis for "Speech Sounds." Butler's concern about the state of the world was palpable, and she truly wondered if we humans would adapt or die. However, the story's bus setting is important not just because it was part of Butler's lived experience. The bus symbolizes forward movement and progress. And when the bus is stalled by several forms of violence, Butler's message reverberates: adapt or die. Two men riding on the bus with limited and different forms of communication begin a fight that causes the bus driver to pull over. Rye speculates that the bus driver is waiting for the fight to blow over so he can continue his route. The driver plans to adapt to the situation. But Obsidian, a man who is described as wearing a "Los Angeles Police Department uniform complete with baton and service revolver," has other plans.[31] He throws a gas canister into the bus to subdue the passengers who were responsible for the "trouble aboard the Washington Boulevard bus."[32] Instead of adapting to the situation, Obsidian causes more harm. He stops the fight, but his action leaves passengers scrambling off the bus, "choking and weeping."[33] It also disrupts the bus driver's route and impacts his livelihood because, as Rye thinks, "if his bus did not run, he did not eat."[34] Obsidian exists as an agent of chaos under the guise of being helpful, and though the story focuses on Rye's internal thoughts, Obsidian becomes our clearest cautionary example. Towards the end of the story, Obsidian sees a woman being pursued by a man wielding a boning knife. Obsidian approaches them both, attempting to ward off the woman's attacker, and fails. The man stabs the woman, and Obsidian shoots the man. The man, thought to be dead, grabs Obsidian's gun and shoots him in the head.

The orchestrators of violence in this story are all men: the two men fighting on the bus, the bus driver, Obsidian, and an unnamed male pursuant. Each man has a communication impairment because of the mass-disabling event, so they exert their masculinity to exert and express their dominance, control, or superiority over others to compensate for their disability. The bus driver can access a bus to provide public transportation for a fee. The two men on the bus have their strength, and their brawl is an expression of their frustration and masculine prowess. Obsidian has the conferred power and privilege of an LAPD uniform, including its baton and firearm. We can only presume that the unnamed male pursuer who kills his intimate partner and leaves two children as witnesses exerts the privilege of being male. If, as masculinity theorist Elizabeth Fish Hatfield remarks, "men's multiple performed masculinities grapple for power a long a continuum,"[35] then in a world that requires adaptation and change in the face of an illness that modifies or disrupts long taken-for-granted speech patterns, these men rely on violence to compensate for their disability. Violence becomes their only means of grasping at power—whether economic power like the bus driver, for bragging rights like the two bus fighters, for social control like Obsidian, or for the mantle of manhood like the unnamed male pursuer. Though the men have adapted to their change in speech patterns, they all hold on to old ways of thinking, many of which result in violence and, in two cases, death. Obsidian's death by gun violence after he fails to save another woman from a male pursuer seems to suggest that if a society is to move forward, there is no space for expressions of hegemonic masculinities, including violence or unsanctioned policing. His LAPD uniform is more than a defunct relic of law and order. It symbolizes his refusal to adapt to new ways of life and release the old. Obsidian's death and the knife wielder's death both offer readers a grisly warning: adapt or die. Their commitment to hegemonic masculinities—Obsidian's as a warrior, protector, and enforcer, and the knife-wielder as apparent batterer and abuser—ultimately gets them killed. Their demise suggests such old ways of thinking and living are not viable for a livable way forward.

Though "Speech Sounds" warns about failures to adapt and reject hegemonic masculinity and violence, the story offers hope. Significantly, as one scholar notes, the representation of authority and power in the story is "neither absolute nor phallocentric. Rye also carries a gun and knows how to use it. Rye can maintain control and exert authority when needed."[36] The difference? Rye knows *when* to use a gun to exert control or authority. Through Rye, readers learn that adaptation, pragmatism, and education are the keys to rebuilding society. All the men's violent actions are contrasted by Rye's pragmatic ones. Before the bus driver slams on the brakes to break up the fight on the bus, Rye, familiar with bus drivers' methods, "braced herself."[37] When the bus stopped, Rye was on her feet, off the bus, and though she "intended to wait until the trouble was over," she also wanted protection from a tree "if there was shooting."[38] After Obsidian throws a gas canister onto the bus, Rye "caught an old woman who would have fallen" and "lifted two little children down when they were in danger of being knocked down and trampled" and "caught a thin old man."[39] After the knife-wielding man kills the woman and shoots Obsidian, Rye "shot the wounded man as he was turning the gun on her."[40] Her pragmatism and ability to adapt to various quickly changing situations help prevent as much harm as possible. She prevents the elderly and children from being harmed, and she prevents her own death by acting in self-defense. Significantly, the deaths of Obsidian, the unnamed woman, and the knife-wielding man are contrasted against Rye's survival and her discovery of two children who can speak—just like she can. In an instant, her world seems to shift. Rye muses that she is both protector and teacher and instead of protecting only herself, she concludes that she will "keep them alive."[41] The short story ends on a hopeful note with the possible creation of a haven that is pushed forward by a woman who, in the span of a single day, was willing to adapt to her surroundings. And perhaps the story's hopeful ending is foreshadowed by her full name: Valerie Rye. The surname, "Rye," is a "homonym for 'wry,'" Sandra Y. Govan explains, and is "appropriate for her character" but also "fits the meaning of the word (contrary, distorted, twisted) and fits her personality and situation" since her world "has become twisted and distorted."[42] The name Valerie, Govan continues, "derives from the French and suggests valor, courage, bravery, and strength," all things Rye has displayed throughout the story and attributes she will need as a survivor, mentor, teacher, and protector.[43] Ultimately, "Rye will care for the children and guard the future," Gerry Canavan writes, "in the process staving off suicide by living through others."[44]

Clay's Ark and "Bloodchild"

If *Wild Seed* and "Speech Sounds" are ambivalent in executing the adapt or die refrain, *Clay's Ark* and "Bloodchild" are not. *Clay's Ark* is the third chronological book of the Patternist series, offering readers the origin story of the Clayark disease and the Clayark race that become antagonists in *Patternmaster* (1976). Written in the third person point of view and set in the year 2021, *Clay's Ark* is divided into six sections: Physician, P.O.W, Manna, Reunion, Jacob, and Epilogue. Apart from the epilogue, each section is divided into chapters that shift between the past and the present. In the chapters titled "past," readers learn about Eli Doyle, a voyager on a space shuttle and the main disease-carrier of *Clay's Ark*, who returns from an alien planet with the disease and conflicting desires to both spread it and keep it contained. Eli actively fights against and fights for the insatiable need to taste and spread his disease, called the clayark disease organism. We learn that Eli is unable to die by suicide and that the clayark organism has given him an enhanced sense of smell, speed, and strength. Although Eli has a compulsion to spread the disease, he tries to choose only those who would survive his infection. He tries to infect intentionally but selectively by isolating the spread. In the chapters titled "present," readers are introduced to Blake Maslin, a white man, and his biracial twin daughters, Keira and Rane, who are traveling through the desert to fulfill Keira's dying wish: to see her grandparents in Flagstaff, Arizona one last time before she succumbs to leukemia. The Maslins are captured by Eli and his partners, Meda and Ingraham, and taken to Eli's desert settlement where he introduces the Maslins to his family, including the human-animal hybrid children. Eli attempts to explain the clayark disease, selective infection, and the importance of isolation. The Maslins are infected, and Keira, who is living with leukemia, benefits from the clayark organism, which strengthens her and cures her cancer. Despite the evidence around them, Blake cannot fathom being isolated. Violence erupts. An escape is attempted. Rane is captured and killed. Blake temporarily escapes, manages to infect a cross-country truck driver, and suffers fatal wounds. *Clay's Ark* explores the necessity of adapting to change or dying.

Clay's Ark emphasizes the importance of empathy, compassion, and acceptance as necessary for the creation of new worlds and the survival of existing ones. Keira possesses a strong ability to empathize and accept all differences. Keira suffers from leukemia, and it is her own experience with illness and disability that allows her to accept Eli's community, adults and children alike, despite their physical appearance. When Eli first captures Keira and her family, he tries to explain to them that he is still human, "just . . . different."[45] Keira whispers in response, "And sometimes you hurt."[46] This moment of understanding between two people is a hallmark of compassion and empathy. When Keira meets one of Eli's children who has a sphinxlike, cat-like appearance, she responds with kindness, curiosity, and compassion. Keira's response to the appearance-based differences around her emerges from the "ugly reactions" she experienced while walking between her Black mother and white father in public.[47] Keira does more than look beyond surface-level prejudices; she actively participates in the creation of a diverse community by embracing Eli, his people, and their farm community. Regardless of race, gender, physicality, profession, or past transgressions, once they are welcomed onto the farmland with the other infected people, nothing else matters. For instance, Ingraham originally tried to attack and rape Meda during their first encounter. Eli recalls the situation musing, "That was another life . . . We don't care what he did before. He's one of us now."[48] They all look out for each other in a way that no longer exists in this new world Butler creates since, in that world, gated communities separate all people. Those who can afford gated communities (like the Maslins) are protected, and the rest are subject to housing insecurity and violence, leading to the creation of violent groups of people called rat families.

If *Clay's Ark* emphasizes empathy, compassion, and acceptance as necessary, it cautions those who reject the creation of new worlds and cling to old ones. Where Keira is empathetic and embracing of Eli's community and their children, her father and sister are not. Keira's compassion is contrasted with Rane's revulsion: "I can't stand them . . . they're not human."[49] Keira thinks of the clayark children as "beautiful" and "perfect"; Rane describes them as "monsters," compares them to animals, and admits she would be "willing to abort it with a wire coat hanger" all because the child looks different.[50] Rane's anxiety and fear are rooted in her fear of something different and unfamiliar, and this theme is at the heart of the "adapt or die" trope. Rane's admission—that she would abort a child because its appearance would not look *normal* in the way she thinks it should—is partially rooted in her own ableism. Unlike Keira, Rane has never experienced health issues. She derisively calls Eli's people "stick people" and places herself and her definition of normal and healthy above anything different.[51] Her words echo past and present attempts at euthanizing disabled people in utero or allowing them to die because their lives are perceived as less valuable. Rane's ableism is perhaps closely linked to her skin color, upbringing, and "personality resembling [her father's]."[52] She is described as having lighter skin than Keira, was raised in a gated community, and, like her father, refuses to accept and adapt to her new surroundings. When presented with evidence that the disease is medically inexplicable, Blake refuses to accept it. He furthers his resolve to escape and seek medical attention. His hubris and stubbornness make him the catalyst for a worldwide pandemic. He scratches and infects a long-haul trucker and becomes patient zero, responsible for spreading the clayark disease worldwide. Both Rane and Blake are punished for their refusal to adapt. Rane is gang raped and decapitated, and though Blake escapes from his captors (his birthdate of July 4, 1977, foreshadows his inclination toward liberty), he is killed in a hit-and-run. However, such mentalities are not limited to Blake and Rane's. Butler reinforces such mentalities with her characters' names. Badger is the leader of the rat pack family that captures Rane, Keira, and Blake. Sherryl Vint points out that the name "Badger" strengthens the link between the negative traits of animals and humans. This connection is evident when Badger and his pack commit various violent and sexually predatory acts, influenced by their poverty, outcast status, and craving for sadistic pleasure.[53] The physical violence associated with Badger, the epistemic violence associated with Rane, and Blake's violent act of spreading the clayark organism worldwide seal their fates: there's no time to adapt. Instead, they die. Keira survives, and the epilogue ends with her pregnancy. Through Keira, Rane, and Blake, readers are presented with a clear message: the new future has no place for old ways of thinking. If Rane and Blake's fates offer a grisly warning, Keira's pregnancy, relationship, flourishing hair, and health (she is now cancer-free) offer glimmers of hope.

Butler's "adapt or die" messaging continues in her 1984 short story "Bloodchild." The story's opening line, "My last night of childhood began with a visit home," marks it as a coming-of-age story and hints at the speaker's impending transition from child to adult.[54] The central narrative of "Bloodchild" involves Gan, the protagonist, and his relationship with T'Gatoi, a high-ranking Tlic official. The Tlic are an alien race (sometimes described as "caterpillar people"[55]) that allow the humans, called Terran, to live in their community. The Terran are immigrants and refugees from a dying home world on Earth. In exchange for a place to live, the Terran must offer up one of their male children to a Tlic family as a host for Tlic children. The central conflict of "Bloodchild" centers on Gan's loss of innocence, his desire to negotiate the power dynamics between him and T'Gatoi, and his future goal of negotiating transparency in the birthing process for all Terrans.

Gan's transition from childhood to adulthood is a five-step process that first begins with his loss of innocence. After Gan witnesses T'Gatoi perform a Caesarian section on a man named Bram Lomas, he is no longer the same child that he once was. Gan watches as T'Gatoi places her claw "just below the left rib," witnesses Lomas's body's stiffening, and watches as T'Gatoi's claw opens Lomas' abdomen. Gan describes his feelings as a co-conspirator in Lomas's "torture."[56] Gan's exposure to unexpected and traumatic labor and delivery marks his loss of innocence. Gan had never seen a live birth before; T'Gatoi shared with him "diagrams and drawings" as a matter of transparency, but Lomas's stiffening, convulsing body, the inhuman sounds he made as T'Gatoi "lengthened and deepened the cut" were a collision of sensory awareness that Gan was unprepared for.[57]

After witnessing Lomas's labor and delivery, Gan realizes his uncritical acceptance of birthing T'Gatoi's children has been predicated on secrecy and limited disclosure. Gan suggests that his relationship with T'Gatoi is predicated on deception, omission, and manipulation. Gan challenges T'Gatoi to ask him for his consent to bear her children: "No one ever asks us," "You never asked me," and "Ask me, Gatoi." Gan reveals that the Tlic expect Terrans to birth their blood-sucking babies, yet T'Gatoi's only direct responses to Gan's questions are: "[Shall I ask you] for my children's lives?" and "Would you really rather die than bear my young?"[58] After Lomas's delivery, the ongoing dialogue becomes steeped in the power play, with each species trying to maintain its ground. Gan challenges T'Gatoi to consider the possibility that humans are nothing more than breeding stock for the Tlic, and he demands that she ask him to decide if (not when) he wants to harvest babies. Gan ultimately decides to bear T'Gatoi's young, a resolution of his internal conflict that results in a dual act of brotherly love and jealous rage that spares his sister, Xuan Hoa, from alien impregnation, and is also the second step that marks his transition to adulthood.

Gan's third step towards adulthood is his first attempt at getting T'Gatoi to "accept the risk" of having a partner. After agreeing to bear T'Gatoi's young, but before their intercourse, Gan initiates a conversation with T'Gatoi. "'Leave it here!' Gan tells T'Gatoi, referring to the rifle. "If we're not your animals, if these are adult things, accept the risk. There is risk, Gatoi, in dealing with a partner."[59] Gan asks T'Gatoi to allow his family to possess an illegal firearm, a rifle. He uses her own phrasing, "these are adult things," against her. Gan's negotiation suggests that if risks are inherent in the birthing process on his part, then T'Gatoi, and by extension, the Tlic, must be willing to accept some risk to themselves as well. This conversation also demonstrates how his decision to become pregnant indicates his awareness of the power dynamic between himself and T'Gatoi and his attempt to leverage that power to his advantage. Gan witnesses first-hand the risk associated with being pregnant with bloodsucking Tlic grubs, but he accepts that risk on the condition that T'Gatoi accepts the risk of Terran possessing firearms. The fourth step of Gan's transition to adulthood is T'Gatoi's impregnation of him. "I let her push me out of the kitchen, then walked ahead of her toward my bedroom," he begins, "I undressed and lay down beside her. I knew what to do, what to expect. I had been told all my life."[60] Sex functions as a rite of passage, and this impregnation, coming on the heels of Lomas's traumatic birth experience, doubly functions as Gan's abandonment of childhood notions and entrance into adulthood.

Although T'Gatoi ultimately receives Gan's concession and impregnates him, the consummation bed may still function as Gan's site of resistance or, at the very least, a site of negotiation. It marks the fifth and final step of Gan's shift from child to adult. Though the consummation bed initially seems to be a site of power for T'Gatoi as she exerts her desire to inseminate, in the moments post-coitus, Gan advocates for showing Terrans what they will endure after T'Gatoi comments that Terrans ought to be "protected from seeing" live births. "Not protected," Gan tells her, "Shown. Shown when we're young kids, and shown more than once. Gatoi, no Terran ever sees a birth that goes right. All we see is N'Tlic—pain and terror and maybe death."[61] Gan's request suggests that his position as a partner to T'Gatoi may be a source of empowerment if he can encourage T'Gatoi to suggest to other Tlic that Terrans see the birthing process as a matter of transparency. The suggestion, if implemented, would allow for other Terrans to see the birthing process as Gan did and allow them to make informed choices, whether those choices mean participating in the life-threatening birthing process, suicide, or harboring firearms. Thus, Gan's post-coital request and suggestion offer some semblance of balance in their relationship, demonstrating that romantic partnerships, even when steeped in power hierarchies, may be subject to negotiation and compromise.

Gan's ultimate acceptance of T'Gatoi is a reproduction of Butler's "adapt or die" mantra from *Clay's Ark*, yet scholars approach "Bloodchild" in varying ways regarding Gan's "mutual dependency" and "shared helplessness."[62] Some suggest that because both T'Gatoi and Gan depend on each other, their intercourse is neither coerced nor tantamount to rape.[63] Others suggest that the power dynamics at play mark the relationships as reminiscent of slavery and sexual exploitation.[64] Certainly, the relationship between the Tlic and Terran is one of exploitation. The Terrans are not allowed to possess firearms or mobile transportation; they are kept secluded in an area called The Preserve, and each Terran family is required to supply a Tlic with one male child per generation. Additionally, the Terrans are plied with sterile Tlic eggs that subdue them while also providing longer life spans. However, Butler described this story as a "paying the rent" story and vehemently disagreed with any interpretation of "Bloodchild" as akin to chattel enslavement.[65] "The only places I am writing about slavery," Butler writes in the afterword to the story, "is where I actually say so."[66] Butler's insistence that "Bloodchild" was not about slavery was evidence of her "how stubborn she could be when it came to sticking to her aesthetic principles,"[67] her friend Nisi Shawl shares. Instead of slavery, Butler thought of "Bloodchild" as "a love story."[68] Qualifying "Bloodchild" as a love story is decidedly uncomfortable precisely because of the deeply rooted elements of control and power embedded in the relationship. As one critic notes, Butler's "transactional view of love"[69] can act as a bargaining chip for the Terrans that aids in their survival, but its role can also alter relationships that are imbued with an unequal power dynamic. Thinking about "Bloodchild" as a love story unsettles our assumptions about love and what comprises love; it helps us think differently and more deeply about romantic relationships and the power hierarchies inherent in even the most loving relationships.

Yet thinking about "Bloodchild" as a love story circles us back to Butler's "adapt or die" refrain. While brotherly love is certainly one reason Gan chooses to become impregnated by T'Gatoi (thus sparing his sister), his emotional connection with T'Gatoi betrays him. Gan also feels jealousy towards his sister. "The thought of her doing it to Hoa at all disturbed me in a different way now, and I was suddenly angry," Gan reveals as the coitus begins.[70] That mélange of emotion sparks Gan to accept the risk and accept the relationship with T'Gatoi; otherwise, he risks losing the relationship he shares with her. The use of the moniker "Gatoi" is reflective of the intimacy he shares with her, and the threat of that severance, that death of a relationship, is more than enough for Gan to accept T'Gatoi his role as T'Gatoi's host and birther of her children.

"The Evening and the Morning and the Night"

With her 1987 publication of "The Evening and the Morning and the Night," Butler returns to the ambivalent adapt or die refrain characteristic of "Speech Sounds" and *Wild Seed* and subsequently offers another story with an explicit dramatization of disability. "The Evening and the Morning and the Night" depicts the lives of people living with Duryea-Gode Disease (DGD). DGD is a fictional genetic disease in which people find themselves marginalized by society because of its lasting effects. The disease manifests after folks who were cured of cancer bore children who were born with the disease. DGD comes with physical side effects—tendencies to "drift" and "dig"—forms of self-harm that may leave them physically mutilated or dead. The story follows Lynn, a third-year university student who is a double DGD, the daughter of two parents with the disease. Because of their tendency to harm themselves or others, DGDs are required to wear emblems that mark them as DGD, maintain a special diet which are derisively described as "dog biscuits" and have relatively short life spans.[71] To avoid being "lepers twenty-four hours a day," Lynn rents a house with several other DGDs.[72] They live together in harmony, with Lynn acting as the house mother, reminding them to clean and do chores. One of Lynn's housemates, Alan Chi, wants to go visit his mother in Dilg, a DGD ward, and Lynn accompanies him. They are met by Dr. Beatrice Alcantara, who reveals that at Dilg, DGDs live long lives, create art, machinery, and weapons. They do not drift. They thrive. In Dilg, Lynn learns that as a double DGD female, she secretes a pheromone that makes other DGDs susceptible to her influence. As one critic notes, "DGDs are able to do their work at Dilg only by living in community and under the influence of pheromones produced by double-DGD women."[73] For the first time, Lynn sees a path forward for her life—she can help create new Dilg communities where she and other DGDs can eat savory food, live unencumbered by the non-DGDs, and thrive.

Given Butler's interest in history, awareness of current events (she frequently described herself as a "news junkie" in interviews and author biographies),[74] and habit of "[pulling] out of the newspapers"[75] content for her work, it is reasonable to believe that she was aware of the independent living movement that began, for one historian, when Edward Roberts, a polio survivor and wheelchair user, sued the University of California at Berkely for "access and integration."[76] Schalk remarks that it is "absolutely necessary" to read Butler's representation of Lynn's group home, Dilg, and other DGD wards as "an engagement with the deinstitutionalization movement."[77] Lynn's description of the lawn maintenance at her group house further highlights Butler's awareness and understanding of public opinions about disabled people: "I went to one of my windows and stared out at the weeds. We let them thrive in the backyard. In the front we mowed them, along with the few patches of grass."[78] Weeds tend to grow where they are not wanted, and if left unchecked, they can wreak havoc on the surrounding plants and flowers. Lynn's weeds thrive in the backyard, an area typically concealed from public view and the decision to mow the weeds in the front reflects an effort to keep Lynn's group home presentable and socially acceptable to observers. The juxtaposition of the manicured lawn's visibility and the unmanicured lawn being hidden is an apt characterization for non-DGDs and DGDs, the abled and disabled. Like the thriving weeds hidden from public view, DGDs are marginalized, institutionalized, and stigmatized. They are required to wear an insignia to mark them as different *and* dangerous. While the story does not reveal that DGDs are killed (or mowed down) when they appear in public, it does reveal that DGDs are avoided and stared at, that DGDs experience legalized discrimination, and when DGDs become "undesirable" by digging and physically mutilating themselves, they are placed in poorly kept observation facilities, hidden from view.

Yet the imagery of the weeds thriving in the background also points to covert resistance. Lynn's group home and the Dilg ward she visits become safe houses for DGDs. They self-segregate to circumvent social stigma and free themselves from impunity and disregard. These safe havens or "pocket universes" become hallmarks of Butler's fiction. Anyanwu's New Orleans plantation, Lynn's group home, Beatrice's Dilg ward, and the desert enclave in *Clay's Ark* are not only spaces where minoritized groups can thrive in a world that seeks to harm them socially, physically, and institutionally but they are also pockets of resistance against ideas that their lives are not worth living or protecting. Lynn's shared home and the Dilg ward are "place[s] of possibility . . . offer[ing] a chance at life"—one that is beyond mere existence and survival.[79]

By returning to disability in "The Evening and the Morning and the Night," we can see that from "Speech Sounds" to "The Evening and the Morning and the Night," Butler's disabled characters reject the ableist assumption that dependence on others means a lack of agency. Both stories rally around the importance of interdependence. In "Speech Sounds," Rye assists people who need help getting off the bus, and she laments Obsidian's loss, knowing that her brief time with him was important. And the two children are glimmers of hope that encourage her to forgo her suicide. Beatrice's Dilg ward suggests that controlled DGDs thrive, but their being influenced by a pheromone does not limit their agency. Adapting to our surroundings, whether through interdependent living conditions like the Dilg ward or Lynn's group home or adapting to newfound circumstances, like adopting two orphaned children—is necessary. The characters have options to choose from. Rye chooses the children, instead of suicide, Lynn appears to find new hope in the possibility of helping herself and others, and Alan? His fate is ambiguous. Will he adapt to the new knowledge that he can live a life free of the digging that harmed his mother and killed Lynn's parents, or will he choose his path to suicide? Like "Speech Sounds," the "adapt or die" refrain is posed as a question—rather than an ultimatum—in "The Evening and the Morning and the Night." Readers are left wondering whether Alan will accept the pheromone induced control or if Lynn will accept her role as one who can influence and change others.

The Xenogenesis Trilogy

The "adapt or die" refrain persists in The Xenogenesis Trilogy. The Xenogenesis Trilogy, which became known as Lilith's Brood in 2000, includes *Dawn* (1987), *Adulthood Rites* (1988), and *Imago* (1989). The trilogy explores the story of humans preserved by an alien species after a human-led nuclear war destroys Earth. Butler's inspiration for the trilogy? President Ronald Reagan. "Early on in his administration he used to talk about 'winnable nuclear wars' and 'limited nuclear wars,'" she tells an interviewer.[80] "I thought, 'The American people put these idiots in positions of power—and they're going to kill us! If people actually fall for this crap, there must be something wrong with the people!' So I set out to figure out what might be wrong with us."[81] From there, the Xenogenesis Trilogy was born. Readers of the trilogy are introduced to a small group of human survivors of a nuclear war are discovered by the Oankali—an alien species of three sexes: male, female, and ooloi (or third sex). The Oankali retrieve the humans, placing them in "suspended animation"—a state of deep. The Oankali are gene traders. They change themselves with the genetic material and cultural diversity of any species they encounter, including humans. As the humans remain in suspended animation, the Oankali alter the humans' bodies: they improve memories, strength, and life span. Most importantly, for the Oankali, they correct the human genetic defect, what they refer to as the "Human Contradiction" a combination of intelligence and hierarchal behavior that makes humans prone to destroying themselves. Additionally, the Oankali sterilize humans to make sure that any children born will be a product of human-Oankali intercourse. The Oankali restore Earth and plan to allow humans to return. The expectation is that humans will begin a new society and fend for themselves.

In *Dawn*, the Oankali choose Lilith Iyapo, a Black woman, to teach and convince the humans to accept the Oankali's offer of hybridity, interdependence, and symbiosis—much like T'Gatoi asks Gan. Lilith's task? To be a "parent" to the first group of awakened humans. Much like Alanna from *Survivor* (1978), Lilith will act as a mediator to help the human survivors accept interspecies intercourse as the only way to conceive and survive. Because of Lilith's task and her eventual role as mother to a new hybrid species, scholars draw parallels between Butler's Lilith and the Lilith from Jewish religious literature.[82] According to Jewish lore, Lilith was Adam's first wife; she considered herself his equal, and after refusing "to lie under him during sex" and leaving the Garden of Eden, she was met with an ultimatum: "return to the Garden or one hundred of her demon children are to be killed every day."[83] Rather than submitting, Lilith chooses exile. Lilith has become a representation of men's fear of a powerful woman especially as they relate to male fears related to impotence, loss of female companionship, and the loss of a patriarchal line.[84] In other words, "Lilith is monstrous, and must be constructed as such, precisely because she chooses to contest the authority of patriarchy—to challenge divine masculine right."[85] The mythical Lilith is typically regarded as the antithesis of Eve. Whereas Eve is described as the great "enabler," one who is the epitome of the helpmeet discourse and sacrifices themselves for others, Lilith is described as the antithesis to the patriarchy.[86] Yet Butler's Lilith is also "significantly 'Eve-like,'" Michelle Osherow writes, noting that Butler's Lilith is an enabler, though her position "as enabler was thrust upon her by her captors" making her "essential" to and responsible for the survival of both the Oankali and the humans.[87] In addition to being connected to the mythical Lilith and the biblical Eve, Butler's Lilith is also connected to the biblical Judas. Lilith repeatedly laments that the Oankali have positioned her as a "Judas goat" or a "Judas."[88] Although linked to the myths of Lilith, Eve, and Judas, scholars tend to position Lilith Iyapo as a sympathetic character who "resists tyranny, is independent, bold, and curious."[89] Lilith's Oankali-imposed task also marks her captivity like that of enslaved Black women, making choices that appear inevitable. Burdened with her task, *Dawn* ends with some humans being transported to earth and Lilith begins a second awakening process, vowing to tell the next group of humans to "*Learn and run!*"[90] Her vow is met in the second book of the trilogy.

Adulthood Rites reveals that human resisters have rejected the Oankali's trade offer. The novel follows Akin, who is the human-Oankali son of Lilith and

Joseph, her human partner who was murdered by other humans in *Dawn*. In *Adulthood Rites*, resisters steal human-looking children and build weapons in hopes of defending themselves from the Oankali. Akin is among the abducted. Captured as an infant, the novel follows his transition to adolescence. Once he loses his human appearance, he leaves the resister colony, attempts to convince the Oankali that the humans need a world of their own, free from Oankali interference. As a young child, Akin recognizes that the forced human-Oankali relationships, the Oankali enforced sterility of resister humans is punishment. Akin seeks to mollify this relationship. He successfully lobbies the Oankali to give the humans a world of their own and restore their fertility. In many ways, Akin takes on the role of mediator in the same way his mother takes on the role of mediator in *Dawn*. But where Lilith is likened to the biblical/religious Lilith, Eve, and Judas, Akin "[mirrors] Christ's dual divine-human nature," according to one scholar, and he becomes for another scholar, a "sacrificial victim" who exists as a "redeemer of the resisters," despite humans' "rejection of his difference"—much like a Christ figure.[91]

Imago introduces siblings, Jodahs and Aaor, and their accidental discovery of a colony of fertile, Earth-born humans after they are exiled from the Oankali community for becoming an unexpected entity after their metamorphoses. Unlike *Dawn* and *Adulthood Rites*, *Imago* is written from the first-person perspective of Jodahs. Part I of the novel, "Metamorphosis," opens with Jodahs in the throes of its maturation from child to adolescent. Jodahs emerges from its transition as the first construct-ooloi: a human-ooloi hybrid, the first of its kind. Aaor becomes the second. Whereas Akin is a human-Oankali child, meaning he fits into a recognizable gender binary, Jodahs does not. As a human-ooloi hybrid Jodahs can change its appearance to that of a human male or female—of any racial or ethnic background—at will. Jodahs and Aaor usher in a new dawn of the Oankali species. If Lilith is a conflation of Lilith, Eve, and Judas, and if Akin is analogous to a Christ-like redeemer, Jodahs and Aaor represent the new heaven and the new earth and are the harbingers change, or perhaps more appropriately, the apocalypse. "The word apocalypse means revelation," says L. Michael White, "That which is uncovered. It comes from the Greek word which literally means to pull the lid off something."[92] Jodahs and Aaor threaten to destroy the genetic makeup the Oankali, stoking the Oankali's fear of the unknown change. The Oankali exile Jodahs and its family to preserve the homogeneity and predictability of their existence and their offspring, hoping to stave off the apocalyptic ending of their world as they know it. *Imago* positions the Oankali as intolerant of difference which is reminiscent of the repulsion Lilith and other humans first experienced in *Dawn*. By the trilogy's end, Jodahs has discovered a hidden resister colony of fertile humans, a discovery that positions Jodahs the Antichrist. In opposition to Akin's redeemer role and as bringers of the apocalypse, Jodahs as the Antichrist figure is one who takes on a "regenerative role," that initiates a new world instead of redeeming or saving the old one.[93] Jodahs, with its sibling, ushers its family into the dawn of a new era, destroying their old ways of life. Not only do they create something new, but they are also something new.

Broadly, the idea of "adapt or die" is at the core of the Xenogenesis Trilogy. Either the humans can reproduce with the Oankali, or they can remain sterile or be placed in perpetual suspended animation. The choice feels illusory. But the "adapt or die" refrain goes beyond reproduction. The trilogy asks readers to consider what belief systems they are willing to give up and what new ways of thinking they are willing to adapt for them to survive. Butler wanted to explore "what might be wrong with us,"[94] and one problem she noted was deeply rooted ideas about sexuality. Lilith encounters her first human, a Black man named Paul Titus, who has lived with the Oankali for an untold number of years, but she learns he still possesses the mentality of the fourteen-year-old boy when he was first Awakened by the Oankali. As Lilith and Paul converse, she learns that he has been involuntarily celibate and that the Oankali deny him human contact—sexual or otherwise. When Lilith rebuffs his sexual advances, Paul becomes enraged, and he violently beats her and attempts to rape her. He screams, "They said I could do it with you . . . And you had to go and mess it up!"[95] Through Paul's rage and forced abstinence, Butler suggests that a Puritanical approach to sex and sexuality, including abstinence-only education, procreative only sex, and men's rights to women's bodies, does not provide any solutions. Butler's warning comes during a time when Congress adopted the Adolescent Family Life Act (AFLA) in 1981, which funded abstinence-only education and rejected (or underfunded) comprehensive sex education. The Oankali place Paul in a rehabilitative sleep that will be "healing to non physical wounds,"[96] but rehabilitation is not comprehensive sex education. Paul's near-rape of Lilith is a warning: if we fail to adapt comprehensive ways of thinking about sex and sexuality and if we do not teach the development of healthy sexualities, we will sanction unhealthy ideas about sex, sexuality, and intimate partnerships—all of which tend to harm the most vulnerable: children, queer people, and women.

Paul's rape attempt is inextricably connected to hypermasculinity, and in *Dawn*, the investments in hypermasculinity turn deadly. When Peter, Curt, and Gregory, attempt to sanction the rape of a woman, Lilith publicly humiliates them. She physically overpowers them and verbally chastises them, calling them "cavemen," "garbage," and "human garbage."[97] Yet Peter's investment in hypermasculinity is perhaps the most severe and readers see it progress slowly. Peter adheres to what Paul Kivel coined as the "Act Like a Man Box." The Act Like a Man Box refers to the "*enforcement* of a narrowly defined set of traditional rules for being a man. These rules are enforced through shaming and bullying, as well as promises of rewards, the purpose of which is to force conformity to our dominant culture of masculinity and to perpetuate the exploitation, domination, and marginalization of women and people who are queer, genderqueer and transgender."[98] We learn of Peter's diminishing position within his social circle after his attempt to facilitate a rape fails: "Peter himself was replaced by Curt."[99] Peter's unsuccessful rape attempt highlights his inability to enforce the man box, so he is removed from his subject position as leader. His domination of a woman is thwarted by a Black woman, and in the post-rape attempt melee, Peter's arm is broken. When he awakens to find his arm healed overnight, we witness Peter's further isolation as his "own people looked askance at him" because they feared he might be not quite human.[100] In addition to isolation, Peter's investment in hypermasculinity and the "act like a man box" results in his own death. After being drugged by the Oankali, Peter "decided he had been humiliated and enslaved" because he "accepted union and pleasure" that made him believe he had "demean[ed] himself in alien perversions."[101] Peter reasserts his masculinity and humanity through violence; he punches an ooloi, activates its defensive reflex, and ends Peter's life. But the investment in hypermasculinity and "The Man Box" has implications beyond harm to self. Curt murders Joseph, Lilith's lover. Joseph does not conform to the scripts of masculinity; he is suspected of being queer, and once evidence that Joseph has allowed himself to be altered by the Oankali emerges, Curt decapitates him. Butler's warnings are clear: if men cannot adapt to new surroundings and escape the cages of their own making that confine them, they will destroy themselves and others.

These cages the humans find themselves in also highlight the harmful effects of imprisonment throughout the series. Undoubtedly, a legacy of imprisonment that appears in *Dawn* is through isolation, solitary confinement, and nonconsensual medical experimentation. For instance, Lilith's initial encounter with the Oankali reflects the non-consensual medical experimentation performed by prison doctors on prisoners. Lilith was "cut" and "stitched" without her "consent" or "knowledge."[102] Lilith was also kidnapped and tortured with silenced and questions. Yet Lilith's physical imprisonment is contrasted with cages of her own making, when her xenophobia—her intense fear of Jdahya, the Oankali instructed to introduce her to her new surroundings—makes her want to "[retreat] into her cage—like a zoo animal that had been shut up for so long that the cage had become home."[103] Though Lilith overcomes her xenophobia, Thomas Foster remarks that her initial "resistance to exposure to difference is represented as another form of captivity—confinement within the familiar, the human."[104]

This confinement within the familiar, this refusal to be exposed to difference is not Lilith's alone. Her human counterparts and Oankali allies also place themselves in cages, confining themselves to the familiar. Extending from this theme of captivity and confinement is the necessity of interrogating our assumptions about sex and gender. The introduction of the ooloi, the third sex, disrupts the gendered order that Lilith and other humans are aware of. Though Lilith has "taken their word for what they are," Paul Titus admits he "never really lost the habit of thinking of ooloi as male or female."[105] His "deliberate, persistent ignorance" strikes Lilith as "foolish," especially since Paul has chosen to live among the Oankali.[106] Paul's refusal to see beyond the binary is part of his attempt to rape Lilith, which results in harm to herself and his placement in a vegetative state for rehabilitation. Paul's refusal to see beyond the rigid sex binary he knows reappears among the Oankali, though the implications appear more positive. Jodahs's metamorphosis into a new entity that the Oankali are unfamiliar with, presents a problem and becomes the central conflict in *Imago*. The Oankali are male, female, and ooloi, but Jodahs will be able to "create new forms, new shells," disrupting the gendered order the Oankali have grown accustomed to.[107] When Nikanj asks Jodahs, "Do you still want to be male?" Jodahs internally asks, "Had I ever wanted to be male? I had just assumed I *was* male, and would have no choice in the matter."[108] Jodahs's opportunity to choose, or to practice gender fluidity, plagues it. As the ooloi child of Nikanj, Jodahs decision impacts Nikanj. "I want to be your same-sex child, but I don't want to cause the family trouble."[109]

These consequences of refusing to interrogate sex or gender may not be the literal death of those who refuse, but they can adversely impact the quality of life for those who are historically marginalized. Lilith suffers the implications of Paul's refusal. Jodahs worries about the backlash its family might receive because their opportunity to practice gender fluidity disrupts Oankali norms. At the time these novels were published, in vitro fertilization (IVF) treatments were finally being touted as miracles, but in the early 1970s, IVF was highly taboo. Although ethical concerns regarding "designer babies" and uncertainty about IVFs safety and effectiveness were some reasons for skepticism about IVF, conservative religious and moral beliefs were the main detractors to IVF. Those holding these beliefs believed that conception should occur "naturally" through sexual intercourse and other methods of conception were against God's design for people's lives. The refusal to move beyond rigid ideas about sex/gender, about what it means to be a person who births, what is a "natural" or "unnatural" conception or birth had the potential to stymie IVF research.

Years after these scientific developments, Butler poses these ideas in her trilogy, and we find ourselves bearing witness to harm once again. Failures to interrogate our assumptions about sex and gender are responsible for the twenty-first-century rollbacks of legal protections for transgender people and the criminalization of drag shows—just to name a few.

If the books of the Xenogenesis trilogy are best described as Creation (*Dawn*), Incarnation (*Adulthood Rites*), and Apocalypse (*Imago*),[110] we can understand the trilogy's "adapt or die" refrain and its implications as mimicking where humanity, in all its shifting and changing forms, should grow. Out of the creation in *Dawn* emerge new possibilities for humans to learn, adapt, and run. Through the incarnation in *Adulthood Rites*, Akin prepares a new world for the resister humans to see if they can develop into something new, something livable without interference. And from the apocalyptic discovery in *Imago* that Jodahs is something new, something that its Creators never imagined, emerges a new world for both humans and Oankali. Throughout the trilogy, change is constant. From Lilith to Paul to Peter to Curt to Joseph to Jodahs, Butler's refrain, adapt or die, reverberates. As we move through the trilogy, we have important questions to ask ourselves. Where are we? Are we in the Creation stage, succumbing to base desires? Or are we in the Incarnation stage, being provided opportunities to adapt or start over? Or have we reached the Apocalypse stage, where the old has indeed passed away and something entirely new emerges? Who adapts? Who resists? Who dies? And what lessons can we learn from each of them?

The End of a Decade

Butler's work shifts in the 1980s, largely because of her feelings about *Survivor* (1978). She did not like the novel because the humans got to escape. She made the novel too easy, she believed. It was not a mistake she made again. Over and over in her works from the 1980s, humans are faced with difficult choices about how they will adapt and survive or choose to die. Whether reimagining an Old Testament narrative, exploring disability, or considering alien invasions, Butler's 1980s fiction prompts readers to consider what sacrifices, concessions, or negotiations we are willing to make for a viable future and whether we can live with the implications of rejecting such change.

CHAPTER 4

1990–2006
A (Bitter)Sweet 16

The last sixteen years of Octavia E. Butler's life were fraught with what she calls "literary menopause"[1]—her term for writer's block. She was preoccupied with hypertension, waning libido, ongoing depression, the death of her mother, and her writing—or lack thereof. But other things plagued Butler, too. "I pay attention. And I care," she told *The Crisis* in 1994. "One of the horrifying things I'm noticing is that younger kids . . . they're raised with a contempt for caring . . ."[2] She echoes these sentiments two years later in an interview with Stephen W. Potts: "It really distresses me that we see these things happening now in American society when they don't have to."[3] Her 1993 novel *Parable of the Sower* explores this widespread investment in a lack of caring, and she tries to counteract it with a fifteen-year-old protagonist who can do nothing but care. She has a condition called "hyperempathy syndrome," a mental delusion that causes her to think she feels the pain and pleasure of others. The sequel, *Parable of the Talents,* published in 1998, warns about the growing danger of a fascist presidential regime, Christian extremism, environmental destruction, police brutality, economic devastation, and food and housing insecurity. She imagined these scenarios hoping for better. Even though she consumed the news a lot—"more than I should, more than is good for me, I suspect," she even admitted—the works published in the last sixteen years of her life are evidence of that hope.[4]

Perhaps this is why *Sower, Talents,* and *Fledgling* (2005) each have a "from hell to paradise" or Egyptian phoenix motif that betrays Butler's sensibilities. Though she described herself as "a pessimist if I'm not careful,"[5] her works *are* hopeful, and her use of the phoenix—a bird that resurrects itself after burning—exemplifies that hope. Across all three novels, fire destroys but also promotes growth, and the fire that was meant for destruction ultimately births something that becomes immortal. In *Sower*, a fire destroys the protagonist's gated community and becomes the spark that births the protagonist's everlasting Earthseed religion, whose destiny is "to take root among the stars."[6] Similarly, the fiery murder of the protagonist's family at the beginning of *Fledgling* births her resurrection; she emerges from a smoky cave blinded, burned, and as an amnesiac. The two additional attempts to kill her and her allies by fire fail and catapult her as the dawn of a new era, the potential savior of her species. Both protagonists are tested and tried by fire, and though they do not emerge unscathed, they do emerge and leave an immortal legacy and a blueprint of a way forward. They offer readers hope.

We can see further evidence of Butler's hope for a better world in her only two short stories published in the final years of her life, "Amnesty" and "The Book of Martha." Although these two stories do not have the "from hell to heaven" motif or the phoenix narrative, they showcase two Black women protagonists who lobby for better worlds using the tools they are provided. One must choose between her livelihood as a writer or the survival of humankind, and the other tries to help humans in an economically depressed world access secure employment opportunities with aliens whom they loathe. Though the circumstances are not ideal (they never are, in Butler's creative mind), the women play the cards they are dealt. And that's what Butler writes about this decade. Playing the cards we are dealt. Her Black women and girl protagonists, Lauren Olamina, Noah Cannon, Martha Bes, and Shori Matthews, are everyday heroes and change agents who make a way out of no way and who embody the words, "we are a harvest of survivors."[7]

The Parable Duology

The distress Butler experienced in the 1990s and the distress that caused her to write her Parable Duology became a collective distress for many Americans in 2020. *Sower* begins in the year 2024, and readers witness ineffective police, police brutality, company towns, drug-addiction-fueled crime, non-livable wages, debt slavery, and more. But after the murder of George Floyd in May 2020, *Sower* became a *New York Times* best-seller, and it is not difficult to understand why. *Sower* resonated with so many because of its clairvoyance. She thought of it as a cautionary tale,[8] a warning about what could happen to the United States if religious fundamentalism, global warming, prison industrial complexes, police brutality, throw-away labor, non-livable wages, unaffordable housing—and more—remain ignored. Its sequel, *Talents*, which was published in 1998 but begins in 2032, readers witness a presidential candidate who runs on the slogan "Make America Great Again," who wins the presidential election, and who inspires his followers to violence without seeming to incite—or condemn—it.

Despite the eerie similarities of the series to the lived experiences of many of her United Statesian readers, the novel begins relatively benignly: the protagonist is Lauren Olamina, a teenager in the process of thinking through a new religion she is calling Earthseed in response to the devastation, corruption, and complacency she witnesses around her. At the novel's opening, she is undergoing "a crisis of faith" because her Baptist minister father plans to baptize her.[9] Because *Sower* is an epistolary novel, readers learn about Lauren's crisis of faith through her journal entries and her Earthseed poetry. Her journal and Earthseed verses guide her, and eventually, she compiles her Earthseed verses into a religious tome: *Earthseed: The Book of the Living*. The progress of Lauren's story places *Sower* in the category of a bildungsroman, showing Lauren's moral and spiritual growth and development. Lauren's loss of innocence is gradual over time, and it happens "in the face of corporate, governmental, and general human violence and stupidity."[10] After the murder and mutilation of her brother, Keith, the death of her two-year-old neighbor Amy Dunn by gunfire, the disappearance of her father, the burning of her gated community in Robledo, California, and her separation from her stepmother and three younger brothers, Lauren heads north, determined to live, to survive, and spread her Earthseed philosophy. Along the way, she collects Harry and Zahra, two members of her now burned gated community, her future lover, Taylor Franklin Bankole, and a host of others. Her journey is more than a physical trek northward; it becomes her pilgrimage.[11] Through her trek forward and her collection of followers, she becomes "a fisher of humankind," invoking "the biblical parallels to Jesus and His disciples."[12] Lauren and her followers "become a modern underground railroad" as they make their trek north and settle in an enclave they call Acorn.[13]

Talents follows the parallel lives of Lauren (now Lauren Olamina-Bankole) after she and her road-weary travelers arrive at Acorn and the life story of her daughter, whose birth name is Larkin and whose adopted name is Asha. In the novel, which is structured after journal entries written between 2033 and 2035, we learn of Lauren and Bankole's marriage, the birth of their daughter Larkin, and the growth of Acorn and Earthseed. Earthseed is targeted by Andrew Steele Jarrett, a presidential candidate whose slogan is "Make America Great Again" and who condemns the violence his followers enact "in such mild language that his people are free to hear what they want to hear."[14] The followers call themselves the Crusaders, and they are part of the Church of Christian America. Shortly after Lauren births her daughter, Acorn is attacked by Christian America Crusaders, renamed Camp Christian, and their enslavement begins. Seventeen months after her enslavement, a natural disaster allows Lauren and the rest of the captives to emancipate themselves, kill their enslavers, and burn Camp Christian to the ground. Lauren embarks on twin journeys to find Larkin and spread Earthseed. As such, *Talents* is a coming-of-age story for Lauren as a religious leader and, more importantly, for Earthseed as a global religion. After liberating herself from Camp Christian, Lauren has several door-to-door missionary moments that help her recruit new believers. One of her new believers publishes her *Earthseed: The Books of the Living* on the Internet, and the widespread availability of the material garners her paid speaking invitations to colleges and universities. New Earthseed settlements emerge, garnering the support of politicians. They fund schools, build homes, and offer scholarships. The novel ends with Earthseed coming of age and sending out its first shuttles into space to help spread the destiny of Earthseed to the stars.

The Parable Series is her first series with a sustained emphasis on the act of writing and her only set of epistolary novels. The likely culprit? Writer's block. She wrote that poetry helped her escape writer's block, and her affinity for journaling was a natural outlet for that poetry, much of which appears in the duology. As epistolary novels—novels that are written in the form of personal documents, including letters, diaries, and newspaper clippings—the significance of writing in *Sower* and *Talents* cannot be overstated. The act of writing becomes a thematic consistency across both novels as both Lauren and Asha call attention to their writing practices. Across Butler's body of fiction, writing has five functions, but all of them appear in *Sower* and *Talents*: (1) writing as freedom or freedom of expression; (2) writing as a catalyst for change; (3) writing as currency; (4) writing as a path to healing; and (5) writing as an archive.

Lauren's writing is her ticket to freedom—freedom of the mind—because journal writing allowed her to think about, develop, and express her Earthseed philosophies, which she would eventually publish and share with others. Lauren writes, "I felt on the verge of talking to her about things I hadn't talked about before. I'd written about them. Sometimes, I write to keep from going crazy. There's a world of things I don't feel free to talk to anyone about."[15] As the daughter of a Baptist minister, Lauren's ideas (which many of my Christian students have difficulty grappling with") will likely not be welcome. Her trepidation is confirmed when confiding in her friend Joanne about plans to leave and survive once the world crumbles, which earns her father's reprimands and censure. However, the desire for freedom of expression persists long after Lauren leaves Robledo. "I've hidden my writing papers, pens, and pencils away in our prison room" is one of Lauren's earliest confessions after she has been enslaved at Camp Christian.[16] Hiding her writing material is a form of resistance rooted in freedom, especially when connected to historical accounts of enslaved Black people who were forbidden to read and write.

The concept of writing as a catalyst for change is closely connected to writing as freedom. Lauren writes not just to freely express her thoughts in ways that she does not feel safe speaking but also because she hopes to become a catalyst for change. Lauren closes her Saturday, April 26, 2025, journal entry with, "Then, someday when people are able to pay more attention to what I say than to how old I am, I'll use these verses to pry them loose from the rotting past, and maybe push them into saving themselves and building a future that makes sense."[17] Lauren's plan to use her verses for the future exemplifies her forward-thinking, future-oriented, visionary point of view. In this way, writing is emblematic of Lauren's visionary thinking. By the end of *Talents*, Lauren's writing, which has been compiled as *Earthseed: The Books of the Living*, is distributed online for free, providing open access to a wide audience. The distribution allows for the free exchange of ideas, helps fund her Earthseed start-ups, and helps lift her and Earthseed out of the shadows and into the limelight.

A third function of writing is that it becomes a form of currency or economic exchange. In *Sower*, Keith discloses that he's permitted to stay among the locals outside the gated community because of his ability to read and write. Lauren documents this conversation with Keith in her June 25, 2026, journal entry. Four months later, in her Saturday, October 31, 2026, entry, Lauren muses, "I wonder if there are people outside who will pay me to teach them reading and writing—basic stuff—or people who will pay me to read or write for them. Keith started me thinking about that."[18] Inspired by Keith, Lauren begins to see the value of writing as currency, as a skill that could generate income. As does Marcos, who, in *Talents*, wrote "rent receipts" to avoid being harassed by law enforcement for squatting.[19] Immediately after her enslavement, Lauren earns her living "sketching, teaching, reading, and writing for people."[20]

Lauren also expresses her need to write even when she does not want to because it comforts her. Her scriptotherapy, or therapeutic writing, becomes a fourth function. "I haven't been able to write a word since Wednesday. I don't know what to write," she writes in *Sower*, and she continues, "I don't want to write about this, but I need to. Sometimes writing about a thing makes it easier to stand."[21] In two journal entries dated Wednesday, November 18, 2026, and Saturday, July 31, 2027, Lauren says, "I have to write."[22] In the first instance, in 2026, she writes it only once. But in the second instance, in 2027, she repeats it three times in a matter of lines. Connecting both moments is that her declaration of "I need to write" is propelled by revelations that she saw a "more squalor, more human remains, more feral dogs" and "ash-covered corpses" which were "burned or half blown."[23] This need to write is echoed in *Talents*. "I need to write about Bankole," she writes after learning of his death, "I meant to do that when I began. I need to but I don't want to. It just plain hurts too much."[24] In each instance of Lauren's written declaration of *needing* to write, Lauren writes as a way of making sense of the world around her. She writes as a form of catharsis and comfort because she does not know what else to do. Writing offers a tenuous path to healing, "Once I've written this, perhaps I can begin to heal. I don't know."[25] Her writing as compulsion is inextricable from her writing as comfort; in both instances, writing functions as catharsis and a path to healing, allowing her to process unpleasant emotions and grisly scenes of the dead or dismembered. Lauren's writing as lamentation that honors the dead likely stems from Butler's own use of writing as a form of grief management. When the Central Library in Los Angeles burned down in 1986, Butler herself writes about the loss of the library as a dear friend, as a form of grief management. This form of writing as healing is a referent to Butler's own knowledge that writing for her was life-giving and life-affirming and that without it, Butler would die. Like Lauren, Butler "needs to write" because of the violence, terror, and death around her to express her grief and offer her some comfort when she has nothing to be comforted by.

Early in *Talents*, readers witness writing as a form of archival memory. Lauren writes, "Here, for our infant Earthseed archives, is what I've learned so far . . ."[26] Later, she encourages her brother to "talk or write" about what happened to him while he was enslaved.[27] Lauren transcribes his story and the records of the slave collars, the forced prostitution, rape, and the fate her their family after they left the gated community in Robledo.[28] Marcos's time as a child preacher has a two-fold function: to document what happened during the reign of Christian America and set the stage for Marcos and his later betrayal of Lauren. Further, Asha, as the narrative voice of *Talents*, is an archive in and of itself. She preserves the lives, words, legacies, and worlds of her mother, her father, and her uncle, all while weaving her life story in between theirs as an exercise in self-understanding. As I discuss in chapter 5, Asha's archive is reminiscent of the work that the Federal Writers Project completed during the post-emancipation period in compiling the stories of the formerly enslaved.

The significance of writing is also evident in the structural shift from *Sower* to *Talents*. Unlike its prequel, *Talents* is more than Lauren's journal entries interspersed with Earthseed verses. It is a compilation of five different sources: (1) Lauren's journal entries from 2032, 2033, and 2035; (2) *Earthseed: The Books of the Living*; (3) Taylor Franklin Bankole's *Memories of Other Worlds*,

(4) Marcos Duran's *Warrior*; and (5) eye-witness accounts from informants, who are former Camp Christian prisoners and Christian America adoptees. This source material is compiled by Asha Vere, the captured, adopted, and renamed daughter of Lauren and Bankole. In compiling this material, Asha acts as a narrative guide. Not only does she offer commentaries on each person's writing throughout, but she also introduces readers to her life growing up as an outcast in a Church of Christian America home. Because Asha's perspective is the lens through which we enter the novel, we not only learn of Asha's reactions to her mother's life and life's work, but through Asha's eyes, we witness Lauren's journey, her enslavement, her insurrection, her escape, and her determination to spread Earthseed.

Asha's role as archivist reinforces her commitment to privileging patriarchal perspectives and voices over her own and her mother's. *Talents* is divided into five sections: prologue, 2032, 2033, 2035, and epilogue. As with *Sower*, each section is framed by an Earthseed verse, and each chapter includes an Earthseed verse as an epigraph. The chapters then include journal entries from her biological parents, excerpts from her uncle's book, and her own commentary. Chapters one, three, and four have the following three-part structure: (1) Excerpts from *Memories of Other Worlds* by Taylor Franklin-Bankole; (2) Asha's commentary; and (3) Lauren's journal entries. Chapters seven and eighteen share that same three-part structure but replace Bankole's words with Marcos's: (1) Excerpts from *Warrior* by Marcos Duran; (2) Asha's commentary; and (3) Lauren's journal entries. Conversely, chapters two, five, and six have a two-part structure: (1) Asha's commentary and (2) Lauren's journal entries. When Asha includes excerpts from her father's or uncle's writing, she does not provide any commentary until after their words have been written. But the pattern of speaking before her mother, framing her mother's words with her own, continues in chapters eight through seventeen. Even in chapter eleven, when Lauren's journals describe the invasion of Acorn, Asha comments first.

At first glance, only five of the twenty-one chapters appear to begin with a male authority figure whom Asha respects and trusts. However, considering that Asha adopts a patriarchal voice, every chapter in *Talents* begins with a patriarchal voice. Her adoption of this voice is directly connected to the abuse she experienced with her adoptive family, the Alexanders. Mrs. Alexander verbally and emotionally abuses Asha, and Mr. Alexander molests her. In Asha's estimation, Lauren's commitment to Earthseed and refusal to leave Acorn is responsible for Asha's upbringing. Asha links her mother's abandonment and the Alexanders' abuse to her ignoring the counsel of two patriarchal voices: her husband, who wanted to leave Acorn for a more secure settlement, and her brother, who wanted her to join Christian America. Therefore, Asha does not frame her father or uncle's words with her own because she reveres them as trustworthy authority figures who want the stability of organized living, whether in an established town or in a widely respected religion. Asha aligns herself with the patriarchal voices of her father and her uncle to punish her mother for her abandonment.

Asha's alignment with her uncle also symbolizes her Oedipal-style attachment to him. Twice in *Talents*, Asha admits that she was "more than half in love" with him and describes him as the "handsomest man" who was "good looking" and "beautiful."[29] Before she learns he is her uncle, she admits she had "quite a crush on" the Reverend Marcos Duran.[30] Asha's infatuation with her uncle and resentment toward her mother is simultaneously rooted in her abandonment trauma and indicative of an Oedipal complex, which is described as "a desire for sexual involvement with the parent of the opposite sex and a concomitant sense of rivalry with the parent of the same sex."[31] As one critic notes, Asha "cannot bear to turn a sharp critical gaze"[32] onto her uncle, who is likely the reason Acorn was attacked. Though there is no explicit textual evidence that Marc reveals the location of Acorn to the Church of Christian America authorities, his body language in his last conversation with Lauren before he leaves Acorn and in his first conversation with Lauren after she escapes from Camp Christian is evidence of his ill intent and his guilt.[33] Asha, who is a sharp critical reader and writer when she wants to be (she is perceptive enough to infer that her uncle was a closeted gay man), refuses to entertain the possibility that her uncle is an informant who betrayed his sister and her community to Christian America authorities. Her denial reinforces her willful ignorance and deeply-rooted anger toward her mother.

My students frequently wonder if the daughter-to-mother resentment is indicative of Butler's real-life relationship with her mother. The answer is no. Sure, Butler eschewed her mother's Christian beliefs, but she credits her mother with her love of reading and writing, noting that "she didn't know what she was setting us both up for."[34] She describes her relationship with her mother as "good." In fact, in her journals and interviews, she often reiterated that she wanted to make enough money to support herself and her mother. Butler's mother passed away in 1996, two years before the publication of *Talents*. Butler was deeply affected by her mother's passing, not writing for nearly a year. She admits that *Talents* became a different story after her mother's passing. "In a sense," Butler writes, "[*Talents*] "was my mother's last gift to me."[35]

Butler invites readers to be skeptical of Asha's investment in heteropatriarchy, and her characterization of Marcos "Marc" Duran offers a warning about the danger of investing in heteropatriarchy. When Marc leaves Acorn, he is angry because he believes Lauren has conspired against him so that others "don't see him as a minister," yet he refuses to express his anger, instead offering Lauren a "weary, irritating, *honest* smile" before he unconvincingly "forgives" her for requiring that he be subject to the rules of speaking at Gathering.[36] Lauren describes his body language: "For a long moment, he stared at me. I watch him get angry—very angry. Then he seemed to push his anger away. He refused to react to it. He shrugged."[37] When she explains this to him further, Lauren notes that he still expresses no anger. "Yet he was furious," she writes. "He wouldn't show it and he wouldn't talk about it, but it came off him like heat."[38] Before he leaves, Lauren observes his body language once again: "He shrugged . . . He smiled. And he was gone."[39]

His controlled body language—shrugging, smiling while furious, refusing to admit his anger—resembles "psychic self-mutilation," a process where men "kill off the emotional parts of themselves" in service to the patriarchy.[40] Marc's resentment toward Lauren emerges from his refusal to see her as a person trying to survive in a world that has brought her (and him) nothing but violence. Instead of seeing her as someone who rescued him from slavery and cared for him, he saw her as competition that needed to be quelled. He wanted to be the victor. "Men who win on patriarchal terms end up losing in terms of their substantive quality of life," bell hooks writes.[41] "They choose patriarchal manhood over loving connection, first foregoing self-love and then the love they could give and receive that would connect them to others."[42] Marc "chooses patriarchal manhood over loving connection"; he becomes the most prominent minister in the Church of Christian America among English and Spanish-speaking communities, and his popularity had some believing he should run for president. Yet, his only connection was with Asha. He remained unmarried and unattached romantically because he "had said without ever quite saying it that he preferred men sexually."[43] Because the Church of Christian America denounced same-gender loving relationships as a sin, Marc opted to abide by that doctrine, leaving him without companionship. Marc's desire to have it all, to rid himself of the shame and trauma of his enslavement and rape, and to be victorious over his sister causes him to participate in psychic self-mutilation, choosing the patriarchy over "loving connections," even going so far as to lie to his niece about her mother, telling her that her mother is deceased.

Marc invests in heteropatriarchy, but his attempts at psychic self-mutilation fail him when he is confronted with the pain of his past as a sex-trafficked rape victim. After seventeen months in slavery at Camp Christian, Lauren escapes, and she discovers that Marc is a minister in the Church of Christian America. She approaches him for help finding her kidnapped daughter, and when she reveals that she and others "were captured, collared, and used for work and for sex," he expresses disbelief.[44] When she reveals their escape, including the murder of their Christian America enslavers, Marc's aghast, "You killed people . . . ?" is met with Lauren's retort, "Their names were Cougar, Marc. Every one of them was named Cougar."[45] Lauren's invocation of "Cougar" and all the psychological, physical, and sexual violence he embodies, triggers Marc; he "wrenched himself around as though he had to uproot himself to move."[46] The trigger and the harsh reality that similar violence was inflicted on his sister and those who once considered him community prevent Marc from adopting the psychic self-mutilation. His earlier attempts of being a "self-contained person" who "knew how to be unreachable" fail.[47] The result is a violent outburst. "He hit me," Lauren writes. "I never expected it, never saw it coming. Even when we were kids, he and I didn't hit each other."[48]

Marc's psychic-self mutilation and investment in heteropatriarchy have far-reaching impacts beyond him and his physical blow to his sister. When teaching *Talents*, I share with students that Lauren's "I never expected it" admission always strikes me as her subconscious "Aha!" moment, her realization that Marc "isn't to be trusted,"[49] and her suspicion that he has "hit" her—or targeted her—in more ways than one. Marc's physical violence here, coupled with the fact that the blow was unexpected and uncharacteristic of Marc, always seems to me confirmation of his unconfirmed treachery: Marc reported Acorn to the Christian America authorities; he is responsible for the murder, the rape, the enslavement, the torture, the kidnapping that Acorn residents endured. Marc's untrustworthiness marks him as the patient zero responsible for the devastation of several people through death, rape, enslavement, and kidnapping. His contagious disease? His investment in white Christian heteropatriarchy. His psychic-self mutilation and desire to have it all while recovering at Acorn lead him to participate in patterns of harmful behavior. He internalizes Christian American ideologies and becomes an informant on Acorn and Earthseed since they are considered a "heathen" cult. But when confronted with the consequences of his psychic-self mutilation, he cannot disentangle himself and adopt his earlier methods of psychic-self mutilation resulting in guilt that expresses itself through physical violence.

The violence meted out against Lauren, the Earthseeders, and anyone deemed antithetical to the Christian America ethos is Butler sounding the alarm bells about the dangers codifying sameness vis a vis investments in Christian heteropatriarchy, which result in queer antagonism, misogyny, misogynoir, racism, ethnocentrism, and "aporophobia," which is the fear and rejection of the economically disenfranchised.[50] Butler's warnings did not occur in a vacuum; she warned of the dangers of Christian fundamentalism as early as *Survivor* (1978), and in *Dawn* (1987), she warns that men who refuse to rid themselves of the "Act Like a Man Box" will destroy themselves and others. In *Survivor* and *Dawn*, which I discuss in chapters 2 and 3, the investments in heteropatriarchy occur when humans are exiled on other worlds. In *Talents*, the rape, murder, enslavement, sex-trafficking, and kidnapping happen in the United States, sanctioned by high ranking political and religious leaders. By extending the warnings proffered in *Survivor* and *Dawn* and placing them in a believable setting, Butler highlights what is probable if such investments continue to be endorsed and rewarded.

"Amnesty" and "The Book of Martha"

Like the Parable duology, the last short stories Butler published in her lifetime, "Amnesty" (2003) and "The Book of Martha" (2003), pay homage to previously published works with meditations on food insecurity, job scarcity, economic depression, human-alien contact, biotechnologically superior alien life forms, social contracts, violence, and addiction, among others. Such an assessment may confirm Butler's fears—she was terrified that she would be writing the same things over and over largely because much of her work after *Talents* emerged from her failed attempts to continue the Parable duology. But her fears were unfounded. The political concerns she revisits never become stale. Butler's realistic cautionary Parable novels seem to diverge from the last of the works published in the 1980s—the Xenogenesis trilogy and the extraterrestrials—but her affinity for out-of-this-world encounters returns in "Amnesty" accompanied by a dose of the realism that floods the Parable series. In "Amnesty," the human government cooperates with aliens, called The Communities, recognizing them as legal persons by the U.S. government in exchange for employment opportunities to combat food insecurity, job scarcity, and economic depression. But it was not always like this. "Amnesty" follows Noah, a Black woman who lives inside a dome called The Bubble with the aliens and works as a recruiter. She interviews humans for potential work within The Bubble. This interview process recalls the interview process Lilith undergoes in *Dawn*. Noah reviews dossiers, selects potential candidates, and endures their questions and their anger at the aliens' takeover of "their world." Upon their initial arrival, The Communities kidnapped and experimented on humans. We have seen this before in *Survivor* (1978) and *Dawn* (1987). But after The Communities learn they are addicted to the physical contact the humans provide, they free the humans who wish to return home. Noah is among the first to leave, but she is kidnapped, tortured, and experimented on by humans before she is released to her family. After attending college, Noah decides to return to work for The Communities in hopes of doing what both

Black women protagonists from *Survivor* and *Dawn* do: teach humans how to coexist and survive with the aliens.

"Amnesty" reinforces that the future is neither all white nor all male. The multiracial group Noah recruits in the story is reminiscent of the multiracial group Lauren forms in the Parable duology. Noah's recruits include James Adio, a Black man; Rune Johnson, a blond, white male; Piedad Ruiz, a Latinx woman; Thera Collier, a red-haired woman; and Michelle Ota, who is arguably of Japanese descent as "Ota" is a Japanese word/surname. Sorrel Trent's racial or ethnic identity is not described, but she is the religious fundamentalist of the group. For some, the aliens in "Amnesty" "amount to just another brutal corporate employer in a broken-down world where "almost nobody else' is hiring,"[51] thematically linking "Amnesty" back to *Sower* and *Talents* with the economically depressed world, company towns, and forced labor. And it also connects back to the wage slavery Dana describes in *Kindred* (1979) and Jane's employment in "Crossover" (1971). But for others, "Amnesty" is Butler's version of "new realist utopian politics."[52] For Claire Curtis, a new realist utopia requires "traditionally oppressed" protagonists, like Noah and Lauren, who "see the worlds in which they live and aim to make those worlds visible to others" by "[finding] a space" to educate others about the world they live in.[53]

Importantly, Noah tells her story; she functions as one who has agency. She expresses her past victimization at the hands of the Communities and humans and looks for a way forward. Like so many other Black women characters in Butler's fiction, Noah positions herself as a change agent. "I can [change them]. Community by Community, human by human. I would work faster if I could."[54] Like Lilith from *Dawn* and Alanna from *Survivor*, Noah, our change agent, wants to bridge the chasm between humans and The Communities. In many ways, Noah reinforces the "adapt or die" mantra from *Clay's Ark* and "Bloodchild," and even the "Learn and run" mantra Lilith vows at the end of *Dawn*. One important way Noah encourages adaptation is by encouraging the recruits to "learn the language."[55] This positions her as a forward-thinking visionary and an Afrofuturist, and using the logic of Afrofuturism, she knows that sign language may have the potential to get the recruits access to certain benefits. Learning the language provides Noah with the freedom to have a compassionate employer. She gets to wear clothing (others are refused clothing), and she can ask for human comforts, like comfortable chairs.

Certainly, though, these benefits rely on the benevolent paternalism of the aliens, and to Butler's chagrin, this could be likened to enslaved Black people who did work to please white enslavers to gain benefits for themselves and their families without uprooting the existing system of dominance. Admittedly, the aliens are extremely controlling and repressive of the humans, "monitor[ing] and polic[ing] their "every move,"[56] but humans monitor, police, and harm other humans, too, as the bruises on one recruit's body reveal. and Noah's own experiences of torture and experimentation by her human captors. For Noah, learning the language becomes a freedom technology, which one scholar defines as "any kind of practical knowledge that helps black people solve problems with their environment and in their society, abetting their escape from physical and psychological bondage and thereby allowing them control of their own actions."[57] What the short story does not posit is an anti-labor movement. What if we just stop working? What if humans refuse to allow themselves to be enfolded by The Communities? Instead of feeding The Communities' addiction, what happens if the humans just refuse? Some characters broach these questions and more. They ask about fighting against The Communities. But the reason "Amnesty" does not posit an anti-labor movement is the same reason that the human government decided to cooperate with The Communities: refusal to work would be unsustainable. An anti-labor movement would be unsustainable. If the humans just refused to work, The Communities would resort back to abducting the humans since they are indeed addicted to them. As Noah notes, "It was a short, quiet war. We lost."[58]

If "Amnesty" ends with what feels like resignation—Noah's "we lost" is followed by an invitation to meet their prospective employers—"The Book of Martha" seems to end with hope. In "The Book of Martha" God asks a Black woman named Martha Bes to come up with some way to save humanity from their destruction. Asking Martha to keep the stories of Noah, Job, and Jonah in mind when making her decision, God assigns her this task and tells Martha that she has been chosen "for all that you are and all that you are not."[59] God also tells her that any damage she causes with her decision will not be undone, though God does allow her to ask questions and engage in conversation before she decides. The task is certainly anxiety-inducing and a huge responsibility. Why would God ask a human to do this work? God's responses appear paradoxical, hovering between a child-like curiosity and a nonchalant, devil-may-care attitude. Essentially, God behaves like a scientist, engaging with Martha's hypotheses on how to alter humanity and offering scientific insights into the pros and cons of her suggestions. Ultimately, Martha chooses to save humanity by satisfying them all the only way she knows how with intense, lucid dreams.

Critics observe that "The Book of Martha" combines Biblical allusions, science fiction, and Afrofuturism.[60] Like "Amnesty," "The Book of Martha" is sprinkled with remnants from Butler's earlier works. The intense dreams that Martha asks for may function as another form of sedation, like the sedation Tlic eggs provide in "Bloodchild" or the sedation that Jane numbs herself with in "Crossover" or the Virtual Reality and Dream Masks that become common in *Talents*. As one of the last works published in her life, the story is about a conversation between a Black writer and God. The conversation is, Marlene Barr notes, unsurprising because "The protagonist articulates Butler's political concerns" and "shares Butler's circumstance."[61] In fact, "The protagonist is Butler," Barr explains.[62]

Of all the things Martha does in this story, one thing is clear: Martha shapes God. God initially appears to her as a Towering Michaelangelo God (white man), then God appears as a life-sized white man, and then a life-sized Black man. Finally, God appears as a Black woman, a mirror image of Martha herself, noting "we look like sisters."[63] When God is a large white man, the way we read his request of Martha is as a burden, where he wants to use her just because she grew up poor and Black and woman. Initially, readers may feel as though Martha is being put upon, as if she is a mule. But, as she and God engage in conversation, God and Martha become peers—not equals—but in the same peer group which is demonstrated in the second and third images of God: God as a regular-sized white man and God as a Black man. Finally, when God appears as a mirror image of Martha, her shaping of God aligns with her comfort level. This mirror image of God as Martha is "very similar to the God theorized by Lauren Olamina," who repeats that "God is Change," that God "exists to be shaped," and that "We shape God."[64] The final image of Martha and God as mirror images is symbolic of a cultural shift where Black women were seeing themselves in God. It may echo Ntozake Shange's "I saw God in myself / and I loved her fiercely" from her 1973 choreopoem *for colored girls who considered suicide / when the rainbow was enuf*. But it also reflects the ways Black feminists and womanists were disrupting deeply entrenched dominant narratives about God, notably those that God was male.[65]

"The Book of Martha" also helps expose the fallacy of redemptive suffering and the burden of strength that is often imposed on Black women. Redemptive suffering posits that suffering is God's will, and it is God's purpose or desire to reward those who endure suffering.[66] Proponents of redemptive suffering believe that suffering is a form of creative exchange, that it transforms the sufferer and the oppressor, and that it allows for nonviolence.[67] Detractors of redemptive suffering maintain that it demands an oppressed person's silence and complicity, allows oppressed people to justify and tolerate their suffering, and places focus solely on Jesus's suffering and not enough focus on Jesus' radical life and ministry.[68] Martha will suffer because of her decision. Martha opts to give people more intense dreams, and she learns that she will likely have to choose another profession because her career as a writer will cease and desist because of the dreams. "I know," she tells God. Martha's creativity and livelihood will suffer because she has been tasked with saving humanity from destruction—and even manipulated because God says he would choose someone else to do it, someone who might be power-hungry and not think of the consequences. As one scholar observes, Martha's "critique of the redemptive suffering matrix" invites us to consider one of Butler's consistent critiques of Christianity: "if there is a god who is on the side of the oppressed and is all-powerful, all-knowing, and all-good, then why do oppressed people even exist?"[69]

The redemptive suffering that Martha experiences highlights her multiple levels of trauma. First, she gives up her power as a creator. When writer and poet Alice Walker recalls her own mother working in a garden, Walker describes her mother as "radiant, almost to the point of being invisible—except as Creator: hand and eye. She is involved in work her soul must have. Ordering the universe in the image of her personal conception of Beauty."[70] As a writer, Martha shapes and orders the world through her idea of beauty: "For hours, she'd been spilling her new story onto paper in that sweet frenzy of creation that she lived for."[71] The "sweet frenzy of creation" that Martha "lived for" will no longer be possible with her decision to save humanity. "I think you'll have to find another way of earning a living," God tells Martha. "Beginning again at your age won't be easy."[72] God's pronouncement is a sad reversal of Martha's rejection of God's earlier claim that she would be returned to Earth and be placed on "the bottom level of society."[73] "I was born on the bottom, but I didn't stay there," she tells God, "And I'm not going back there!"[74] Yet, the loss of her creative drive and vocation combined with her age certainly spells the loss of income and opens the door for potential financial insecurity.

The second trauma? Martha asks God to remove her memory of their encounter and her participation in causing possible harm to herself and to others: "I'm afraid the time might come when I won't be able to stand knowing that I'm the one who caused not only the harm, but the end of the only career I've ever cared about. I'm afraid knowing all that might drive me out of my mind someday."[75] The potential of trauma, of being driven "out of [her] mind someday," is reason enough for Martha to ask God for dissociative amnesia, which psychologists classify as "a disorder characterized by retrospectively reported memory gaps"[76] that is often brought on by traumatic experiences. By requesting dissociative amnesia, Martha rejects the burden of strength that is often imposed on Black women as a side effect of redemptive suffering. Black womanist theologians explain the burden of strength as a phenomenon that "... continues to conceal the authentic experiences and needs of Black women, that encourages women to deny and ignore themselves ..."[77] The Strong Black Woman archetype "developed as an identity with three defining attributes: caregiving, emotional strength/regulation, and independence ... and were to be consummate caregivers, morally upright, selflessly devoted to the needs of others, and capable of enduring struggle without complaint."[78] Martha refuses to embody this archetype. Her request to God that she does not want to remember the part she played in transforming humanity is significant. Martha does not want to bear the responsibility for such a humanity-altering decision. In choosing not to remember, Martha rejects responsibility or the consequences of things that have been forcibly imposed on her and rejects the harmful assumptions that Black women should bear the burden of strength (instead of seeking help for various harms they live through).

Though Martha did have the option to opt-out, she chose to persist for the common good, even if that common good came at her own expense. Here Butler's "adapt or die refrain" (discussed in chapter 3) comes back into our purview. If Martha refuses God's task, God plans to send her back. "After all," God tells her, "there are millions of human beings who would give anything to do this work."[79] Martha's choice? Adapt to her new task or risk having God choose someone who would "make even worse choices" without thinking or caring about the consequences.[80] Much like her literary predecessors, Lilith from *Dawn*, Alanna from *Survivor*, and even Gan from "Bloodchild," Martha chooses life. By sacrificing part of herself to give humanity a fighting chance, Martha gives others a chance to survive. As a Butler stand-in, Martha's fate suggests that if given the opportunity to save humanity from itself, Butler would sacrifice her writing career if it meant making the world a better, safer place.

Understanding "The Book of Martha" through the lens of redemptive suffering offers a pessimistic view of the story, but in the story's afterword, Butler says it was her attempt at creating a utopia story. Yet one scholar maintains that "The Book of Martha" rejects the traditional premise that literary utopias are founded on. For Tarshia L. Stanley, literary utopias are created by writers from historically centered positions (white, cisgender, economically elite, abled men) who create utopias that support their privileged positions, thus making historically minoritized readers and writers suspicious of their attempt at utopia.[81] Butler does not subscribe to such narrow perceptions of literary utopias. As a skeptic of utopias, Butler defies this trend. In "The Book of Martha," she does not allow her protagonist to access solutions based on the traditional, narrow center; instead, Martha's life as a (formerly) poor Black woman allows her to consider the consequences of the utopia for everyone who occupies it, not just the elite.[82] Butler creates Martha as one concerned with communal change rather than her own individual desires. Martha creates a utopia that rejects the positions of the historically elite and instead includes the various needs of all people and the planet. Part of creating that utopia relies on Martha's changing image of God. God's transformation from a twelve-foot-tall white man to an average white man and finally to a Black woman is a "direct challenge to Eurocentric expressions of civilization," which informs her choice to change humanity by centering those on the margins rather than those who are often already centered.[83]

In addition to all that "Amnesty" and "The Book of Martha" do, they also solidify Butler's commitment to returning to old habits. Noah is a Black woman who, much like her biblical namesake, builds a community to make space for herself and her fellow humans in the new world that is destroyed by hubris rather than flooding. Butler admits she "was thinking of the story of Mary and Martha in Luke" and thought, "well, this character can be Martha, one of the workers who served the Lord."[84] Her return to biblical names, like the use of Mary and Rachel in *Mind of My Mind* (see chapter 2), and narratives, like the Genesis narrative adopted in *Wild Seed* (see chapter 3), demonstrates her investment in using things around her as reminders to us readers that adaptation and growth are necessary for our survival.

Fledgling

Although her final novel published during her lifetime does not use biblical references, Butler does use circumstances around her to shape the narrative. The persistence of racism is a key influence in the underlying plot of *Fledgling*, and the novel suggests that divesting from racism is essential for the survival of any species. Published in the same year as Stephenie Meyer's *Twilight* (2005) and J.R. Ward's *Dark Lover* (2005), Butler's first and only vampire novel was born to shake her out of her writer's block. Some describe the novel as "erotica," a descriptor Butler admitted she thought was under the umbrella of "just fantasy."[85] *Fledgling* centers on Shori Matthews, a Black girl vampire who forms sexual relationships with men and women who appear much older than she is, all the while trying to find out who has murdered her family and nearly murders her—and why. Notably, Shori has the appearance of a ten-year-old child. As the novel's first-person narrator, readers journey alongside Shori as she wakes up in a cave blind, naked, badly burned, and devoid of any memory. Once her body heals, she leaves the cave, encounters a twenty-two-year-old white man, Wright Hamlin, drinks his blood and researches what she is. She learns she is a vampire-human hybrid with "dark" skin, which results from a consensual genetic experiment involving a Black woman's DNA. After meeting with her father, Iosif, she discovers she is Ina, a vampire species that has historically and genetically been all white, and she learns that her family is being murdered by racist Ina families and their allies because they oppose the species' miscegenation or the mixing of Black human DNA and white Ina

DNA. In the process of defending herself and finding out who attacked her and her family (and why), she develops into an intelligent member of the Ina community, and she collects human partners called symbionts. These symbionts become addicted to her vampire venom, transmitted through her vampire bite, affording them sexual pleasure, longer than normal human life spans, slowed again, and increased resistance to disease. The novel ends with the Council of Judgement, an Ina legal proceeding, to determine the guilty parties of the murders of Shori's family and symbionts and mete out a decision for these crimes. Beyond callbacks to her previous work, *Fledgling* asks readers to think about the think through genre, assumptions about childhood sexuality, and the persistence of racism.

Butler admits she wrote *Fledgling* to break out of her writer's block, and the varied genres she uses in the novel are evidence of that. The novel certainly reads as a detective story, as Melody Jue observes, and Theri Pickens writes that the first half of the novel follows the trajectory of a *Law & Order* television episode (which would not be surprising given that Butler, by her own admission, consumed lots of television).[86] *Fledgling* also "offers striking similarities" to *The Furies,* the third play in Aeschylus's Oresteia trilogy, because both revolve around "a series of intra-familial murders" where "citizens surrender vigilante justice to a (presumably) impartial judge."[87] Others even characterize *Fledgling* as a postmodern neo-slave narrative.[88] But the novel is also a paranormal romance. I remember the first time I asked my students to think of *Fledgling* as a romance novel. There were uncomfortable laughs. An awkward squeak of a shoe against the tile floor. Averted glances. And then, as I pressed them with a raised eyebrow, the ideas flowed. We began compiling a list of romantic tropes we see in movies—love at first sight, enemies to lovers, insurmountable odds, happily ever after—and then we began to map those onto *Fledgling*. It was an uncomfortable exercise given that the novel explores pedophilia, the sexualization of a Black girl child, and addiction, among other things.

While criticism of the novel based on the age differences between Shori and Wright exists and is worthy of exploration, Shori's sexual relationships with Wright and her symbionts must be understood within the broader context of Butler's work and the vampire genre. Critics of *Fledgling* cite the hypersexualization of Black girlhood through Shori and the apparent pedophilia the novel sanctions. However, significant age gaps in sexual relationships are a pattern across much of Butler's fiction. In *Clay's Ark*, Keira is sixteen, and Eli is "in his early thirties,"[89] "yet their relationship is sexual. Although there are no clear ages provided in "Bloodchild," we do know that T'Gatoi, a high-ranking political official, was raised alongside the mother of the boy she plans to impregnate. In *Kindred*, Dana and Kevin Franklin have a twelve-year age difference (Dana is twenty-six, and Kevin is thirty-eight). Lauren is eighteen when she begins her sexual relationship with fifty-seven-year-old Bankole in *Sower*. While the perceived twelve-year age difference between Wright and Shori is not the widest age gap among Butler's characters, it is perhaps the most shocking because it becomes difficult to divest the relationships from the optics of pedophilia.

But these optics are where Butler toys with her readers and our perception of the vampire genre. Typically, in vampire lore, the seducing vampire is a white male who appears to be in his teens (but is at least a century old) and who falls in love with a human teenage girl. Notably, "the vast majority" of vampires in paranormal romance novels and TV shows are "old—though young looking—accomplished and attractive, white men" who are "modernized into the current decade" by the woman with whom they fall in love.[90] Edward Cullen from *Twilight* (2005, 2008), Angel from *Buffy, the Vampire Slayer* (1997–2001), and Stefan and Damon Salvatore from *The Vampire Diaries* (2009–2017) are some examples. The optics of pedophilia do not appear as pronounced because the vampire looks to be of a similar age as their love interests. Historically, the vampire has represented the outsider, the other. But in the 1990s, the vampire took on a sympathetic tone, the most popular being *Buffy*, *The Vampire Diaries*, and The *Twilight* Saga. Paranormal romance novels, like J.R. Ward's Black Dagger Brotherhood Series, "divorce the vampire from their Otherness."[91] In these mainstream, popular texts, the vampire moves from representing the undesirable Other to becoming the desired partner.[92]

Fledgling disrupts the existing trends in vampire romances. First, Shori's Black human DNA and her amnesia doubly mark her as an Other, an Outsider. The Ina vampires, who have historically been white and abled, view her Black human DNA and her impairment as marks of inferiority. Second, though Shori is marked as an outsider by many Ina, she is the object of desire by humans and Ina alike. Joel, a twenty-one-year-old Black human man, wants to be one of Shori's symbionts. He grew up around Ina and wanted to be part of her community. The Gordon family also wants Shori to become a mate to their sons so she can eventually bear their children. And Theodora, an older white woman who thought Shori was going to be "a tall, handsome, fully grown white man," also wants Shori.[93] Shori has no shortage of admirers, much like her white male vampire counterparts in paranormal romances. Third, whereas vampires like Edward and Damon are young-looking but are at least a century old, Shori is young and young-looking. She has the physical appearance of a ten-year-old human child, and as a fifty-three-year-old Ina vampire, she is a child, as some of the oldest Ina are over three hundred years old. She is the Black girl revision to Edward or Damon; the Black vampire girl child seduces, entices, and enthralls adult humans and vampires alike. Finally, unlike Edward or Damon, Shori does not lie to her symbionts, nor is she intentionally manipulative. Edward withholds information from Bella Swan just as Stefan and Damon withhold information from Elena Gilbert under the guise of protection. Shori keeps her partners informed, knowing a lack of information is dangerous and that being informed can allow one to make choices that ensure their relative safety. Shori does not abuse, coerce, or glamour her symbionts into sex or submission. Shori is, as one character describes her, an "ethical little thing."[94]

Regardless of Shori as the Black girl revision to leading white vampires in paranormal romances, the optics of pedophilia among Shori and her partners are clear, and Butler refuses to shy away from this comparison or its unsettling implications. Wright's clear insistence that he should not want to be with Shori sexually, calling her "Jailbait. Super jailbait," and another character's quip, "That would make things legal, at least," in response to Wright's hope that Shori is eighteen or nineteen, are invitations to examine the relationship through pedophilia.[95] But why? One answer lies within the genre. Butler despised being pigeonholed into one genre or another. And she uses *Fledgling* to poke fun and to interrogate the power dynamics of male/female relationships through the vampire genre. She uses the existing conventions of the vampire genre and bends them. *Fledgling* debunks ideas about vampires, crucifixes, mirrors, and immortality, and in doing so, she places a Black girl vampire at the center of the narrative, one who is the seducer, rather than the seduced. Shori is granted agency even though she is belittled, ridiculed, and as one scholar notes, the subject of both racist and ableist assumptions.[96] It is important to see *Fledgling* as a subversion/inversion of the dominant Western (white) vampire narratives, including paranormal romance.

A second answer lies within our own assumptions about childhood sexuality and agency, which the novel calls us to question. In the United States, childhood is shaped by several cultural, historical, and social factors, and it is often categorized as a time of innocence. That innocence is rooted in the absence of children's agency and sexuality. "There seems to be a widespread belief that children do not know or should not know anything about sexuality," writes Emma Renold. "Moral panics and public concern that children are not innocent enough hinges primarily upon issues of 'early sexual maturation.'"[97] Renold goes on to explain that through the myth of childhood sexual innocence: "Sexuality is reinscribed as the property of the adult where adult power erases any notion of children's sexual agency in matters of consent and sexuality rights more widely.[98] In other words, we have it in our minds that children are and should remain "innocent of sexual desires and intentions," even going so far as to assume that children are heterosexual.[99] *Fledgling* rejects this. We see Shori as sexual early on. Even in her amnesia, she recognizes her need for blood and her sexual desire for Wright, and she tells him, "I'm old enough to have sex with you if you want to."[100] And Shori's bisexuality and polyamory are clear in her choice of male and female symbionts. In addition to the myth of sexual innocence, Childhood is also marked by a lack of agency; children are deemed powerless. We do not think of children as people but as pets or puppets who must be controlled or protected. *Fledgling* rejects this, too. Shori is not without power. She rejects Wright's attempt to take her to a hospital early on in the novel, and her first encounter with Theodora uses the language of rape to describe Shori's drinking of her blood: "I . . . covered her mouth with my hand as she woke. I held on to her with my other arm and both my legs as she began to struggle . . . She struggled wildly at first, tried to bite me, tried to scream . . . when she gave no more trouble, I let her go."[101] Though Shori is a child in her vampire community and has the appearance of a ten-year-old human child, Butler does not allow her to subscribe to the widely held beliefs about children as inherently devoid of agency.

    The questions raised by *Fledgling* regarding the myth of the sexually innocent child may prompt readers to reevaluate conventional beliefs. Are readers prepared to accept the scholarly assertion that "Any notion of Shori's youth as a legal and ethical barrier to sexual consent is negated by her vampirism"?[102] Some may readily embrace this idea, while others will remain skeptical. Nevertheless, the novel provides an opportunity to critically engage with these uncomfortable complexities. At the very least, the novel calls into question our complicity in upholding the "myth of childhood sexual innocence" and prompts us to reflect on why we selectively accept certain conventions within the vampire genre when the conventions of sex and sexual desire fit what we deem to be appropriate.[103] But more than that, *Fledgling* reminds us that fantasy vampire worlds are not exempt from racism. Shori is referred to as a "murdering black mongrel bitch," and her racist Ina detractors lament the pollution of the Ina species with the question, "What will she give us all? Fur? Tails?"—a clear nod to the very human belief that Black people were animals.[104] In vampire worlds white vampires have ties to the Confederacy; Bill from *True Blood* (2008–14), Damon from *The Vampire Diaries*, and Jasper from *Twilight: Eclipse* (2007, 2010) are three popular examples. And typically, those ties are peripheral to the story, and discussions of race or racism seem to be eerily absent from these stories. But like so many topics, Butler does not shy away from the obvious. *Fledgling* refuses to seduce readers into believing that racism and speciesism do not matter—even in a fictional vampire world.

A Bittersweet Transition

In the remaining sixteen years of her life, Butler was plagued by hypertension, depression, grief, and writer's block. Compared to her previous literary output, we might be tempted to declare the last years of her life as lean ones. But this is also the time where she was awarded the MacArthur Fellowship. In 1995, she became a MacArthur Genius Grant recipient—the first science fiction writer to ever win the award. With this award she was, for the first time in her life, not worried about money. Though her health issues, grief, depression, and writer's block no doubt contributed to her slower writing pace, I do like to think that for the first time in a while that she had the opportunity to rest. After all, she does say that she was writing just that it was not anything worthwhile. Despite the circumstances that contributed to her writer's block, she remained deeply concerned about social issues, addressing them in the Parable duology, "Amnesty," "The Book of Martha," and even *Fledgling*. The Black women and girl protagonists echo Butler's earlier heroic women, and their circumstances recall earlier themes from previously published work. Yet Butler writes about them in fresh ways, steadfastly committed to hoping for a better world—even if it is only one she can imagine. Her final works guide us. *Sower* and *Talents* are the stories that are most frequently recommended in the wake of the COVID-19 pandemic, the nationwide bans on books, drag shows, Critical Race Theory—and so much more. Though her life and writing career ended so abruptly, she left us with gifts that keep on giving. A bittersweet transition indeed.

Part II

Writing across Genres

Butler's Literary Range

CHAPTER 5

"Where I actually say so"
Lessons from Her Freedom Narratives

"The relocation of slavery into the contemporary present is typical of black speculative fiction,"[1] writes Maisha L. Wester, and Octavia E. Butler's writing is no exception. However, Butler was reluctant to accept literary critics' assertions that her 1984 story "Bloodchild" bears any resemblance or thematic comparisons to slavery. "It amazes me that some people have seen 'Bloodchild' as a story of slavery," she writes in her afterword to the story. "It isn't."[2] "The only places I am writing about slavery," she tells Stephen W. Potts in a 1996 interview, "is where I actually say so."[3] Butler would agree that she writes about slavery or its legacies in *Kindred* (1979), *Wild Seed* (1980), *Parable of the Sower* (1993), and *Parable of the Talents* (1998). However, this chapter does not explore *Wild Seed*. Certainly, *Wild Seed* explores the experiences of enslaved Black Americans. The novel depicts the brutal reality of slavery specifically in its focus on The Middle Passage and the Transatlantic Slave Trade. The destruction of the main characters' villages and the division of families at seaports in West Africa are historically accurate descriptions of enslavers raiding African communities and dividing people for profit. The female protagonist makes the perilous journey from Africa to the Americas, and in her loneliness, she nearly casts herself into the sea to escape the stifling loneliness—reminiscent of historical records that show enslaved Black people jumped from ships and died in the Middle Passage. This same character's arrival in New York at the Wheatley Plantation brings another reference to Black American enslavement. "Wheatley" is an allusion to Phillis Wheatley Peters, who was enslaved by John and Susanna Wheatley, and who published *Poems on Various*

Subjects, Religious and Moral in 1773, making it the first published volume of poetry by an enslaved Black person.

Though *Wild Seed* does deal directly with slavery, it does not do so in the tradition of first-person narratives of enslavement. In this chapter, readers will understand how *Kindred*, *Sower*, and *Talents* participate in the African American literary tradition of narratives of enslavement, resistance, and freedom. In the spirit of African American resistance, this chapter has several purposes. The first section, "Slave and Neo-Slave Narratives: A Tradition and Its Legacies," describes the format, goals, and characteristics of slave narratives and neo-slave narratives. The second and third sections explain how *Kindred* is a neo-slave narrative and, in the tradition of slave narratives, indicate how *Kindred* offers readers lessons on how to act. The fourth and fifth sections explore the Parable duology in the tradition of enslavement, resistance, and freedom, and how they pay homage to enslaved Black people and their legacies in the United States.

The Tradition and Legacies of Slave Narratives

Kindred, *Sower*, and *Talents* exist within the tradition of the nineteenth-century African American slave narrative which scholars also refer to as emancipatory narratives or freedom narratives.[4] The nineteenth-century African American slave narrative is a first-person account of a formerly enslaved person's life as an enslaved person and their journey or escape to freedom. nineteenth-century narratives of enslavement existed to advocate for the abolition of slavery. The goal of these narratives was to expose the inhumanity of the slave system, to encourage abolitionism by providing an eye-witness account of the enslaved person's experience, and to provide evidence of enslaved Black people's humanity.[5] Readers witness this purpose and function at work in Frederick Douglass's *Narrative of the Life of Frederick Douglass, an American Slave, Written By Himself* (1845), or Solomon Northup's *Twelve Years a Slave* (1853). In addition to those goals, emancipatory narratives written or dictated by enslaved Black women, such as Harriet Jacobs's *Incidents in the Life of a Slave Girl* (1861) or Mary Prince's *A History of Mary Prince* (1831), had an additional goal: to "collectively specify the harshness and severity of slave women's diverse forms of labor, chiefly field-work (to raise livestock, to produce tobacco, food, clothing, and other consumable goods), domestic service, childcare and child rearing, sexual work (from concubinage to breeding), and textile manufacture (from spinning to sewing)."[6]

Nineteenth-century African American slave narratives follow a specific format. These narratives begin with authenticating material—a short letter or preface to the reader, written by a white benefactor who attests to the reliability and good character of the formerly enslaved author. This authenticating material also calls attention to what the narrative will reveal about the moral abominations of slavery. William Lloyd Garrison authenticates Douglass's 1845 narrative, Lydia Maria Child authenticates Harriet Jacobs's 1861 narrative, and David Wilson authenticates Solomon Northup's 1853 *Twelve Years a Slave*. After the prefatory authenticating material comes the formerly enslaved person's telling of their story that indicts enslavers ethically and morally and depicts slavery as hell on earth.[7] Frederick Douglass explores how slavery corrupts the enslaved and the enslaver; Harriet Jacobs reveals how pretty enslaved Black girls are subject to unwanted sexual advances and punished if they refuse them, and Solomon Northup's narrative reveals that freeborn Black folks are often enslaved on the word of white men with no legal recourse to defend themselves. Often, there is a personal crisis that jumpstarts the enslaved person's decision to run away, and the writers rely on their faith in God to provide the strength for their freedom journey.[8] Typically, this segment of the narrative uses typology, a theological perspective that maintains that Christian beliefs in the New Testament are symbolized in the Old Testament. Enslaved Black people used biblical typology to explain their lived experiences and present conditions. For instance, many enslaved Black people considered their enslavement in the context of the Old Testament book of Exodus, as a way to analogize their experiences of bondage with the biblical narratives as a reminder that the God of the Hebrews was a deliverer of the oppressed and a destroyer of the oppressors. We see such examples in Paul Laurence Dunbar's poem "An Antebellum Sermon" (1895), David Walker's *Appeal to the Coloured Citizens of the World* (1831), and William and Ellen Craft's *Running a Thousand Miles for Freedom* (1860). After the narrative's climactic point, readers witness the former slave's arrival to freedom, and upon that arrival, the formerly enslaved person either re-names themselves or dedicates their future to antislavery activism (or both).

In addition to a similar narrative structure among nineteenth-century slave narratives, one key feature of one of the most celebrated nineteenth-century slave narratives is the "scene of instruction"—the scenes in emancipatory narratives where the formerly enslaved narrator learns to read and write,[9] or where enslaved Black people teach others to read and write. Douglass's 1845 narrative features three such scenes. In the first, his master's wife, Sophia, teaches a young Douglass how to read, and Mr. Auld admonishes her saying, "'A nigger should know nothing but to obey his master—to do as he is told to do. Learning would spoil the best nigger in the world. . . . It would forever unfit him to be a slave."[10] In the second, Douglass makes friends with white children, and "as many of these as I could," he writes, "I converted into teachers."[11] In the third,

Douglass reveals he learned to write by challenging white boys, telling them that he could write better than they could, which allowed him to practice his writing when they challenged his claim. Butler's fiction is replete with scenes of instruction, all offered by Black women. In *Kindred*, Dana teaches an enslaved Nigel to read in secret, and when caught, she is beaten for it. After escaping her burned gated community, Lauren teaches Zahra to read in *Sower*, and in *Talents*, after escaping from Camp Christian, Lauren relates how she taught children to read and write, having them write their alphabet on the ground. In each of these works, this education as freedom is linked to the elements of the nineteenth-century slave narrative and Black resistance more broadly because enslaved Black people were legally forbidden to learn to read and write because learning "would *spoil* the best nigger in the world."[12]

Understanding the nineteenth-century slave narrative, its structure, and its key features, is key to understanding *Kindred*, *Sower*, and *Talents*, not because they are nineteenth-century slave narratives, but because each novel fits into the African American literary genre of the neo-slave narrative much like Margaret Walker's *Jubilee* (1966), Toni Morrison's *Beloved* (1980), and Assata Shakur's *Assata: An Autobiography* (1987). A neo-slave narrative is a "modern narrative of escape from bondage to freedom" that is published in the mid-twentieth century or later and is often, but not always, set during the enslavement era.[13] Neo-slave narratives either depict the experience of chattel enslavement or the effects of chattel enslavement in the United States. *Kindred* is a neo-slave narrative in the most traditional sense: the novel was published in 1979 and is set in antebellum Maryland on a plantation. The modern relationship between Kevin and Dana demonstrates the effects of chattel enslavement in their contemporary moment. *Sower* and *Talents* are examples of neo-slave narratives that, while set in the future, are directly impacted by the chattel slavery past. *Sower* demonstrates the residual danger of chattel enslavement, and *Talents* offers a vision of the frightening implications when that past is re-implemented.

Kindred as Neo Slave Narrative

Written in first person, the novel's opening line, "I lost an arm on my last trip home,"[14] positions *Kindred* within the tradition of the slave narrative, but not without its own revisions. For example, *Kindred* is a novel, so there is not a white person who writes a preface that authenticates the forthcoming narrative. However, the arrival of Dana's husband, Kevin, in the past functions as authentication. Before joining Dana at the Weylin Plantation, Kevin has his doubts about Dana's time travel remarking "I don't know what to think" after her disappearance and reappearance happen the first time.[15] But, on Dana's third trip back, once Kevin arrives on the plantation with her, he exclaims, "It happened! It's real!"[16] This moment is important for Kevin, but it is also important for us as readers. Without Kevin's validating voice, readers might be left wondering if Dana is hallucinating or if maybe she has made it all up. It is no coincidence that the person who authenticates Dana's travels is a white man. Dana's second trip to the Weylin Plantation offers readers their first opportunity to witness slavery as hell on earth. Dana witnesses a group of drunken white patrollers beating an enslaved Black man in front of his free Black wife and daughter. Dana watches as the man is tied to a tree as one of the drunken men cracks a whip midair, "apparently for his own amusement," before bringing the whip on the man's back causing convulsions. Dana could "literally smell his sweat, hear every ragged breath, every cry, every cut of the whip" and "see his body jerking, convulsing, straining against the rope as his screaming went on and on."[17] Although Dana's first trip to the Weylin Plantation allows her to act as an eyewitness observer like Douglass's eyewitness account, a later trip finds her in a similar position as the enslaved Black man she witnessed being beaten. Dana recalls, "They took me to the barn and tied my hands and raised whatever they had tied them to high over my head. When I was barely able to touch the floor with my toes, Weylin ripped my clothes off and began to beat me. He beat me until I swung back and forth by my wrists, half-crazy with pain, unable to find my footing, unable to stand the pressure of hanging, unable to get away from the steady slashing blows."[18] The inclusion of Dana's personal experience of violence is important for modern readers of *Kindred*. Whereas Dana's repeated time travel trips back to the Weylin plantation are real enough, the marks on her body that remain when she returns to the present serve as proof of her eyewitness experience of slavery as hell on earth. In the same way that formerly enslaved Black people write about their experiences of enslavement, Dana's experiences of enslavement are made visible by the scars and physical markings that she bears on her body.

Dana's repeated trips back to the Weylin Plantation also underscore the collective "harshness and severity of slave women's diverse forms of labor"[19] that enslaved Black women wrote about in particular. Tess, an enslaved Black woman who performs manual labor on the plantation, is the clearest example in *Kindred*. In addition to completing daily tasks to help the plantation run smoothly, Tess is required to sexually submit to Mr. Tom Weylin. But when Tom is "tired of her as a bed mate,"[20] he gives Tess to Jake Edwards, a white overseer. A weeping Tess laments, "'You do everything they tell you . . . and they still treat you like a old dog. Go here, open your legs; go there, bust your back. What they care! I ain't s'pose to have no feelin's!'"[21] Tess's description of her experience, being split between manual labor and sexual labor, demonstrates her position as a "fragmented commodity," a term Barbara Omolade uses to describe the unique conditions of enslaved Black women who are commodities for their multiple forms of labor.[22] Tess, however, seems to be a failed fragmented commodity. Tess is sold, and Dana suspects it is because "She'd had no children."[23] Readers never learn the actual reason Tess is sold, but Tess's physical labor on the plantation is overshadowed by her lack of human reproduction. Because she fails to bear children—by either an enslaved man or by an enslaver—she is a failed fragmented commodity.

Like formerly enslaved nineteenth-century narrators, Dana endures several personal crises that inform her decision to escape. Arguably, each time Dana returns to 1976 from the nineteenth century it is an escape. For instance, when Dana returns to 1976 the first two times, she does so because she believes her life is in danger; a gun is pointed at her head the first time, and the second time, she believes that after being beaten by a patroller she will die. But there are two incidents of Dana's *intentional* escape. The first is when she runs away from the Weylin Plantation after she discovers that Rufus has lied about sending her letters to Kevin. Her discovery of Rufus's deceit spurs her decision to run away from the plantation. Her unsuccessful escape attempt results in her capture, beating, and return to the Weylin plantation. The second intentional escape occurs after Rufus punches her in the face. His physical abuse of her leads Dana to slit her wrists, a near-death experience that sends her back to 1976. Contemporary readers may not want to think of death by suicide as an escape; however, it was a tactic enslaved Black people used. African American Spirituals and Sorrow Songs, like "Swing Low, Sweet Chariot," "Oh Freedom," and "Steal Away," employ a double meaning. The lyrics suggest a plot for freedom by "stealing away" and escaping the bondage of their captors; however, freedom through death and reunification with Christ who comes to "carry them home." The mass suicide at Igbo's Landing, where newly enslaved captives drowned their white captors and then at the behest of their leader walked into the sea and drowned to escape slavery, invokes this death as a freedom tradition. For Dana, however, death by suicide was a gamble. Either she would slit her wrists and die in the antebellum South, or she would slit her wrists and it would return her to the twentieth-century present. Unlike nineteenth-century emancipatory narratives that use biblical typology, there is no clear use of biblical typology in *Kindred*. Dana admits she long ignored the Christian teachings of her aunt and uncle; however, it might be argued that Dana uses history as a sort of typology. She uses her existence in her 1976 present and her being pulled back to save Rufus as the reason or the justification to explain why she travels back in time. In that way, the "typology" is her connection to Rufus as her several times removed grandfather. Finally, the renaming of self that is characteristic of slave narratives is not a literal renaming but a symbolic renaming in *Kindred*. Dana is a new person, marked by slavery with a physical impairment—her amputated arm. Dana's amputated arm is "a kind of birthmark, marking her identity,"[24] allowing her to be "reborn into the present" with the past "inscribed" on her body,[25] as a reminder that "she will always bear the mark of her kindred."[26] Though Dana is not a new person in name, she is a new person, reborn and touched by slavery, leaving her irrevocably different from who and what she was before.

Kindred's Three-Pronged Lesson for Contemporary Readers

Beyond teaching readers about the importance of history and demonstrating that the past is more than a prologue, that it is a specter that haunts and dwells with us each day, *Kindred* also reminds us about the value and necessity of allyship. In an unpublished interview, Butler offers some insight into her thought process for her characterization in *Kindred*. She says, "The comment I heard most often repeated by white people after the first showing of ROOTS on television was 'But they didn't show any good white people.' I always felt this was like someone watching a movie about Auschwitz and complaining that there were no good Germans in it. Slaves, like Jews in Auschwitz were likely to find good captors, good masters few and far between. Nevertheless . . . Kevin's existence is to please those looking for good white people."[27] Butler's word choice is worth exploring. She says Kevin's inclusion is an attempt to please those looking for good white people, but she never says that Kevin is good. She does say that "Kevin is a decent man who decided where he stood long before the time trips began."[28] But the word choice—*decent*—also suggests room for improvement. Kevin's inclusion has some instructional value for well-meaning white people who want to be or claim to be allies. Jay Dodd defines an ally as one who is ". . . willing to take on the stigma of being the "other," willing to not be complacent in the reproduction of discrimination, willing to remove yourself from the center . . ."[29] Therefore, one thing that *Kindred* does is encourage good white people to become allies. To be an ally means first coming to an understanding of privilege, and the best character to recognize this trait in is Kevin.

As readers, we witness Kevin coming to understand his whiteness so he can function as an ally. For example, while in the nineteenth-century past, he remarks to Dana, "This could be a great time to live in. I keep thinking what an experience it would be to stay in it—go West and watch the building of the country, see how much of the Old West mythology is still true."[30] When Dana bitterly responds, "West . . . That's where they're doing it to the Indians instead of the blacks," she notes that Kevin looked at her "strangely," remarking that

"He had been doing that a lot lately."[31] Later, when Dana and Kevin witness the Black children on the plantation pretending to sell each other on the auction block, Dana is horrified, but Kevin says, "Dana, you're reading too much into a kids' game."[32] Dana challenges him yet again to see with his eyes open when he says he's only seen one whipping but that "this place isn't what I would have imagined. No overseer. No more work than the people can manage . . ." until Dana cuts in: ". . . no decent housing . . . Dirt floors to sleep on, food so inadequate they'd all be sick if they didn't keep gardens in what's supposed to be their leisure time and steal from the cookhouse when Sarah lets them. And no rights and the possibility of being mistreated or sold away from their families for any reason—or no reason. Kevin, you don't have to beat people to treat them brutally."[33]

Kevin rationalizes and minimizes enslaved Black peoples' conditions, and Dana offers the following in response, "You might be able to go through this whole experience as an observer . . . It's protection. It's nineteen seventy-six shielding and cushioning eighteen nineteen for me. But . . . I can't maintain the distance."[34] Early on in his venture to the past, Kevin requires a lot of explaining, and Dana holds him accountable, calling him to see life not through his eyes of privilege. Kevin's relative comfort with what he sees around him is a hallmark of his complacency, one that echoes the Rev. Dr. Martin Luther King Jr's words on complacency in his "Letter from A Birmingham Jail." In it, King says the biggest stumbling block in the civil rights movement is the white moderates because of their complacency, writing, "Shallow understanding from people of good will is more frustrating than absolute misunderstanding from people of ill will. Lukewarm acceptance is much more bewildering than outright rejection."[35] Dana's frustration at Kevin's shallow understanding is evident. Kevin teaches us that we *all* have growing to do and that we need to heed the voices who continue to hold us accountable, just as Dana does.

But *Kindred* also suggests that being held accountable is not enough. After five years in the nineteenth century, Kevin changes physically, mentally, and emotionally. He witnessed a child born dead because it was whipped out of his mother, and he also saw the mother die. But unlike before, where he was a passive observer, he becomes an active participant, moving from ally to accomplice. He participated in abolitionist and anti-racist work while stuck in the past, stealing slaves and helping them to freedom. Kevin's move from ally to accomplice is important because it teaches us that a return to "normalcy" in the wake of a series of devastating, life-altering events is not possible. Upon returning to his 1976 life, Kevin cannot focus because his confrontations with the past have disrupted everything he sees in front of him. His comfort with "toys" (like an electric pencil sharpener) seems pointless. Having come to an understanding of whiteness and the brutality he escaped because of his whiteness does not allow him to cope well with his present. He wants to rid himself of the past, but he cannot. He, like Dana, is marked by the past; physically, he has a scar, he has a hint of a Southern accent, and he even has a look that bears a striking resemblance to the "closed and ugly" visage of Tom Weylin.[36] What Kevin teaches us is that when we confront the past, our comfort with the present and our ideas about what is normal must be disrupted for us to work against oppression and advocate for oppressed groups.

As the novel's heroine, Dana is another character to examine through the lens of allyship. Dana thinks about allyship before she is transported back in time, remembering a conversation she had with Kevin after he asked to marry her. Dana tells Kevin to go talk to her sister, but she warns him that he may not be prepared for his sister's response. And he wasn't. Kevin laments his confusion at his sister's racist response to his desire to marry Dana, remarking: "The thing is, there's no reason for her to react this way. She didn't even believe the garbage she was handing me—or didn't used to. It's as though she was quoting someone else. Her husband, probably. Pompous little bastard. I used to try to like him for her sake."[37] When Dana asks if her future sister-in-law's husband is prejudiced, Kevin admits, "Her husband would have made a good Nazi. She used to joke about it—though never when he could hear."[38] But it is Dana's response that tells us a key component of allyship: "But she married him."[39] Dana's comment, "but she married him . . . " lets us know something more about being an ally: you cannot be an ally if you are married to a bigot. In other words, Dana lets us know that who we are linked to matters. In addition to Dana being a conduit for us to understand how allyship works, she was also an ally. On her earliest trips back to the past, Dana allies with the enslaved Black people on Weylin's plantation. Dana seeks real, practical change in the quality of life for those around her who are being oppressed, notably evident in teaching Nigel and Carrie to read.

At the same time, however, even Dana's fondness and commitment to understanding and helping Rufus may get in the way of her full support for and an alliance with the enslaved. After Dana travels back in time and the longer she stays in the nineteenth century, the more she seems to wrestle with this idea of allyship. Dana tries to maintain her identity as a free, intelligent Black woman. But despite being enslaved and abused by Rufus, she is forced to continually help and save him if she wishes to live in the future, which involves thoughts and actions that do not seem to align with the characteristics of an ally. She faces the moral tension that saving Rufus means she lives at the expense of the brutal degradation and oppression of dozens of slaves. What's clear, then, is that Dana's morals and ethics are continually compromised because she thinks she must persuade Alice to submit to Rufus sexually. Dana goes beyond her call of duty to simply keep Rufus alive on her return trips. Why? Because she fears that if she does not keep Rufus alive and get Alice pregnant, she will not exist in her present time. Dana says to Alice, "Goddamnit, Alice, will you slow down! Look, you keep working on him the way you have been, and you can get whatever you want and live to enjoy it."[40] Dana's comment to Alice at this moment in the text recalls an earlier moment in *Kindred* where Dana thinks to herself, "It was so easy to advise other people to live with their pain."[41] Alice is continually raped, and Dana waits for the birth of Hagar, of whom she is a direct descendant. Once Hagar is born, Dana's hamartia is that she does not try to help Alice, and she doesn't drum up a plan to free Alice. Instead, she tells Alice not to leave, and in many ways, she aligns herself with Rufus and becomes complicit in supporting a slave master mentality. When Dana invests herself in preserving her lineage, it "only serves to draw her into deeper and deeper complicity with the horrible past of slavery that created her future."[42] Neither Dana nor Kevin is perfect; in fact, what we can conclude is that both teach us that allyship is a continuous process.

Allyship, while necessary, is not enough. *Kindred* reminds us that civil disobedience is crucial. Butler is not the first Black writer to champion civil disobedience, but it permeates *Kindred*. Civil disobedience, which is "said to fall between legal protest, on the one hand, and conscientious refusal, revolutionary action, militant protest and organized forcible resistance, on the other hand," appears in subtle forms throughout *Kindred*.[43] One of Dana's earliest forms of civil disobedience is teaching enslaved Black children to read noting that there is "nothing more subversive than that."[44] She asks herself, "Why couldn't I just turn these two kids away, turn off my conscience, and be a coward, safe and comfortable?"[45] Her insurrectionist act is met with bodily harm—a whipping. A second act of civil disobedience occurs when, after returning to the Weylin Plantation for the fourth time, Dana's "complacency" with her condition "was brought to an end."[46] After Rufus punches her in the face—violating the unspoken agreement that Dana would keep him alive and Rufus would not harm her—he orders her to go inside the Big House. Dana engages in a "conscientious refusal" that is characteristic of civil disobedience when she "turned [her] back and went to the cookhouse, deliberately disobeying."[47] After ignoring Rufus' order, Dana slits her wrists, which nearly kills her, but it does allow her to travel back to her twentieth-century present, escaping him, if only temporarily. A third act of civil disobedience is Dana's self-defense. Nearing *Kindred*'s end, Rufus tries to rape Dana, and she defies her own "mandate"—one that says she will always save Rufus's life—by killing him. Though she kills Rufus, she loses her left arm in the process. What does Dana teach us about civil disobedience? Each act of civil disobedience causes Dana some form of bodily harm, though she undermines systems of oppression at every turn. It suggests, then, that although there is power in civil disobedience, civil disobedience does not come without a price. Are we willing to pay for it?

In addition to allyship and civil disobedience, the gendered nature of *Kindred* and nineteenth-century slave narratives make the case for the importance of women-centered networks. If Black women-authored nineteenth-century slave narratives offer vivid accounts of Black women who struggle to survive in the chattel slave system, *Kindred* highlights how Black women's survival, safety, and sanity are in jeopardy because they are "caught between" opposing forces. The phrase "caught between" appears three times in *Kindred*, and each time it is used to describe a Black woman. Exploring the "caught between" highlights the complexities of Black women's lived experiences, from the nineteenth century to Dana's twentieth-century world and our twenty-first-century present. In chapter six of "The Fall," Sarah tells Dana, "You're caught between," referring to Dana being caught between loving Kevin and avoiding Margaret Weylin, who is sexually attracted to Kevin and insulted by Dana's presence.[48] In chapter two of "The Fight," Dana shares, "Today and yesterday didn't mesh. I felt almost as strange as I had after my first trip back to Rufus—caught between his home and mine," describing her feeling of being out of sync in her 1976 home.[49] In chapter six of "The Fight," Dana describes Sarah as "caught between anger and concern, not knowing which one to express," referring to Sarah's concern for Rufus who had just been beaten by Alice's husband for raping Alice.[50]

These three uses of the phrase "caught between" reveal three key truths: Black women are often caught between something that is theirs and a jealous white woman who believes they should not have it; Black women are caught between inexplicable circumstances, two different worlds, that may leave them feeling out of place; Black women are often caught between divided loyalties. Sarah is caught between anger and concern, but Dana is also caught between encouraging Alice to go to Rufus while simultaneously telling Alice that Dana would not go to Rufus in her position. We learn from this concept of "the caught between" that their survival, safety, or at the very least, sanity is maintained through women-centered networks. One example is the aftermath of Liza's betrayal of Dana. Dana's escape attempt is foiled when Liza secretly reports her to Tom. In a show of solidarity with Dana, Tess, Carrie, and Alice ensure that the "next time" Liza sees Dana—or anyone—attempting to flee the Weylin Plantation Liza will "keep her mouth shut."[51] Liza appears before Tom Weylin "bruised and battered" and "black and blue all over" and Alice tells Dana, "Now she's more scared of us than of Mister Tom."[52] Another example is Dana's offer to "stall Rufus" and give Alice a head start if she intends to run away instead of submitting to his sexual conquests. These two examples, among others, stress to Black women today the importance of cultivating and maintaining these Black women-centered networks for our survival, safety, and sanity.

The call-to-action tradition that *Kindred* participates in also emerges through Butler's conflation of the nineteenth-century past with the global twentieth-century present. *Kindred* reminds us of the importance and necessity of linking global movements for liberation. Dana's experiences of state-sanctioned violence in the nineteenth century are drawn into sharp relief when the state-sanctioned anti-Black violence emerges in an international context. On the radio, Dana hears "a story about South Africa—blacks rioting and dying wholesale in battles with police over the policies of the white supremacist government" and she muses that "South African whites had always struck me as people who would have been happier living in the nineteenth century, or the eighteenth. In fact, they were living in the past as far as their race relations went."[53] In drawing parallels between her time in the past and her time in the future, we are once again reminded that the past is more than a mere prologue. The past is present, and if we are not careful, the past will become our future.

Traditions, Hush Harbors, and the Federal Writers' Project in the Parable Duology

If *Kindred* warns us that our past will become our future, *Sower* and *Talents* warn us that Butler's future will become our present if we do not heed her cautions. *Sower* participates in the emancipatory narrative tradition, through its homage to emancipatory narratives and themes that link to chattel slavery though it does not resemble a neo-slave narrative in the same way that *Kindred* does. *Sower*, a first-person epistolary novel, is concerned with bondage and freedom. While the novel offers us a semi-fictional future-oriented dystopia, there are several allusions to nineteenth-century chattel enslavement in the novel. Lauren's quip that she and her group are like the "modern underground railroad," the conversations about debt slavery, and references to ex-slave resistance are just a few examples.[54]

In addition to its homage to emancipatory narratives through themes and references that link to chattel slavery, Lauren Olamina's disguise as an able-bodied Black man takes on a deeper significance when understood in the context of Ellen Craft. In 1848, Ellen and William Craft, an enslaved husband and wife duo, fled from a Macon, Georgia plantation, and arrived in the North. They wrote about their journey in *Running a Thousand Miles for Freedom; or, the Escape of William and Ellen Craft from Slavery* (1860), and the success of their escape was rooted in Ellen's ability to pass as a disabled white man. "Knowing slaveholders have the privilege of taking their slaves to any part of the country they think proper," William Craft writes, "it occurred to me that, as my wife was nearly white, I might get her to disguise herself as an invalid gentleman, and assume to be my master, while I could attend as his slave, and that in this manner we might effect our escape."[55] Ellen's very fair skin allowed her to pass as white, and after shearing her hair, she could pass as a frail man. The disguise of white maleness was not enough for Ellen, however. Because she was passing as a white gentleman on a train, the expectation is that she should be able to write, speak, and socialize. Because Ellen could not read or write, she faked a hand injury and bound her jaw, so that if a white person approached her for conversation, she could signal to her jaw (which would hide her voice) and point to her injured hand so she would not be required to write anything, allowing her husband, posing as her enslaved manservant, to speak for Ellen. Further, Ellen's disguise as a disabled white man was necessary because, given the proprietary conventions of the time, it would have been too dangerous for a white woman to be traveling alone with an enslaved Black man. Ellen passed as a disabled white man with her husband posing as an attending slave. I intentionally mention Ellen's constructed disability because Lauren is impaired by her hyperempathy. Hyperempathy is a disorder that causes the afflicted to believe that they share the pain and pleasure of others. If Lauren sees someone in pain, she feels their pain. If Lauren shoots someone in self-defense, she feels the gunshot wound until the other person dies. Lauren sees her hyperempathy as a weakness, yet she adopts a masculine persona, shears her hair, and she chooses not to disclose her disability because both her maleness and perceived able-bodiedness make her safer while traveling on the road north. For both Lauren Olamina and Ellen Craft, the adoption of the masculine persona was about access to certain spaces and about preserving their safety. Ellen Craft adopts a masculine persona and a disability because they make her safer and minimize the risk of exposure. Conversely, Lauren adopts a masculine persona and hides her disability because both of those things make her safe, also minimizing the risk of exposure to harm. Thinking through Lauren Olamina's disguise and her trek to freedom in the context of Ellen Craft who does indeed pass as a disabled white man in the same way that Lauren passes as an able-bodied Black man to ensure her safety, coupled with the deliberate, intentional language of enslavement firmly places *Sower* in the neo-slave narrative tradition in African American literature.

Talents, like its prequel, includes references to nineteenth-century chattel slavery. As Lauren describes her world, readers learn that the past is more than a mere prologue. The past has awakened and saturated the present in full force.

Lauren writes, "Indenturing indigents, young and old, is much in fashion now. The Thirteenth and Fourteenth Amendments—the ones abolishing slavery and guaranteeing citizenship rights—still exist, but they've been so weakened by custom, by Congress and the various state legislatures and by recent Supreme Court decisions that they don't much matter."[56] As the novel progresses, readers learn that slavery becomes a punishment for a crime, which could mean vagrancy, being non-Christian, or being the "wrong" kind of Christian. Despite protests that it was illegal to collar non-criminals, force people to work without pay, confiscate property, or separate children from families, readers learn about slave auctions and new torture tools, the slave collars, that go around a person's neck and transmit electromagnetic shocks or lashings when orders are disobeyed, and witness the enslavement of Lauren and her Earthseed community.

Although the references to enslavement permeate *Talents*, the novel also explores elements of covert resistance characteristic of enslaved Black people during the antebellum period. The creation and flourishing of Acorn, the settlement Lauren and her followers establish, is best understood as a hush harbor. During the antebellum period in the United States, the hush harbor also referred to as a brush arbor, was "a secluded informal structure, often built with tree branches, set in places away from masters so that slaves could meet to worship in private."[57] Notably, hush harbors allowed enslaved Black people to practice syncretism, where they combined African and Christian worship practices.[58] "In the secrecy of the quarters or the seclusion of the brush arbors ('hush harbors'),"historian Albert J. Raboteau wrote, "the slaves made Christianity their own."[59] This secrecy was paramount for Acorn. Though the religion practiced was Earthseed, a syncretic version of various religions, the seclusion of Acorn was necessary for its survival. At Acorn, not only did Lauren and other followers of Earthseed practice their beliefs, but they also lived unmolested by government officials, raising their families, practicing environmental sustainability, and cultivating a thriving community.

However, the religious fervor sweeping the nation made Acorn a target. Just as enslaved Black people "faced severe punishment if caught attending secret prayer meetings,"[60] so too did those who were not part of President Jarrett's Christian America. "We at Acorn," Lauren writes, "were told that we were attacked and enslaved because we were a heathen cult."[61] After six years at Acorn, the Earthseed community was attacked by men, called Crusaders, in armored trucks who neutralize them with tear gas and fasten slave collars around their necks. Acorn gets taken over by members of the Church of Christian America, and they rename it Camp Christian, which becomes a conversion camp or twenty-first-century plantation where the formerly free perform manual labor, are forced to attend conversion church services, are raped by their enslavers, are denied reading and writing material, and are subject to countless human atrocities. The enslavement of free-born citizens at Acorn recalls the "slavery as hell on earth" component of nineteenth-century slave narratives but it also calls back to the harrowing experiences of Solomon Northup. Northup, born a free Black man, was drugged, captured, and sold into slavery for twelve years, the result of which is his narrative *Twelve Years a Slave: Narrative of Solomon Northup, a Citizen of New York, Kidnapped in Washington City in 1841, and Rescued in 1853*. Though Northup is rescued, Lauren and her community rescue themselves. Seventeen months after their enslavement, in resistance like that of Nat Turner, the enslaved at Camp Christian kill their enslavers and burn Camp Christian.

Structurally, the novel mimics the epistolary format of its prequel; however, as I discuss in chapter 4, *Talents* is Asha Vere's compilation of various first-person stories including eyewitness accounts from Camp Christian's formerly enslaved persons. The clear references to slavery combined with polyvocal narrative framing liken Asha Vere's compilation of *Talents* to an edited critical edition that exists within the tradition of post-emancipatory field reports and subsequent collections associated with the Federal Writers' Project. The Federal Writers' Project was a government initiative that sought to alleviate the effects of the Great Depression by sending out-of-work writers to interview people and transcribe their life stories. In 1937, John A. Lomax, the National Advisor on Folklore and Folkways for the Federal Writers' Project, was impressed with the narrated stories of formerly enslaved Black people and he requested more of their work. By 1941, Lomax's successor, Benjamin A. Botkin, compiled the interviews and narratives into *Slave Narratives: A Folk History of Slavery in the United States from Interviews with Former Slaves* (1941).[62] Much like a writer for the Federal Writers' Project, Asha uses informants to talk about the brutalization people, whether enslaved or adopted, endured under Christian America. One informant tells her about a Matron, a Christian America wife who adopted and later killed a seven-year-old child.[63] Another of Asha's informants is Cody Smith, a former Camp Christian slave, who shares about her life and the lives of others. Cody shares about Day Turner, a man whom Lauren admired and whose name is an allusion to the nineteenth-century insurrectionist Nat Turner. Day plots an unsuccessful slave insurrection at Camp Christian and is subsequently executed. She uses her mother as an informant through the inclusion of her journal entries, particularly those that describe her experience of enslavement. Where *Kindred* and *Sower* more readily mimic the nineteenth-century slave narrative—and therefore fit the widely accepted definitions of neo-slave narrative—*Talents*, with its homage to hush harbors and allusions to the Federal Writers Project, also exists within the neo-slave narrative tradition, keeping alive the tradition of telling enslaved peoples' stories and, like its prequel, offering seeds of wisdom for readers to continue planting and building and flourishing—just as Lauren would have wanted.

Rebuilding as We Climb

"What does that say about our culture?" Butler asked, raising concerns about the increasing prevalence of prisons, nuclear facilities, and toxic waste dumps across the country.[64] This question was posed to Jelani Cobb in 1994, one year after the publication of *Sower*, and Butler's ongoing worries about the prison system persisted. Butler's fascination with the prison industrial complex and her participation in a call-to-action African American literary tradition allows us to think about the Parable series as a meditation on how we rebuild a society that is built on the prison industrial complex and the government's selective protection and provision for its "desirable" citizens.

Historians like Michelle Alexander and prison abolition advocates like Bryan Stevenson have noted how the prison industrial complex is a legacy of slavery. The prison industrial complex is "much more" than jails and prisons Angela Y. Davis tells us; rather, "It is a set of symbiotic relationships among correctional communities, transnational corporations, media conglomerates, guards' unions, and legislative and court agendas."[65] As Stevenson explains, "central to understanding this practice of mass incarceration and excessive punishment is the legacy of slavery."[66] The prison industrial complex's expansion is directly tied to slavery's abolition, the sociopolitical gains made by Black people during Reconstruction, and the civil rights movements of the 1960s and '70s.[67] In *Talents*, the imprisonment and enslavement of citizens are tied to those who are deemed a problem or criminal, who are labeled "allies of Satan," "heathen purveyors of false and unchristian doctrines," "seducers of our children" or those who do not conform to restrictive beliefs of Christian America.[68]

The Parable duology has a protagonist who looks to the past to imagine a different present that will transform the way she looks at her future. In reading *Sower* and *Talents*, Lauren's journey forces us to ask: What might a world without policing look like? What might a world without prisons look like? In *Sower*, Lauren notes how the police officers and law enforcement are ineffective; how they price gouge or are likely to arrest, rape, and murder just as much as the "maggots" outside are. Her father tells Lauren and others who have recently been robbed that "The police . . . may be able to avenge you, but they can't protect you."[69] In short, law enforcement is ineffective, untrustworthy, and harmful. In *Talents*, Lauren's established Earthseed community, named Acorn, is positioned as a viable alternative; they offer protection, food, and medical care to all who join them. Those who join are expected to contribute to the community—through education, sustainability, training, and work.

The Parable duology also offers several solutions to building and rebuilding communities after government failures to provide care for its citizens. First, they tout the value of community organizing through supportive, interdependent relationships. We see this early on in Lauren's gated community in Robledo, where they set up neighborhood watches and work together to put out fires or run off thieves. Lauren continues this throughout her journey in *Sower* and *Talents*, informing new followers, "But if you travel with us, and there's trouble, you stand by us, with us."[70] In *Talents*, we learn that Earthseed "offered full scholarships to poor but gifted students" and as part of their acceptance, they would "spend seven years teaching, practicing medicine, or otherwise using their skills to improve life in the many Earthseed communities."[71] Second, the Earthseed community advocates for an ethic of care. They give people care regardless of their political beliefs or their disposition toward others. This does not mean that one must believe in Earthseed, but one must be willing to contribute to the care and well-being of the community. The best example of this is Marc, Lauren's brother, who later becomes a preacher for Christian America. Marc is accepted into the Earthseed community and provided medical care and food, regardless of his insistence that Earthseeders believe in false doctrine. Third, the Parable duology suggests that the best way to help others is to offer means for them to help themselves, whether through literacy training, sustainability training, or gardening. Fourth, open access to information is promoted in the Parable duology as evidenced by the digitization and distribution of Lauren's *Earthseed: The Books of the Living* freely on the Internet. Finally, the Parable duology promotes network building. We see this most clearly in *Talents* when Lauren begins to establish a series of safe houses or networks to rebuild Earthseed not as a secluded alcove or hush harbor but as an organized social network that grows to fund scientific exploration, grade schools, and scholarships. She secures financial commitments from those to develop and sustain new Earthseed communities. Ultimately, the Parable duology continues the tradition of the nineteenth-century slave narrative, with its call to action at the end. The Parable series takes us on the journey of one woman who seeks to change the world and offers readers practical steps for envisioning and obtaining a just future for all.

The Tradition Lives On

At the end of the 2003 edition of *Kindred*, Robert Crossley remarks that "the most powerful and valuable [thing] for readers of *Kindred* is the simple reminder that all history occurred not so very long ago" and *Kindred* reminds us that "historical progress is not a sure thing."[72] Though Crossley refers only to *Kindred*, his observations apply to *Sower* and *Talents* as well. Revealing that the more times change, the more they stay the same, these novels grapple with the past, present, and potential futures. Published fourteen and nineteen years apart, the novels are a portal into worlds of possibility and failure, hope and despair, and freedom and bondage made possible because of their connection to and engagement with the past. Dana and Lauren teach us that "we've been here before," and we are certainly in that "here" now. In the more than forty years since the publication of *Kindred* and the more than thirty years since the publication of *Sower*, what we read about in *Kindred* and the Parable duology, we see today unfolding before our very eyes. Wage slavery. Mass incarceration. Economic exploitation. Political Corruption. And so much more. As neo-slave narratives, these works exist within an African American literary tradition that does more than just tell a compelling story; these works, like their nineteenth-century predecessors, should spur their readers to take actions that will liberate the oppressed. If the purpose of nineteenth-century slave narratives is to spur white readers to participate in ending chattel enslavement, what do *Sower*, *Talents*, and *Kindred* as neo-slave narratives teach us beyond those connections to nineteenth-century enslavement? *Kindred* can teach us and inspire us on what to do regarding allyship, civil disobedience, and women-centered networks, and the Parable duology underscores the necessity for coalition building, multicultural communities, and care to ensure our collective survival. In the African American literary spirit and tradition of resistance and freedom, these three works stand the test of time, offering us insights, strategies, and paths forward. Are we willing to heed the warnings?

CHAPTER 6

"This time, I want a love story"
Her Early Romance Novels

"This time, I want a love story—a story of deep emotional ties, devotion, and intense sexiness."[1] Octavia E. Butler wrote these words in December 1998 as she prepared to write an article for *Writer's Digest* on writer's block while she was navigating through the muck of writer's block herself. She wants to write something "sexy" to help pull her out of the murk. She will publish *Fledgling*, her final novel, in 2005, and it was, for her, sexy. But her desire to write a love story existed long before she wrote those words in 1998 and long before she published *Fledgling*.

"At eleven, I was writing romances," she reveals to Charles Brown in 2000, "and I'm happy to say I didn't know any more about romance than I did about horses."[2] Butler never married, and interviewers never seemed to ask about her romantic relationships,[3] but she spoke about reading and writing romance at a young age. As I combed through her archives, I came across some of her earliest writing. She penned a revision of Adam and Eve's first encounter in one of her early notebooks, writing in careful cursive and using black ink. Her version, which focuses on their physical intimacy and the sensations they experience, uses vivid imagery, sexually explicit language, and perhaps jarringly so, an AABB rhyme scheme that is often associated with nursery rhymes.[4] It is one of several attempts at writing love stories during her school-age years. Throughout her archived materials, she made it clear that she desired romantic relationships. She sought companionship, planning dalliances at conferences, writing lists on improving her appearance, and even going so far as to question her heterosexuality and consider same-gender relationships as a solution to her loneliness (she eventually determined she was not a lesbian).[5] Butler's insecurities surrounding her "social anxiety" stunted "not only her career opportunities" but also her ability to form "[connections] to other people" whether platonic or romantic.[6] Although Butler's desire for a long-term romantic companion never materialized—her journals make that quite clear—she never shied away from incorporating her personal life or desires into her writing: her emphasis on matriarchal power, the absence of father figures, and her protagonists' left-handedness all correlate with Butler's life: she was raised by her mother, grandmother, and aunts; her father died while Butler was still very young; and Butler was left-handed. Butler's repeated pattern of incorporating autobiographical tidbits in her work can also be seen in how she hints at her romantic desires. The recurrent romance tropes and erotica that appear in her fiction stem from her desire to learn more about herself. "That's one of the things I do in my writing," she once said, "either I find out certain things about myself or I write to create some context in which I can explore what I want to be."[7]

But Butler as a romance novelist? Whether you are new to Butler or not, this might come as a surprise to you. Certainly, common biases and misconceptions concerning romance novels abound. Romance is "the most popular [and] least respected" genre, denigrated for its formulaic plots and stock characters, even though it attracts widespread readership—though most of its readership is women.[8] But Butler was no stranger to writing in a genre that was unpopular for her. As a Black woman writing science fiction, she knew she was "a dancing bear, a novelty" and that some thought her writing was "almost a betrayal, a waste of time, at best" because she was not writing what one expected of a Black American writer at the time.[9] Perhaps it surprises you to think about Butler as a writer of romances. Maybe it should not. Butler's writing was also intimately tied to her "sex drive," creating the "erotic practice" that birthed many of her short stories and novels.[10] In her early days as a writer, she did not know how to write about women because they were never active agents in the books she was reading. In an interview with Larry McCaffery and Jim McMenamin, Butler shared, "everything I read that *was* intended for women seemed boring as hell—basically, "Finding Mr. Right": marriage, family, and that's the end of that. I didn't know how to write about women doing anything because while they were waiting for Mr. Right they weren't doing anything, they were just waiting to be done unto."[11] Her desire for intimate, romantic relationships, coupled with her desire to see women as active agents in the books she read, became intertwined with her compulsive desire to write. Her interest in romance, however elusive for her, was one motivating factor for her writing.

Another motivating factor for thinking through Butler as a romance novelist is money. As a child, Butler was swindled out of $61.20 by a fake literary agent, and in her earliest years as a writer, she was "miserable" because she

"THIS TIME, I WANT A LOVE STORY" 111

worked at "grubby jobs" when her writing "didn't sell and didn't sell and didn't sell . . . "[12] She recalls "crying over a smashed jar of Skippy's Peanut Butter" when she was unable to find work and had "only peanut butter, bread, beans, rice, and a pound of ground beef to eat for the week." Butler feared being poor like she was as a child and desperately wanted to "avoid a return" to her "old hand-to-mouth lifestyle."[13] As I reviewed her archival materials, I learned that she studied romance market trends, flagging *The Ladies Home Journal* and Avon as potential publication venues, attempted to train herself to write romance (building her on childhood erotica), and documented a few of interest to her, like Jayne Allen Krentz's *Sweet Starfire* (1986) and Wallace Wood's *Torrid Romance* comics. Though her attempts at writing romance seemed to fail, and though she wanted to write science fiction, Butler was keenly aware of the pitfalls of labeling a work "science fiction" or "fantasy." Consequently, she longed to avoid labeling her fiction because "It's amazing what the absence of a label can do," she shared. "It can get a hard-cover book onto the shelves of bookstores that refuse to carry hardcover science fiction. It can get a book reviewed by reviewers who don't usually handle sf."[14]

Butler's desire for romantic companionship, her concerns about money, and her rejection of labels make this chapter's exploration of *Survivor, Kindred*, and *Wild Seed* as conversant with the romance genre more intriguing. Although *Survivor, Kindred*, and *Wild Seed* were initially published as science fiction or fantasy, they were also published between 1978 and 1980, which may be no coincidence since "By the end of the seventies, the romance was the most significant single category within paperback publishing."[15] Notably, in 1981, one year after *Wild Seed* was published, "romance sales were estimated at upwards of $200 million, representing as much as 40 percent of the domestic paperback business."[16] Butler, ever aware of market trends and determined to succeed as a writer, would have been aware of such things. She writes about being aware of her best interests, her affinity for science fiction, and her rejection of labels. These competing interests signal that her work blurs genre conventions, inviting readers to explore an acclaimed science fiction writer through an unlikely genre: romance.

What Makes a Romance?

Romance Writers of America (RWA), the largest genre writer's association in the world, defines a romance novel as one with "a central love story" and "an emotionally satisfying and optimistic ending."[17] A romance novel, defined by Pamela Regis, is "a work of prose fiction that tells the story of the courtship and betrothal of one or more heroines," which requires eight essential elements; otherwise, it is not a romance novel.[18] These eight elements—the society defined, the meeting, the barrier, the attraction, the declaration, the point of ritual death, the recognition, and the betrothal—can occur at any point in the novel, whether chronologically, through flashbacks, back and forth, out of order, or mentioned in passing rather than narrated.[19] The society that the would-be couple is part of may prevent them from being together, perhaps because the society is "flawed," "incomplete," "superannuated," or "corrupt."[20] Readers must witness the couple's first meeting through direct narration or flashback. After meeting one another, the couple must experience a barrier, attraction, declaration, a point of ritual death, and recognition. The barrier, which can be internal or external, is something that prevents the love interests from marriage, and the removal of the barrier is important because "it usually involves the heroine's freedom from societal, civic, or even religious strictures that prevented the union between her and the hero . . . The barrier's fall is a liberation for the heroine."[21] The attraction between the would-be lovers is "the reason the couple must marry."[22] The declaration is a scene (or scenes) where the lovers declare their love for one another. Another key component of romance novels is the point of ritual death; it can be literal or symbolic, and underlying it is "the myth of death and rebirth" for the heroine; however, the death is ritual, and the heroine does not die.[23] The recognition, which can be internal or external, is new information presented to the would-be couples that will overcome the barriers that prevent them from being together.[24] All romance novels include an accepted marriage proposal.

Romance scholars Candy Tan and Sarah Wendell divide the Modern American Romance novel into two schools of thought: Old School and New School Romances. The Old School Romances appear from the 1970s to the mid/late 1980s. They are comprised of brutal heroes and rape; they are usually coming-of-age stories for the heroine and are typically written from the woman's point of view. Further, conflicts often consist of big secrets, arguments, and misunderstandings, and the brutal hero experiences a "sudden realization of love" when it comes to his female counterpart.[25] New School Romances, which began appearing in the late 1980s, overlapping some with the Old School Romances, continue to exist today. New School Romances consist of gentler heroes, scenes from the hero's point of view, a sexually experienced heroine (which often includes oral sex, birth control, and condoms), and the tacit erasure of rape from the genre.[26] Much of Butler's fiction blurs the boundaries of Old School and New School romances. *Wild Seed*, *Survivor*, and *Kindred* were published on the cusp of when American romance novels were shifting from predatory, brutal male love interests to kinder heroes, from sexually inexperienced heroines to sexually aware women, from the women-centric point of view to the point of view of both men and women. With her sexually experienced Black female protagonists, novels written from the third person omniscient perspective, and conflicted heroes, Butler's work tenuously embraces both Schools of romance.

Connecting Butler's works that have romantic themes, plots, or subplots—*Survivor*, *Wild Seed*, *Fledgling*, *Kindred*, "Bloodchild," "Near of Kin," and "Crossover"—is that all the men (or the phallus-bearing entity in "Bloodchild") exhibit predatory, manipulative, exploitative behavior. Such behavior is reminiscent of the Old School romances from the 1970s and 1980s, like Captain Brandon Birmingham from Kathleen Woodiwiss's *The Flame and the Flower* (1972), who repeatedly rapes the heroine until she falls in love with him. *Kindred*, *Survivor*, *Wild Seed*, and "Bloodchild" are heavily invested in slavery, captivity, and/or colonization, and each text, perhaps excluding "Near of Kin," involves power dynamics that are questionable among the prospective couples. Despite the questionable heroes, both *Wild Seed* and *Survivor* are hybrids of the Old School and New School romance, each with a brutal hero who transforms into a gentler being by the novel's end and with a heroine who is sexually experienced. Conversely, Kevin and Dana's romantic subplot of *Kindred* does seem firmly entrenched in the New School Romance genre, though unsurprisingly, the grim romance subplot of Rufus and Alice, a white enslaver and an enslaved Black woman, is rooted firmly in the Old School tradition of romance.

Discussing Butler and romance would be incomplete without referencing African American romance. African American authors who write romance fiction aim to include the required traits as outlined by the RWA and Regis, but there are key differences. Julie E. Moody-Freedom adds that early African American romance writers included "social uplift" as a key ingredient.[27] Susan Weisser reveals that Black female protagonists in African American romance novels are usually shown "to be more educated, professional, and intelligent" than their white counterparts, the Black male leads are "successful and stable," and she finds a greater degree of "sexual conservatism" in African American romances.[28] Black romance novelists provide readers an escape through a romance that is "devoid of racial conflict, gratuitous sex and profanity," but these romances also "dispel stereotypes" and provide positive or empowering messages discovered often through realistic issues faced by Black readers.[29] Neither *Survivor* nor *Kindred* can accurately be classified as African American romance; they feature interracial or interspecies couplings. But *Wild Seed* is the epitome of a Black love story.

Contextualizing *Wild Seed* as part of the African American romance genre places it firmly within the second wave of African American women's historical romance novels. In contrast to the first wave of African American women's romance novels (1892–1920), which featured fair-skinned heroines and a marriage plot, the second wave of African American romances feature heroines with darker skin, heroines who challenge the Black male protagonist's sexism, and heroines who blend the fulfillment of erotic desire and social uplift.[30] Although second-wave African American historical romance novels began for Rita Dandridge in 1989, the development of African American romance emerged in the 1960s with Frank Yerby's novels, *Speak Now: A Modern Novel* (1969), *The Dahomean: An Historical Novel* (1971), *A Darkness in Ingraham's Crest* (1979), and is solidified with Rosalind Welles' *Entwined Destinies* (1980), which is considered "first-known romance featuring African-American characters written by an African-American author."[31] African American historical romance novels in the second wave include Anita Buckley's *Emily, the Yellow Rose* (1989) and Beverly Jenkins's *Night Song* (1994), *Indigo* (1996), and *Through the Storm* (1998).

These second-wave African American romance novels are set during slavery and Reconstruction, and generally, these writers "depict how free Black populations participated in abolition movements during slavery and in post-emancipation established Black enclaves that had their own businesses."[32] Of importance is the readers' response to romance. Because "African American romance readers are not a monolithic group," the novels require the genre's happily ever after; however, storylines must include some key qualities to appease a broad readership: the inclusion of African American culture and history, the absence of stereotypical representations of Black characters, and positive, empowering messages discovered through realistic issues faced by Black readers.[33] *Wild Seed* matches these patterns and appeals to a broad readership: Anyanwu, a dark-skinned immortal woman who witnesses chattel enslavement, survives the perils of the Middle Passage, manages—despite opposition from Doro, her lover-turned captor-turned partner—to hold fast to her traditional beliefs, practices, and customs, and to create a sanctuary where Black people live freely during the nadir of American enslavement.

Rape, Romance, and Butler

Before applying Regis's eight elements of romance to three of Butler's novels, it is crucial to explore the portrayal of rape in both the romance genre and Butler's fiction. This section discusses depictions of rape that are unsettling, even for this author, and readers familiar with Butler's work may be chagrined about thinking through her work as a romance. The prevalence of rape, forced seduction, sexual exploitation, and other forms of psychological, physical, and sexual abuse throughout her work—whether in *Kindred*, *Survivor*, *Wild Seed*, *Fledgling*, or "Bloodchild"—make the label "romance" disconcerting.

Yet rape, and even gang rape, was all the rage in Old School romance novels, including *The Flame and the Flower*, Rosemary Rogers's *Sweet Savage Love* (1974), and Catherine Coulter's *Devil's Embrace* (1982). Rape was once a defining characteristic of the Modern American Romance genre that was eventually met with resistance by 1981.[34] Part of the reason for the rape-as-seduction element in the genre is that during the 1970s, women were not permitted to desire sex. The only way to allow a woman to express her sexual desires was to have the option taken away from her through rape. And, of course, any "good" woman who is compromised by a "well-meaning" man will certainly be rewarded with true love, gentler sex, and a happily-ever-after.

To be clear, rape was not just limited to romance novels. The most famous rape on daytime American television was Luke's rape of Laura in *General Hospital* in a 1979 episode. What's more, is that Luke and Laura marry in a November 1981 episode in what has been described as a "fairy-tale wedding" that was "seen on television by 30 million people."[35] What might be more disturbing than rape and the highly watched on-screen marriage of the victim to her rapist? The knowledge that the inclusion of rape was done for ratings. The show's producer was threatened with cancellation if she could not bring ratings up in two weeks' time."[36] Rape sells, whether in romance novels or daytime soap operas.

Because rape was so prevalent in the romance genre, romance scholar Angela R. Toscano investigated rape as a narrative device in romance, exploring its "narrative and structural purpose."[37] For Toscano, that purpose is to act as "the external and fated event that brings the lovers together."[38] In the romance genre, rape has three forms: The Rape of Mistaken Identity, The Rape of Possession, and The Rape of Coercion or "Forced Seduction." In *Survivor*, *Kindred*, and *Wild Seed*, rape for the protagonists occurs most often as "the rape of possession," "function[s] primarily to demonstrate to the hero that physical and sexual power cannot make the heroine love him."[39] The Rape of Possession "is about an exchange that requires the hero to acknowledge the heroine as her own person, to meet her on her own terms, to confess his wrongdoing—often in scenes of groveling apology—in order to allow the heroine to choose or to deny him as her lover."[40]

Each of the novels that I explore at length in this chapter uses the rape of possession. It appears in *Survivor* when Diut announces his intentions to have a "liaison" with Alanna simply because he has chosen her, despite her emphatic protest: "I have not chosen you."[41] Alanna's resistance is met with physical violence; he "knocked [her] down again with a single openhanded blow," leaving her to wonder "why he didn't just grab and rape me the way the wild human had. It would be simple enough."[42] Amused at her refusal, admitting that Alanna is "the only woman ever to try and refuse," Diut bargains with her, telling her she will "not be dependent on others to guide or guard" and he "covered [her] . . . as he forced his way into [her] body, an intruder too large and much unwelcome."[43] Alanna chooses Diut as her partner once she realizes she is pregnant; however, his acceptance of her is not assured until he can visually confirm her pregnancy. In *Kindred*, Rufus rapes a free and married Alice, sells her husband South, and enslaves her as punishment. Rufus's machinations to possess Alice sexually and legally are abetted by Dana. Rufus enlists Dana to encourage Alice to submit to Rufus sexually, combining the rape of possession with The Rape of Coercion or Forced Seduction, which is "not simply to rape" but also to "compel an interaction between two speaking persons" and make the victim "complicit with her own violation."[44] The groveling apology comes at Alice's death-by-suicide, and unlike Alanna, Alice never accepts her relationship with Rufus and intends to escape his enslavement with her children. The rape of possession appears most clearly in *Wild Seed* when Doro "made [Anyanwu] undress and lie with him."[45] Like Diut and Rufus, Doro uses beatings, verbal threats, and humiliation to ensure Anyanwu's submission, and Anyanwu, like Alanna and Alice, maintains what dignity she can. Unlike her literary ancestors, Anyanwu escapes Doro, living unencumbered for ninety-nine years. But when their paths cross again, he finds her preparing to die by suicide rather than live with him, and his groveling apology comes forth on the brink of her death—in a panicked attempt to express his love.

Survivor, a Captive Romance

Survivor includes all of Regis's eight elements of a romance novel, yet it is not a romance novel. It does not tell "the story of the courtship and betrothal of one or more heroines."[46] The subplot of *Survivor* explores Alanna and Diut's courtship and betrothal while she is in captivity with the Tehkohn tribe for two years, whereas the main plot explores Alanna's attempts to free the human Missionaries from the Garkohn tribe by forging an alliance with her husband Diut, leader of the Tehkohn tribe. They meet three different times, the third time on the night of their first sexual union, and during each meeting, they express a simultaneous fascination-revulsion with each other that becomes the basis for their eventual sexual attraction, which transitions into mutual respect and sexual desire. Beyond the social barriers of religious dogma that forbid their union, the absence of a child threatens the longevity of their liaison. As a Tehkohn leader, Diut needs an heir, and their union—which amounts to a contract relationship—will dissolve unless an heir is produced. The popular romance convention of accidental pregnancy solves this barrier. The pregnancy is accidental because there was a belief that no child could come of a

Kohn-human union. The confirmation of Alanna's pregnancy prompts Diut to convene the Gathering ceremony, a declaration of love. Their marital union is assured when the witnesses accept the invitation to the Gathering. After their marriage, two moments of ritual death threaten their relationship: the death of their child, Tien, as it is the only thing that legally binds her as Diut's wife and Alanna's meklah readdiction after the Missionaries return her to their settlement. The romance subplot is not incidental or superfluous to the novel's narrative structure; it provides the necessary background for Alanna's attempts to free the Christian Missionaries from the Garkohn tribe in the present day. Presented as a series of flashbacks that transition between the perspectives of Alanna and Diut, the romance subplot is the instrument that facilitates Alanna's full acceptance into the Tehkohn community as a community member, not a captive. Thus, the romance subplot becomes intertwined with the conventions of the captivity narrative, which I discuss in chapter 3.

Kindred's Grim Romance Subplot

Kindred depicts an interracial relationship and eventual marriage between a white man, Kevin, and a Black woman, Dana, in 1970s America, who time travel to nineteenth-century Maryland, finding themselves entangled in the daily affairs of the Weylin family, Dana's ancestors. The novel also includes several instances of enslaver-enslaved sexual relationships and two rape scenes which are both perpetrated by Rufus. As with *Survivor*, it is difficult to think about *Kindred* in terms of romance fiction, considering the novel's depictions of rape, exploitation, ownership, abuse, and manipulation. That *Kindred* exists on the cusp of the Old School and New School romance does little to assuage that discomfort. However, Butler initially pitched the idea of *Kindred* as a romance. *Guardian* was an early draft of *Kindred*, and her handwritten notes about *Guardian* show that Butler was grappling with the idea of romance, describing Rufus and Dana's relationship as "the story of a Love affair. The Emotional Fluctuation Are Those of Lovers. The Final Act Is an act of Love."[47] Although Butler initially was thinking through an earlier version of *Kindred* as a meditation on the love between Rufus and Dana, scholars have learned that she was "terrified" at the prospect of her book being misrepresented or misunderstood as a romance novel.[48] In a letter to her editor, she writes: "You said you wanted to call the novel DANA. (God, no!) I can see a title like DANA attracting the ladies' romance readers, though I wonder how many of them would read past the cover copy. On the other hand, a ladies' romance title like DANA might well keep the more general reader from ever picking up the book."[49] Christine Montgomery and Ellen C. Caldwell note that even though Doubleday (the publishing company for the 1979 edition of the *Kindred*), hired "an artist who was focused on romance novels" to commission the cover art for the novel, Butler's letter to her editor reveals her dismay that marketing her novel as a romance will detract from broad readership—echoing some sentiments and stereotypes about romance novels.[50]

Beyond Butler's vacillation between thinking of earlier drafts of *Kindred* as a potential love story and her horror of it possibly being marketed as a ladies' romance, of note is the striking resemblance between the romantic relationship between Dana and Kevin and Butler's platonic relationship with Harlan Ellison, her science fiction mentor. Butler nursed a one-sided "fierce crush" on Ellison,[51] writing about him in her journals and nicknaming him Elyano. In addition to the obvious (both Kevin and Ellison are white men, and Dana and Butler are Black women), both pairs were brought together by a love of writing, and the twelve-year age difference between Dana and Kevin is only one year shy of the thirteen-year age difference between Butler and Ellison.

Regis's eight elements of romance appear in *Kindred*, and the Dana-Kevin romance subplot juxtaposes the white supremacy of Dana's twentieth-century present with her nineteenth-century past—a signal that the past is more than a mere prologue. The society Kevin and Dana live in is 1976 United States. They face racial prejudice, bigotry from Kevin's sister and Dana's guardians, and during their initial meetings, face crude remarks by a white coworker: "chocolate and vanilla porn."[52] Not only do these same external social circumstances dictate that they not pursue a relationship, but Kevin's paternalism towards Dana—specifically his anger at her refusal to act as his secretary and type his work—is also a barrier that threatens their relationship. Despite these barriers, what continues to attract them to each other, and what eventually overcomes the social barriers, is their sexual chemistry and their shared goal of becoming writers. Although there seems to be no declaration of love pre-marriage, Kevin does pose the question four months after their initial meeting asking, "How would you feel about getting married?" to which Dana responds, "You know damn well we are."[53] After the proposal, a new barrier emerges in the form of their family members' bigotry and anger; Kevin's sister "quotes cliched bigotry," and Dana's uncle is "more hurt than mad."[54] Both recognize that neither one of their families will accept the decision to get married, so they drive to Las Vegas and marry, with the severing of their ties with their families functioning as a ritual social death that allows them to marry.

The romance subplot between Dana and Kevin is juxtaposed against Rufus and Alice, who represent the forbidden love trope in the romance genre. The forbidden love trope depicts two characters who are not supposed to have feelings for each other becoming entangled in a romantic relationship. As a white man, Rufus is forbidden from marrying an enslaved Black woman although the social customs of the time permitted him to pursue a sexual relationship with her. As an enslaved Black woman, Alice should not feel any proprietary feelings toward Rufus. Alice, who loves her husband, an enslaved Black man, is caught in a love triangle that, as Sandra Y. Govan notes, "degenerates into an extraordinarily painful relationship, one compounded by rivalry, passion, guilt, love, lust, punishment, pride, power, and implacable hatred."[55] Rufus rapes Alice, sells her husband further south, enslaves her, and then secures her as a sexual conquest, with the help of Dana who is caught in the middle of their forbidden relationship. Rufus tells Dana, "I begged her not to go with him . . . *I begged her* [. . .] If I lived in your time, I would have married her. Or tried to."[56] Dana tells Alice, "Well, it looks as though you have three choices. You can go to him as he orders; you can refuse, be whipped, and then have him take you by force; or you can run away again."[57] Alice acquiesces to Rufus's demands, becoming "a quieter more subdued person."[58]

When I discuss Alice's rape, whether in the classroom or during presentations, there is always some discomfort about how we characterize Alice's response. Is it acquiescence? Resignation? Complicity? Certainly, Alice's rape is designed to punish her for marrying an enslaved Black man and abetting his escape instead of choosing a white man who has expressed sexual interest in her. But is it possible to understand Alice's resignation as both a forced *and* a calculated move? Whereas widely accepted discourse maintains that enslaved Black women are unable to consent to sexual relationships with their enslavers,[59] others suggest that such assertions remove what little autonomy enslaved Black women had by dismissing their ability to consent to sexual and romantic relationships with their enslavers, especially considering that these relationships could be leveraged to obtain better material conditions for consenting enslaved women and their loved ones.[60] Such was the case for Harriet Jacobs. In her 1861 *Incidents in the Life of a Slave Girl*, Jacobs discusses her calculated participation in a sexual liaison with a white man in hopes of securing her freedom and the two children of their union. It is unlikely that Butler read *Incidents* in her preparation for *Kindred*. Literary scholars did not know that Linda Brent was Harriet Jacobs until Jean Fagan Yellin's 1981 essay, and Yellin's edition of *Incidents*, which would have been available to the wider public, was released eight years after *Kindred*'s publication.[61] However, Butler has a consistent motif in her works: Black women doing what they need to do to survive. This motif precedes Alice; we witness Amber from *Patternmaster* (1976) and Alanna resign themselves to exploitative sexual encounters for their own means. Given this context, we can understand Alice's resignation as multifaceted. Certainly, Rufus's rape of Alice is punishment for her exercises in bodily autonomy. Yet, in the context of Alanna and Amber, Alice's decision masks a subversive agenda: survival and escape. Of course, doing what is necessary for survival does not make a sexual arrangement romantic or mutually satisfying, as Alice's eventual death by suicide makes clear.

The juxtaposition of the Alice-Rufus relationship with the Dana-Kevin relationship is supposed to remind readers of the progressive nature of Kevin and Dana's relationship and the strides made between the nineteenth century and 1976. However, their relationship also serves as a warning to Black women that their interracial marriage may be akin to enslavement. For instance, on her second trip to the Weylin plantation, Dana is beaten and nearly raped by a white patroller. Dana knocks the man unconscious, and he falls across her body. Her fear for her life causes her to return to the present, where she finds herself underneath Kevin. After fighting against him, she exclaims, "I thought you were the patroller."[62] "In this way," one scholar remarks, "Butler connects two oppressors' bodies; both men are powerful white figures, and, although Dana's marriage to Kevin appears to be secure, Butler suggests that, for Black women, interracial heterosexual marriage too might be a form of oppression not unlike chattel slavery."[63] Butler suggests that the progress achieved between Alice's nineteenth-century past and Dana's twentieth-century present is perhaps much narrower than we might be willing to admit.

This warning early in the novel foreshadows the inevitable turn—when Rufus attempts to rape Dana at the novel's end. Throughout the novel, Rufus and Dana's relationship transitions from a savior to a mother figure. From a mother figure to a sibling. And from sibling to a bitter foe. Dana saves young Rufus from drowning and burning down the Weylin plantation. As a young boy, Dana functions as a mother figure after he breaks his leg, teaching him to read, reading to him, and trying to instill basic morals in him. After Rufus enslaves and purchases Alice, his relationship with Dana becomes like siblings. They quarrel, lash out, and threaten each other. As Rufus continues his lust for Alice, his infatuation and protective nature over Dana manifest into jealousy; he sells an enslaved Black man who admits his fondness for Dana. After Alice's death, Rufus tries to breach their tacit agreement by initiating a sexual encounter with Dana. Instead of the novel ending with a coupling, instead of two becoming one in a sexual union, two become one, with Rufus' death at Dana's hands. Dana severs their connection by killing Rufus, effectively cutting off a forbidden encounter before it begins.

Dana and Kevin's romantic subplot survives the novel because the relationship is consensual and mutually beneficial, but the twisted love Rufus feels for

Alice is strangled by the noose of slavery. Rufus does not get his happily ever after with Alice; she chooses death because he has led her to believe that he has sold their two children into slavery as punishment. Kevin and Dana overcome the social circumstances that dictate that their love remains forbidden, but Rufus and Alice do not. Kevin and Dana mutually declare their feelings for each other, but only Rufus declares his love for Alice, and that declaration is rooted in ownership, entitlement, and punishment: "I didn't want to just drag her off into the bushes . . . But she kept saying no. I could have had her in the bushes years ago if that was all I wanted."[64] Rufus admits that he would have married Alice if he lived in a different time, but allowing Alice to live freely and to choose her lover (her husband) freely without molestation from Rufus does not cross his mind. The relationship barriers remain, and a mutual attraction never exists. Although Rufus appears to honor Alice in death—he frees their children, and their son even calls him Daddy—his actions are too little, too late. Butler once described *Kindred* as a grim fantasy, yet the term "grim romance"—a ghastly, uninviting relationship between two lovers—aptly characterizes Rufus and Alice. The evils of slavery are too much for brokered, coerced love to endure.

Wild Seed as a Romance Novel

The elements of romance that are teasingly interwoven in *Survivor* and *Kindred* emerge fully in *Wild Seed* as Butler deftly blends all eight romance elements as the central plot of the novel. Butler's feelings about *Survivor* and her feelings after writing *Kindred* offer insight into why *Wild Seed* is arguably her first—and only—romance novel. Published on the heels of *Survivor*, which she vehemently disavowed and requested that it remain out of print, and *Kindred*, which she described as "a depressing book for [her] to write," Butler admits she "thoroughly enjoyed" writing *Wild Seed*, describing it to interviewers as a pleasurable reward for writing *Kindred*.[65] Of all her published work *Wild Seed* remains the only novel that fully embraces the romance genre. Although *Wild Seed* is chronologically the first book of the Patternist series (1976–1984), some suggest that reading it as a stand-alone book changes the scope of the novel.[66] As a standalone novel, it exists as a Black historical romance, and its plot, a tumultuous, centuries-long, tug-of-war love affair between two beings inescapably caught in each other's web, satisfies Black women readers who longed to see themselves in romances and to witness a Happily Ever After during a time where they did not see themselves represented in the romance genre.[67]

Structurally, *Wild Seed* follows the eight elements of romance Regis defines: the society, the meeting, the attraction, the barrier, the point of ritual death, the recognition, the declaration, and the betrothal. Butler outlines society early in the first section of *Wild Seed*. The Transatlantic Slave Trade has either taken or destroyed Doro's community members and Anyanwu's kin. Doro adopts the paternalism and abuse associated with the Transatlantic Slave Trade, and his quest for seed villages, developed through forced breeding and murder of individuals Doro does not find useful, becomes the flawed society in which Anyanwu finds herself entangled. The Wheatley Plantation, a microcosm of the widespread chattel enslavement from the Middle Passage to the Americas, is the society within the society, and Doro becomes the status quo that Anyanwu confronts and resists throughout the novel.

We witness the account of Doro and Anyanwu's meeting unfolding by chance. Their meeting is propelled by attraction—one instance of one-sided attraction, and four instances of mutual attraction: divine attraction; sexual chemistry; shared longing; and shared goals. Doro is biologically compelled by "something new—an impulse, a feeling, a kind of mental undertow pulling at him . . . He felt that there was something for him farther on, a little farther, just head. He trusted such feelings."[68] His impulses lead him to "discover" Anyanwu. Mutually, Doro and Anyanwu experience divine attraction; they believe that their names, which mean "Sun" and "east—the direction from which the sun comes"—are evidence that their ancestors "named [them] well" and that they "were intended to meet."[69] They also have unmistakable sexual chemistry as she: "[manages] to exhaust his strong young body with lovemaking,"[70] and as immortals who see their communities and children die, they share a longing for community, and by the novel's end, they have a shared goal: to create a community of people like themselves that will, hopefully, be long living.

In *Wild Seed*, five external barriers prevent Anyanwu and Doro from being together: "But Anyanwu had never learned to forgive Doro's unnecessary killings, his casual abuse when he was not courting her, his open contempt for any belief of hers that did not concur with his, the blows for which she could not retaliate and from which she could not flee, the acts she must perform for him no matter what her beliefs."[71] Although Doro's dismissal of Anyanwu as his wife, his breeding of her with other men, and his abuse and manipulation of her are paramount, the largest barrier to their relationship, one that develops over centuries, is Doro's mistreatment of the people who are most loyal to him. He kills them after their usefulness has ended, taking "too much pleasure."[72] The one internal barrier that prevents Anyanwu and Doro from being together is Doro's refusal to admit that he needs Anyanwu. He outwardly threatens to kill her and secretly desires to kill her—despite his son's protestations that they need each other. It is not until Anyanwu reaches her final point of ritual death that Doro's internal barrier falls.

The four moments of ritual death take place throughout the novel. The first and second moments of ritual death arise in 1690 when Doro violates his relationship with Anyanwu by requiring her to marry his son Isaac. In protest, she uses her shapeshifting powers to give herself a tubal ligation by "disconnect[ing] the two small tubes through which her own seed traveled to her womb" to "avoid giving any children at all, to avoid being used."[73] Moments later, after Doro threatens to take Anyanwu's body to get the children he wants from her, Anyanwu participates in a second, advanced form of ritual death by "alter[ing] her reproductive organs further" to make herself "literally no longer a woman, but not quite a man—just to be certain."[74] Because Doro values Anyanwu's womb, her disconnection from it is not just the end of her procreation but also the death of Doro's chances to start and maintain the community he hopes to create. Both the first and second moments of ritual death are soon reversed after Isaac convinces Anyanwu to live so that she can help Doro overcome his internal barrier and so that she can prevent the external barriers—both of which prevent them from living their lives together in harmony—from manifesting in the future. A third ritual death happens in 1741 when Anyanwu flees from the Wheatley Plantation after the death of her husband, Isaac, to the point where it "was as though she had ceased to exist."[75] She disconnects from the only community she has known for fifty years since she met Doro in 1690. Isaac's death allows her the courage to liberate herself from Doro's tyranny. By severing herself from the community she has cultivated as her own, she courageously begins again without any discernible community. The fourth moment of ritual death is a pregnant Anyanwu's decision to die after she gives birth. When Doro asks why she has chosen to die, she responds: "Because of what we have already said. Everything is temporary but you and me. You are all I have, perhaps all I would ever have . . . And you are an obscenity."[76] Anyanwu resigns herself to suicide, unable to continue tolerating his merciless killing of those who faithfully serve him. As he pleads for her life, Doro "knew suddenly that she would die now. Right in front of him, she would lie there and shut herself off."[77] This fourth moment of ritual death results in Doro's recognition of his love for Anyanwu and a renewal of the first covenant Doro establishes with her.

In a reversal of conventions, where "the heroine is at the center of the recognition scene,"[78] *Wild Seed* positions Doro at the center of two recognition scenes. Doro acknowledges and recognizes his intense emotions—emotions he has ignored and sublimated throughout the novel. He realizes that he needs her: "No, all that was important was that she revive [from lovemaking] whole and well. Nothing must happen to her. No amount of anger or stupidity on her part or his must induce him to think again of killing her. She was too valuable in too many ways."[79] His recognition is not met with easy acceptance on his part: "He did not like what she was doing to him. He could not remember a time when his thoughts had been so confused, when he had wanted so badly, so painfully, something he could not have. He had done what Anyanwu had apparently done. He had allowed her to touch him as though he were an ordinary man. He had allowed her to awaken feelings in him that had been dormant for several times as long as even she had been alive. He had all but stripped himself before her."[80] This passage is evidence of Doro's internal barrier. His centuries-long refusal to acknowledge that he needs Anyanwu dissolves, and his feelings and his humanity "awaken." Another realization on Doro's part occurs when Anyanwu threatens to die by suicide because he realizes that he can't live without her.

To this end, *Wild Seed* trades the love-at-first-sight convention for a centuries-long friends-to-lovers to an enemies-to-lovers trope. Towards the novel's end, when Doro's internal barrier begins to wane and he recognizes his humanity, love, and need for Anyanwu as a companion, readers witness his first attempt at declaring his love for Anyanwu in the only way he knows how by promising not to harm her: "Hear and see whatever it is that helps you know I'm being honest with you. I won't hurt you. [. . .] Just lie still and trust me. Believe I mean you no harm."[81] His words come before their metaphysical consummation, which also functions as a betrothal scene and the earliest admission to Anyanwu—and to himself—that he loves her. Doro's second declaration of love is intertwined with the recognition that he cannot live without her. "'Please, Anyanwu. Listen . . . Listen to me. There isn't anything I wouldn't give to be able to lie down beside you and die when you did. You can't know how I've longed . . . ' He swallowed. 'Sun Woman, please don't leave me.' His voice caught and broke. He wept. He choked out great sobs that shook his already shaking body almost beyond bearing. He wept as though for all the past times when no tears would come, when there was no relief."[82] Doro's declaration of love also becomes *his* point of ritual death when he encounters a new barrier (Anyanwu's intent to die by suicide) that will prevent their union. As I describe in chapter 3, Doro's weeping is a baptismal moment, that signals the death of his former self and his rebirth, completed as he awakens in Anyanwu's arms with his head on her "still warm" breast that was "still rising and falling gently with her breathing."[83]

Their betrothal is fragmented into two parts. Soon after their first meeting, Doro suggests: "We would be right together, Anyanwu. Have you never wanted a husband who was worthy of you?"[84] He convinces her that if she leaves her community to join him, he will give her children she will not need to bury. The second proposal appears towards the novel's end, where Doro asks to join with Anyanwu mentally, soul bonding with her, but without killing her, in the most intimate act he could fathom. Doro "enveloped her" and "touched her spirit, enfolding it within himself, spreading the sensation of his touch through every part of her."[85] The language describing their soul bonding is reminiscent of intercourse, and the phrase, "spreading the sensation," reads like a man's ejaculation in a romance novel. The loneliness that drove their soul-bonding consummation scene "formed a kinship between them" and affirms their betrothal.[86] With both Anyanwu's and Doro's ritual deaths avoided, we see the acceptance of the second proposal (and a renewal of the first proposal) in the novel's epilogue, where a new, revised covenant between the two has been established: "Anyanwu could not have all she wanted, and Doro could no longer have all that he had once considered his by right."[87] This compromise is a reversal of the five external barriers that prevented them from being together, and the novel's last line, "She would not leave him," confirms the betrothal.[88]

Through *Wild Seed*, Butler uses the framework and tropes of the romance genre to offer commentary on the necessity of healing, reciprocity, and reconciliation between Black women and Black men. Reading *Wild Seed* as a romance underscores the importance of the partnership between Doro and Anyanwu. The novel's resolution becomes an affirmation for Black couples "that their highest potential is only attainable through partnership."[89] It is important to point out that during his second declaration of love and proposal, Doro inhabits the body of a Black man, and Anyanwu is in her Black woman form.[90] The declaration of love and metaphysical consummation, coupled with the Blackness of their bodies, culminates in a "Black love" marriage by the novel's end. The marriage between two powerful Black beings becomes a vehicle for championing reconciliation, partnership, and harmony between Black men and Black women. The tenuous happily ever after reached in the novel's epilogue becomes a commentary on the importance of reciprocity between Black men and Black women. This nod to reciprocity, harmony, and compromise is a marked shift from the widely held belief systems of the Black Nationalist Discourse of the 1960s and throughout the 1970s that positioned Black men and Black women as antagonists to or enemies of each other. The marriage between Doro and Anyanwu exists in tandem with the then-fledgling Womanist discourse, which began emerging in the 1980s. Alice Walker, famously known for her 1980 novel *The Color Purple*, first uses the term "womanist" in her 1979 short story "Coming Apart," and expands on it in 1983. Understanding *Wild Seed* as a Black historical romance novel unveils the significance of partnership, love, and reconciliation between Black men and Black women, offering a striking commentary that resonates beyond the novel's end and intertwines with the emerging womanist discourse of the 1980s.

Romance on Her Mind

Using the tropes of the romance genre while writing outside of its mainstream allows Butler to ask some compelling questions, especially during the late 1970s and early 1980s. For instance, intimate partner violence was not a crime at the time *Survivor* was published in 1978, yet the novel asks readers to consider how we navigate our romantic relationships while living in a patriarchal society. Is it possible for women and men to indulge in romantic relationships ethically? Butler may have been able to ask these questions without envisioning alternative pasts, presents, and futures. But the science fiction genre offers her leeway to explore what it means to love, to be loved, and the different ways of loving self and others in ways that shock the senses. For example, *Wild Seed* explores the tensions between men and women—men's tendency toward dominance and women's tendency toward being subjected to that dominance—and reframes it through the lens of romance, allowing us to consider how romantic relationships always require a negotiation, one that necessitates for our survival—and for the collective survival of Black people—mutual adaptation, mutual submission, and mutual compromise. Otherwise, we are doomed.

From *Survivor* to *Kindred* to *Wild Seed*, one thing is clear: romance was on Butler's brain in the first decade of her professional writing career. The shift in Butler's use of romance—from the interracial and interspecies romance in *Kindred* and *Survivor* to an epic Black love story that begins in Africa and migrates to New York, Louisiana, and California—underscores the pleasure Butler found from writing *Wild Seed*. But the pleasure ended there. As I discuss in chapter 3, Butler did not feel successful despite her publication output in the 1980s for a variety of reasons—her languished *Black Futures* project, health issues, death, depression, and writer's block. The latter was alleviated only by her publication of *Fledgling* in 2005 which she describes as a "fairly lightweight" novel.[91] Like *Survivor* and *Kindred*, *Fledgling* flirts with elements of romance and even borders on the erotic. The enjoyment and pleasure Butler associated with writing *Wild Seed* reappear as a fleeting glimmer with *Fledgling*. This novel begins a torrid love affair between a twenty-two-year-old white man and a Black girl vampire with the physical appearance of a ten-year-old girl.

That glimmer of pleasure and enjoyment Butler experienced is not lost on some of her readers. ". . . your books are very sexy, by the way!" Marilyn Mehaffy admits to Butler during an interview. "I always think that—that they're a real turn-on—but I never hear anybody talking about their sexiness."[92] "I hope so," is Butler's reply, "because one of the signs—I put signs on my walls as a reminder while I'm writing—is 'sexiness,' not only sexiness in the sense of people having sex, but sexiness in the sense of wanting to reach readers where they live and wanting to invite them to enjoy themselves."[93] Butler's desire to "reach readers where they live" and her invitation to them to "enjoy themselves" is a hallmark of the romance genre and a call back to her own passions. She described writing fiction as the love of her life noting that it was why she wanted to be alive.[94] Butler's romantic visions are bound up in her own declaration of love, her recognition of why she was alive, and her desire to make her reading a pleasurable experience for her readers. Through this romantic lens, Butler freely explored her interests, desires, and passions in a way that satisfied both her and her readers.

CHAPTER 7

Word Weaver, World Maker
The Art of Her Nonfiction

Octavia E. Butler's deftness as a storyteller sometimes overshadows her nonfiction work, perhaps with good reason. She has one published speech, nine essays, one newspaper column, and one book review, ranging from 1980 to 2001. Though the nonfiction she published is relatively little compared to her fiction, there are key trends that pop up. She favors anaphora (the repetition of a word or phrase at the beginning of back-to-back sentences), rhetorical questions (questions asked to make a point, rather than to get an answer), lists (for structuring), and with few exceptions, personal anecdotes. What follows is an exploration of her nonfiction, which I have divided into four categories: early nonfiction, advice to writers, life writing, and writing to enact change.

Early Nonfiction

"Discovery, Creation, and Craft" is Butler's 1983 review of Claudia Tate's edited collection, *Black Women Writers at Work* in tandem with *Confirmation: An Anthology of African American Women*, co-edited by Amiri and Amina Baraka. At first glance, it appears to be an outlier with the rest of her nonfiction, which takes the form of advice to writers, autoethnography, and raising social awareness. Yet to read her review of a book bursting with her contemporaries, it becomes apparent that the praise she affords the contributors of *Black Women Writers at Work* dispels the myth of a monolithic "Black woman writer of the time." Her praise also aligns with her personal aspirations for her writing: she wanted to be a "hell of a good storyteller" without resorting to preachiness or proselytization.[1] Her affirmative review of *Black Women*

Writers at Work offers a glimpse of the writing Butler admired and wrote herself. A biased review? Certainly. But true? Absolutely.

That she wrote such a review at all is thrown into sharp relief if we consider some of the writing advice she received. During her first year of college, Butler's creative writing teacher "told another student not to use black characters in his stories unless those characters' blackness was somehow essential to the plots. The presence of blacks, my teacher felt, changed the focus of the story—drew attention from the intended subject."[2] At eighteen, Butler was unsurprised by this incident in 1965, given that the Civil Rights and Black Power Movements were well underway. "I would never have expected to hear my teacher's sentiments echoed by a science fiction writer in 1979," she offers candidly.[3] But she did hear them. At a science fiction convention. From a writer who "explained that he had decided against using a black character in one of his stories because the presence of the black would change his story somehow."[4] The writer later suggested that if a story needs Black characters "to make some racial point" a better alternative would be "to substitute extraterrestrials—so as not to dwell on matters of race."[5]

The 1979 incident sparks "The Lost Races of Science Fiction," Butler's first nonfiction response to racism in Science Fiction. The essay, published in the Summer of 1980 issue of *Transmission*, allows her to "do a little dwelling" on her contemporary's comments about Black people in Science Fiction.[6] She opens her dwelling with a rhetorical question: "Science fiction reaches into the future, the past, the human mind. It reaches out to other worlds and into other dimensions. Is it really so limited, then, that it cannot reach into the lives of ordinary, everyday humans who happen not to be white?"[7] As with all rhetorical questions, which are asked to make a point, rather than to get an answer, Butler's question points to the absurdity of the writer's claim. The purpose of her essay is to address and rebut the belief that Black people cannot be present in works unless the work is about racial oppression. Butler concedes that Black characters could reshape the focus away from the author's original intent—but only in the hands of an inept, unskilled writer, especially one who is "too restricted in their thinking" to imagine Black people in any other way.[8] She expands further, articulating her annoyance with writers who harbor such restricted mindsets with her anaphoric use of "No writer who": "No writer who regards blacks as people, human beings, with the usual variety of human concerns, flaws, skills, hopes, etc., would have trouble creating interesting backgrounds and goals for black characters. No writer who regards blacks as people would get sidetracked into justifying their blackness or their presence unless such justification honestly played a part in the story. It is no more necessary to focus on a character's blackness than it is to focus on a woman's femininity."[9] In other words, if Science Fiction writers view Black people as human, they will not have any problems creating Black characters without "stereotyping" them. Her essay's three-part structure—identify the problem, interrogate the problem, and offer solutions to the problem—is intended to instruct her audience, white SF writers, and ask them to do better in terms of writing racially inclusive texts with care and intention.

Butler offers three reasons for the absence or near-absence of Black people in science fiction. First, she addresses the claim that "substituting extraterrestrials for blacks" is a viable solution that can make a "race-related point" without causing discomfort to white readers. She counters this point with the suggestion that SF writers should give their readers some credit using the following scenario: "Let's replace blacks with tentacled beings from Capella V. What will readers visualize as we describe relations between the Capellans and the (white) humans? Will they visualize black humans dealing with white humans? I don't think so. This is science fiction, after all. If you tell your readers about tentacled Capellans, they're going to visualize tentacled Capellans."[10] Butler notes that readers of SF may not draw an analogy between extraterrestrials and racial minorities because they are conditioned to imagine what is presented to them. She further debunks the replacement impulse by questioning the prospective readers' politics: "And if your readers are as touchy about human races as you were afraid they might be when you substituted the Capellans, are they really likely to pay attention to any analogy you draw? I don't think so."

Similarly, she addresses the "Why can't blacks be represented by whites . . . leaving readers free to use their imaginations and visualize whichever color they like?" line of thought with three sentences: "Well, remember when men represented all of humanity? Women didn't care for it much. Still don't."[11] Butler surmises that no evidence supports replacing Black people with extraterrestrials or white people as a solution to keep white readers from being uncomfortable about race and racism. Second, she balks at the idea that because science fiction is supposed to be "escapist literature" that allows readers to escape the real world and not be "weighted down with real problems" as the excuse for why Black people are not in SF: "War, okay. Planet-wide destruction, okay. Kidnapping, okay. But the sight of a minority person? Too heavy. Too real," she writes with sarcasm.[12] Finally, she notes that Black people are "out of fashion," at least in film, and will continue to be so "until someone decides to take a chance, and winds up making a damn big hit movie" about Black people.[13]

As with any problem, Butler interrogates it. "Why are there so few Black SF writers?"[14] She offers four reasons: the lack of authenticity of the genre when so many writers imagine white-only worlds; conscious racism in the genre, where most SF has been all white; habit and custom, which she describes as "a more insidious problem than outright racism"; and finally, laziness combined with ignorance, which is the "second insidious problem."[15] Butler notes that "people seem worried about accidentally giving offense," and she counters this fear with a tongue-in-cheek rhetorical question: "But what do authors ordinarily do when they decide to write about an unfamiliar subject?"[16] "They research. They read," she offers in response, in case her audience is unsure.[17] Butler's solution for all of this is for SF writers to remember that they are writing about people. "Authors who forget this, who do not relax and get comfortable with their racially different characters," she warns, "can wind up creating unbelievable, self-consciously manipulated puppets; pieces of furniture who exist within a story but contribute nothing to it; or stereotypes guaranteed to be offensive."[18]

Butler's "Lost Races of Science Fiction" was designed to spur white science fiction writers to move beyond their biases and write women and Black people as if they existed. It comes as no surprise, then, that three years later, she was offering a glowing review of *Black Women Writers at Work*. Though the genre of those writers differed from hers, the possibilities for what could be done with science fiction were on the horizon. She hoped to edit and publish *Black Futures*—an entire anthology of science fiction. It did not come to fruition. But, in 2000, Sheree Renee Thomas' *Dark Matter: A Century of Speculative Fiction from the Black Diaspora* was published. And Butler's work was included. Where her white science fiction contemporaries could not envision Black people in their fiction, others took up the mantle she herself hoped to take up. Her earliest nonfiction offers us a glimpse into who she was: a woman fiercely committed to her craft and preferred genre and who expected her writing cohort to be as careful, nuanced, and expansive in their inclusion of minoritized populations as they were with tentacled Capellans.

Advice to Writers

If "The Lost Races of Science Fiction" is a rebuttal to racist, close-minded thinking, it is also an early form of advice to writers. Butler was often interested in offering advice to writers; she gave talks about the importance of her writing craft, she was an artist-in-residence in places like Tulane University, and she taught at the Clarion Writers Workshop. Both "Furor Scribendi" and "How I Built Novels Out of Writer's Blocks" are extensions of those impulses.

Published in 1993, "Furor Scribendi" is a "how to" essay; it is an advice column or training manual on how to write for publication. She wrote the essay for L. Ron Hubbard's *Writers of the Future* anthology, but in an afterword to the essay, she explains that it was a revised, condensed, and compacted version of a talk she previously gave to fledgling writers. Its tone, business-like and prescriptive, is a departure from much of her nonfiction. She imagined "Furor Scribendi," which was also tentatively titled "A Rage to Write," as "a self-help book for people who want to write for publication" and "for people who want to get their writing into publishable shape, but have not, or for people who don't understand why their work isn't already publishable."[19] Her tri-fold audience and her purpose for writing explains the radically different tone from her previous nonfiction. In a move that is uncharacteristic of her other nonfiction, she abandons her trademarked anecdotal introduction in favor of four declarative statements, the latter of which is "Here are the rules."[20] She hooks her audience with her no-holds-barred rules for becoming published:

1. Read.
2. Take writing classes and workshops.
3. Write.
4. Revise.
5. Submit.
6. Forget inspiration, talent, and imagination.

One look at her journals, commonplace books, and notes to friends and it is clear: this list is not surprising. Butler believed in each rule—even if following them did not exempt her from writer's block.

By the time Butler writes "How I Built Novels Out of Writer's Blocks" for *Writer's Digest* six years later, she was the author of eleven novels. It is no wonder that Dawn Ramirez, the editor of *Writer's Digest* at the time, phoned Butler in December of 1998 and commissioned Butler to write for *Writer's Digest*, offering $0.40 per word. As a community of "Writers helping writers improve their craft, achieve their goals and recognize their dreams—since 1920" with a mission to "help ignite writers' creative vision and connect them with the community, education and resources they need to bring it to life."[21] *Writer's Digest* was the perfect place for Butler, who was eager to help writers and no stranger to writer's block, offer advice.

In "How I Built Novels Out of Writer's Blocks," Butler addresses writers, noting "any writer who's had it knows what I mean."[22] There's a familiarity and collegiality to her writing, where she's baring herself, really hoping to help others. "I've just present almost ten years alternately fighting and using writer's block while working on books . . . ," she admits.[23] She's referring to *Parable of* the *Sower* (1993) and *Parable of the Talents* (1998). Her openness would likely be appealing to her reading audience who would certainly be asking themselves, What caused her writer's block? As if anticipating their question, she answers. With *Sower*, she attempts to distance herself from her character who was a power-seeker because "I had bought into the idea anyone who wanted power probably should have it."[24] But in attempting to distance herself from the character, she found her efforts stultifying. She tried to rectify the writer's block using several tried-and-true techniques—writing from a different point of view, writing in different locations, and reading other writing. These techniques "failed"; she "froze," and she realized "not this time." Her use of short, choppy sentences, "When this failed, I froze" and "Not this time," emphasizes and reinforces the opening line of the article: "Writer's block is a deadness."[25] The short, choppy sentences are offset by longer, intriguing sentences that use em dashes, commas, and parentheses. The apparent deadness is followed by flourishing, and two things—a "change of genre" and "the news" helped Butler break writer's block so she could complete *Sower*.[26]

"I thought I was rolling," is what Butler offers as a follow-up to her seeming defeat of writer's block.[27] Instead of seducing her readers with more tales of success immediately after *Sower*, she reveals that when it came to its sequel, she faced writer's block. Again. Offering readers an additional tale of writer's block after successfully overcoming it establishes her credibility far more than her success as a writer. Maintaining her pattern, she emphasizes her inability to write by narrating with short sentences: "It was impossible," "I couldn't do it," and "Very scary."[28] The solution this time was the same as before—learning something new. Instead of poetry, it was a computer, which she described as "a nastier enemy than the novel had ever been."[29] Whether shifting to write in a new genre, gleaning from the news, or enduring a new technological enemy, Butler's advice for writers experiencing writer's block is simple: use it. It "has been a guide and a goad to me . . . It isn't a tool that I would want to use, but writers can't always be choosers. And if we're serious, we do use everything."[30]

Life Writing

The idea that "writers use everything" was certainly true for Butler. Though she was sometimes reluctant to use too much of her personal life in her writing. In her journals, she toyed with the idea of writing an autobiography, but she had her reservations. How could she lose herself in a character if she was writing about her life and not inventing a new world? Could she really bare herself to her readers? Was her life not incredibly boring? These questions plagued her, and despite the autobiographical tidbits that pepper her characters (she and Dana are both left-handed, she kept a journal just like Lauren Olamina) she was reluctant to commit to the autobiography. Her reluctance did not prevent her from writing, however, and she imagined any memoir or autobiography as a series of essays, and she even toyed with possible titles, including *Trickster, Teacher, Chaos, Clay*. Her essays "Positive Obsession" (1989) and "Eye Witness" (2002) and her speech, "Devil Girl from Mars: Why I Write Science Fiction" (1998), fall under the umbrella category of Life Writing, which includes autobiography, memoir, and autoethnography—and all their variations. An autobiography covers the author's entire life, from birth to present (whatever that present is, usually starting with the parents' marriage and their birth), and a memoir covers a part of one's life with a specific event, date, or focal point as the beginning. Autoethnography is a genre of writing about yourself to explore, understand, and reveal insights about the society you are part of as it relates to your personal experience, which may be a single event or a series of events to interrogate social structures.

"Positive Obsession" was first published in *Essence* magazine in 1989 with the title "Birth of a Writer." But as Butler writes in her afterword to the essay in *Bloodchild and Other Stories*, "I never liked the *Essence* title. My title was always 'Positive Obsession.'"[31] "Positive Obsession" is a creative nonfiction essay best characterized as an intellectual autobiography, where she combines her lifelong obsession with reading and writing with her earliest memory of it: Butler's transition to reading on her own, what she calls her mother's "sneak attack" that jump-started Butler's positive obsession with literacy.[32] Structured as a series of fourteen vignettes, "Positive Obsession" explores her life, intellectual work, and creative process. Her central theme? Her fixation with reading and writing. Her intellectual autobiography sheds light on her earliest experiences with reading and writing; her recognition of her Blackness and how it could bar her access to certain public spaces; her teenage self-assurance that she would be a writer one day; her aunt suggesting that she would need to get a real, practical job (because the writing was a hobby); her frequent job-hopping in factory work; her early morning writing ritual before work; her failure to publish anything for five years after her first short story was published; and her positive obsession with *ars scribendi*—the art of writing.

In the final vignette, she highlights the importance of science fiction for Black people in general, and since her essay was originally written for *Essence* magazine, she may have been targeting a Black women's readership who may have heard of her work or who might have been skeptical about the need for science fiction. "I'm still asked," she writes, "what good is science fiction to Black people?"[33] She offers the following answer: "What good is any form of literature to Black people? What good is science fiction's thinking about the present, the future, and the past? What good is its tendency to warn or to consider alternative ways of thinking and doing? What good is its examination of the possible effects of science and technology, or social organization and political direction?"[34] Her answer combines anaphora and rhetorical questions to underscore the absurdity of such a question and to emphasize the urgency and necessity of material that encourages critical thinking. Her answer belies the very reason she writes science fiction: to explore the what if, if only, and if this goes on. Her questions challenge the assumptions that science fiction is neither useful to nor important for Black people. Instead of answering the question, Butler interrogates the interrogator, inviting readers to participate in critical self-reflection, unpack their genre biases, and imagine "what if I did read science fiction?"

Years later, Butler would answer a similar question, but this time in a public setting with undergraduate students as her audience. Butler was often nervous about speaking in public, but she relied on one key mantra: tell stories and offer personal anecdotes to connect to her audience. And, if there was time, try to wiggle in a bit of humor. Her February 19, 1998, speech, "Devil Girl from Mars: Why I Write Science Fiction," bridges all three. The speech was billed as a conversation starter for a group of Massachusetts Institute of Technology (MIT) students who would later be placed in smaller discussion groups ruminating on the theme, Media in Transition. Unlike Butler's other nonfiction work, this is perhaps the most conversational work. The transcript of this work is available online, and considering how it has been archived, the assumption is that those interested in LGBTQ+ initiatives, Afrofuturism, Science Fiction, and Black Women Writers will find this speech interesting.

The question her speech asks and answers is "What is the media that affected me and my work?" She begins with a personal anecdote about watching a terrible movie—*Devil Girl from Mars*—that led to her interest in writing science fiction. "I can write a better book than that," she tells herself and the audience, which is not only an attention-grabber but also a tone-setter for the rest of the speech—it generates laughter and showcases her humor.[35] Whereas "Positive Obsession" uses formalized storytelling vignettes that are numbered and sectioned, this speech does so in an informal way, given the setting and the medium. The speech moves from this introductory moment to how a series of different moments in the media impacted her writing. In addition to *Devil Girl from Mars* inspiring her to write science fiction, she mentions that science fiction documentaries and movies from school, NPR, editorial cartoons, the news—and more—influence her writing. Nearly all her examples come from *Parable of the Sower* and *Parable of the Talents* though she mentions "Speech Sounds" (1983) by name and offers an oblique reference to the telepaths in her Patternist Series (1976–1984). Butler paints herself as an informed woman who wants others to be informed. As she consumed media and heard more about increased homelessness, prison corporations, vagrancy punishment, global warming, drug-addicted mothers and their infants, the more she created the worlds of her Parable Series. She began writing science fiction because she wanted to tell a better story than *Devil Girl from Mars*, but she continued to write science fiction because she wanted people to pay attention.

If "Positive Obsession" and "Devil Girl from Mars: Why I Write Science Fiction" both delve into Butler's intense dedication to writing, her essay "Eye Witness" (2002) which was published in *O! The Oprah Magazine* keenly analyzes real-world events filtered through her childhood memories. Through these recollections, Butler's disdain for barriers and cages becomes evident— as does her lifelong desire for empathy. By revisiting two pivotal childhood incidents that left an indelible mark on her, she establishes her credibility with personal eye-witness accounts, effectively employs emotional appeals, and positions herself as someone who had to learn about empathy through her experiences as a young Black girl who lived in a world divided by socioeconomic and racial lines.

The essay's full title, "Eye Witness: Octavia E. Butler's Aha Moment!" not only enhances Butler's credibility but also invites readers to invest in their own journey toward self-awareness. Yet the title has three striking implications. An "eyewitness" is often one who observes a crime, but we can also interpret this title as the first-person "I"-witness, signifying someone who testifies or provides evidence for an event, which holds resonance in traditions like Black Church testimonies. As one who writes an autobiographical essay, Butler certainly offers a first-person I-witness testimony about her growth in recognizing dignity in others. Moreover, "eyewitness" underscores the idea that the eyes are windows to the soul. By framing empathy as an "eye-witness experience," Butler urges her audience toward action. They should respond if they have witnessed empathy's absence, which she equates to a criminal act. Conversely, if they experienced empathy, they should share their stories, as she does in her essay.

The essay follows a cyclical pattern. Butler begins by describing a memory she recalls from when she was three years old. She recalls several family members working for a white family, using the backdrop of the white family's house as the canvas on which she paints her narrative. At three years old, she encounters the white family's dog, Baba, in a moment that shapes her perception of difference for the first time. She looks into Baba's eyes and realizes he is different from the humans she knows. For three-year-old Butler, Baba's eyes elicit fear and fascination, becoming an "aha!" moment. From then on, Butler always paid attention to eyes, writing: "Eyes reminded me that someone else was there."³⁶ This declaration about eyes leads to another memory at the age of seven, where she witnesses her classmates taunting a chimpanzee at the zoo. She was "still too young to understand the concept of being ashamed of my species," she wrote, noting that she "felt horrible" and "wanted the chimp to be free."³⁷ Noticeably absent from her recollection of the zoo is the intentional presence of authority figures—whether parents, guardians, or employees. The absence of intervention implies a passive endorsement of her classmates' cruel behavior, and by paralleling this criminal indifference with her initial lack of recognition of Baba's dignity, she offers both an eyewitness account of a crime and an I-witness testimony.

As she transitions back to her three-year-old self, Butler closes with her adult perspective on both incidents, encouraging readers to become their own eyewitnesses to something profound: "I've known since I was barely 3 . . . that it is better—much more interesting—to get to know others and to discover who and what they are."³⁸ While she did not immediately acknowledge Baba's dignity, she eventually recognized it. The act of truly looking into someone's eyes, as suggested by "Eye Witness," has the power to unveil their worthiness. The essay plainly reveals that our inability to truly see others and let ourselves be seen is a barrier to empathy. Through her characterization of Baba as a sentient being and her insight into human indifference and cruelty, Butler affirms her belief that "It is better to look into their eyes with open curiosity," ready and willing to discover the inherent dignity within them.³⁹

Writing to Enact Change

Change is a prominent theme throughout Butler's fiction. Whether her characters adapt to changing circumstances, as we see with Dana in *Kindred* (1979), Anyanwu in *Wild Seed* (1980), or Lilith in *Dawn* (1987), or find themselves rooted in uncompromising, outdated modes of thinking, as we see with Coransee in *Patternmaster* (1976), Blake and Rane in *Clay's Ark* (1984), and Peter in *Dawn* (1987), Butler believed that change was necessary and inevitable. Such impulses extend to her nonfiction work, and she sometimes wrote pieces that were designed to disturb one's conscience, stirring up social awareness and moving people to act—to enact changes before conditions became dire.

In August 1993, "Free Libraries: Are They Becoming Extinct?" was published in the First Word column for *Omni*, a magazine devoted to science and science fiction, featuring articles and short stories related to the subject matter. As is characteristic of columns, Butler expresses her own opinion regarding the existence of and the apparent dissolution of free libraries—and the danger it poses to us as a society. Her audience seems to be those who seem unaffected by the dissolution of public libraries. That she wrote this piece for *Omni* suggests that she was hoping to attract the attention of SF readers and writers who may have been used to scrounging around for books they liked to read. And who likely also relied on public libraries to find affordable (free) reading materials that interested them. To make her claims, Butler weaves her personal experiences, *Sower*, and references to current events happening in the U.S. without specifics. Her goal? To offer a compelling argument about the importance of public libraries and the need to address their current challenges—and the dangers therein if public libraries are allowed to be defunded or underfunded.

Butler opens with her recollection of the Los Angeles Central Library burning to the ground on April 29, 1986. She witnessed the "black smoke pour from the windows" as she stood on the corner of Fifth Street and Grand Avenue.[40] Butler's use of dates and proper nouns sets the stage and the tone for her op-ed. The date, the names of the street corners and the library, coupled with the vivid imagery of black smoke "pouring" from the windows, offer a sense of immediacy, urgency, and foreboding, which underscores the apocalyptic scene she paints as she positions herself as a shell-shocked survivor who witnessed the library meet its end. She offers the rhetorical question, "Free Libraries: Are They Becoming Extinct?" as a warning of the dangers ahead—if changes are not made. She notes that the burning of the LA library in the late 1980s was a microcosm of what was happening in the U.S. seven years later as the library renovations neared their completion. She frames the national library crisis as amidst a larger, near-apocalyptic crisis—capitalism—and the "shortsighted," "expediency," and "neglect" it often brings.[41] The warning about the near-apocalyptic crisis is underscored further when she offers two brief excerpts from *Sower* (though the novel is not mentioned in the article). *Sower* is, in Butler's own words, the story of a protagonist who "lives in a poorer, dumber, near-future time."[42] The public library is "among the best tools" that will help humanity adapt, she writes.[43] Yet the treatment of the public library, she notes, suggests that it is doomed. Butler emphasizes the humanitarian reasons why public libraries matter, describing them as the "open universities of America"; they are free and accessible, they offer special services to everyone, and they offer "worlds of possibilities" to the ignorant and impoverished.[44]

Perhaps because Butler knew that readers may not empathize with an unknown "shut in," vague references to "children" or to the "nonreaders," she makes a personalized connection to the necessity of public libraries: "I'm a writer at least partly because I had access to public libraries."[45] She establishes her credibility, not only indicating that she was a beneficiary of public libraries but that as a Black daughter "of a shoeshine man who died young and a man who was uneducated but knew her way to the library," these spaces were her saving grace.[46] Essentially, without libraries, Butler's earlier works like

Kindred, *Dawn*, and the award-winning "Bloodchild," "Speech Sounds," and "The Evening and the Morning and the Night" may not exist. In 1993, Butler was not shy about discussing her background, but reiterating its importance for *Omni* readers and any others who may have come across the article is key for emphasizing her purpose in writing this article: to sound the alarm, to note that the end is near if we don't act.

In April 2023, thirty years after Butler's piece appeared in *Omni*, the American Library Association issued its annual report with the following words from its director, Traci D. Hall: "Many libraries and their staffs nationwide—school, public, college and university, special, carceral, and consortial—found themselves contending with reduced funding and staffing, threats to personal safety in the form of bomb scares and to professional livelihoods from fringes and job losses, and bills threatening to criminally charge librarians or defund libraries altogether for making certain materials available on their shelves or findable through reference services. Despite these pressures, libraries have proven themselves to be among the most adaptable of public and community-serving institutions."[47] "This is not sensible!" Butler wrote in 1993.[48] And her response to the varied threats against public libraries, including book banning and censorship, and the well-being of their employees, would echo that sentiment. Butler's last lines offer a warning and an emphatic plea: "We're doing ourselves last harm in exchange for the ephemeral good of quick-fix budget cuts," she writes. "It's time we stopped, considered the consequences of our self-destructive behavior, and made the necessary changes."[49] Her essay ends with a call to action. She urges readers to "stop" and "consider" the consequences of neglecting public libraries and the far-reaching impacts of such neglect. The crisis she hoped would be averted in the 1990s is knocking at the proverbial door. The smoke she witnessed pouring out of the windows is back, and this time, the smoke is nationwide. Is the end near? Are free libraries becoming extinct? The signs are there. But so, too, is hope.

Two years after she published her column on libraries, Butler's "The Monophobic Response" (1995) asks a rhetorical "what if" question to indicate that when it comes to dismantling human biases, few humans are ready to confront the implications of their fear of others. What if extra-terrestrials invaded Earth? How would their arrival affect our sense of identity? Would humans unify? These questions—and more—Butler poses in "The Monophobic Response." Originally a talk she gave at the PEN/Faulkner Awards for Fiction, it was later republished in Thomas' *Dark Matter* (2000). The opening of her speech-turned-essay, "For all but the first 10 years of my life, writing has been my way of journeying from incomprehension, confusion, and emotional upheaval to some sort of order, or at least to an orderly list of questions and considerations. For instance . . . ," leads me to imagine it as a stream-of-consciousness letter to future readers, like a love letter tucked away in a time capsule, intended to be found by a future audience.[50] Butler's questions, *What if . . . ? How would . . . ? Would humans . . . ?* would leave the finders of the time capsule thinking we had created an ideal version of ourselves, that we had arrived. However, "The Monophobic Response" seems to solidify what Butler has long believed about humans: we are invested in creating and maintaining hierarchies.

We are the creators of our own hierarchies, a claim Butler reinforces with her use of anaphora, "No wonder we need aliens. No wonder we're so good at creating aliens. No wonder we so often project alienness on one another."[51] She enumerates several attributes that differentiate humans from one another, emphasizing the hierarchies and conflicts resulting from creating aliens of our fellow humans. Whether country of origin or culture, gender or sexuality, race or ethnicity, religion or socioeconomic status, because we are monophobic—because we fear being alone—we create hierarchical communities of ourselves. This fear and our response to it is paradoxical; we create a "sibling rivalry" in an effort to "satisfy our desires for territory, dominance, and exclusivity."[52] "The Monophobic Response" is Butler's effort to highlight the paradox of human nature—we imagine and create fictional aliens to cope with our fear of being alone, yet "we are unable to get along with those aliens closest to us, those aliens who are, of course, ourselves."[53] Instead of working to repair the fissures and cracks we have created, we are invested in maintaining the silos that harm us. And yet Butler ends her meditation wondering about the possibilities: What if extraterrestrials invaded Earth? How would their arrival affect our sense of identity? "What," she asks, "will be born, then, of such a strange and ironic union?"[54]

Five years later, in an essay written for *Essence* Magazine, Butler remains concerned with the "what if?" question, but instead of ruminating on the possibilities of extraterrestrials arriving on Earth, she offers glimpses of how we can predict the future here on Earth. In "A Few Rules for Predicting the Future" (2000), Butler opens with a recollection of an exchange with a student while she was signing books after a campus talk. A student asked her if she believed the future would pan out in the way she described in *Sower* and *Talents*, with their emphasis on drug addiction, illiteracy, wealth inequality, climate change, and more. Her response, that all she did was "look around at the problems we're neglecting now and give them about 30 years to grow into full-fledged disasters,"[55] dissatisfied the student, and he pressed Butler further, desperate for a solution. "There isn't one," she tells him, clarifying, ". . . there's no single answer that will solve all of our future problems. There's no magic bullet. Instead, there are thousands of answers—at least. You can be one of them if you choose to be."[56] To her surprise and chagrin, she discovers the student has offered an "accurate but incomplete" summary of her response in his college newspaper.[57] Butler's peevishness at the student's inaccurate assessment is evident in her reflection, "It's sadly easy to reverse meaning, in fact, to tell a lie by offering an accurate but incomplete quote."[58] She declares that *Sower*, *Talents*, and her attempts to offer warnings are an act of hope. "A Few Rules for Predicting the Future" corrects a college student's misrepresentation of her words by offering and explaining four rules for predicting the future.

Rule Number One? Learn from the past. Butler explains that as she wrote *Parable of the Sower* and *Parable of the Talents*, she wanted to immerse herself in history because she likes to "use past and present behaviors as guides to the world we seem to be creating."[59] She mentions researching Nazi Germany and re-reading William L. Shirer's *The Rise and Fall of the Third Reich: A History of Naz Germany* (1960), and juxtaposes her affinity for learning from the past with her 15-year-old neighbor who knew nothing about Nazis—something Butler discovered as she was helping her young neighbor with her homework assignment. Butler ends her first rule with a dire caution, "We forget history at our own peril."[60] Rule Number Two? Respect the Law of Consequences. Butler opens with another personal anecdote, but instead of writing, she shares a conversation she had with her doctor, where Butler expressed her concerns about the side effects of some medication she was taking. Her doctor offers to prescribe her another medication, one that is meant to counteract the effects of the first and has no side effects of its own. The doctor's assessment made Butler "absolutely certain" she did not want the second medication.[61] Why? "I realized that I didn't believe there were any medications that had no side effects. In fact, I don't believe we can do anything at all without side effects—also known as unintended consequences."[62] In using her exchange with a doctor about medicine and its side effects, Butler points out the absurdity of thinking that we can move through life without side effects, implications, or consequences to our actions. The third rule, Be Aware of Your Perspective, encourages readers to consider the things that play a role in our efforts to predict the future. She parallels her interest in the Space Race of the 1950s and 1960s with her desire to leave her mother's home and explore the unknown-to-her world around her. She "never imagined" that her "wishful thinking" about space exploration would have so little to show for itself.[63] She was hoping lunar colonies would be established and that people would get sent to Mars. Her point? Beware of your perspective—"Wishful thinking is no more help in predicting the future than fear, superstition or depression."[64] The fourth rule, Count on the Surprises, speaks to the unpredictability of the future. She anticipates potential skeptics or naysayers by asking and answering, "So why try to predict the future at all if it's so difficult, so nearly impossible?" Because making predictions, offering warnings, and thinking about what is possible is wise and is a sign of hope. ". . . our tomorrow is the child of today," she closes, "Best to try to shape it into something good. Best to do that for any child."[65] The hopeful end to Butler's essay successfully addresses the college student's distortion of Butler's meaning and offers her readers hope—and four rules to consider.

Yet the hope she espouses with such conviction about changing the future does not extend to her thoughts on expunging racism a year later. The beginning of the United Nations' 2001 World Conference Against Racism, Racial Discrimination, Xenophobia, and Related Intolerance, held August 31–September 2001, in Durban, South Africa, inspired NPR's *Weekend Edition* to ask Butler to respond to the prompt "Can you imagine a world without racism?" Her short essay "On Racism" (2001) was the resulting response. She writes that she initially tried to imagine a world where everyone felt "all the pain and all the pleasure they caused one another" but came to realize that "the threat of shared pain wouldn't necessarily make people behave better toward one another. And it might cause trouble."[66] The result was a single character with these empathic abilities. And then comes the bombshell in her essay. "Nothing. Nothing at all," is her answer to the question, "What would make us more tolerant, more peaceful, less likely to need a UN Conference on Racism?"[67] The finality of such a declaration is reinforced by the way those words appear on the page: as two single lines set apart from the other lengthier paragraphs. The finality of the statement is abrupt and abrasive, yet the declarative statements are followed by an autobiographical interlude: "I say that, remembering childhood, remembering the schoolyard, remembering being a perennial out-kid. At school, I was always taller than the rest of my class, and because I was an only child I was comfortable with adults, but shy and awkward with other kids. I was quiet, bookish, and in spite of my size, hopeless at sports. In short, I was different. And even in the earliest grades, I got pounded for it. I learned that five- and six-year-old kids have already figured out how to be intolerant."[68]

Butler's comments about intolerant children mirror her commentary in "Eye Witness" (2002), where she discusses seven-year-old children who taunt chimpanzees at a zoo. Butler notes that her experience, while unique to her, remains a "familiar experience to anyone who remembers the schoolyard."[69] Here, she invites her readers to reflect on their childhood—a time of supposed innocence—to consider the intolerance around her. "Of course," she offers with a caveat designed to persuade her readers further, "not everyone has been a bully or the victim of bullies, but everyone has seen bullying, and seeing it, has responded to it by joining in or objecting, by laughing or keeping silent, by feeling disgusted or feeling interested. . . ."[70] By showcasing the intolerance of children, Butler notes how it is ingrained in humanity at an early age. Thus, when she concludes that the only way for a world to exist without racism, without multiple forms of intolerance is possible "Only if we want it to. Only when we want it to," she is calling for a re-education.[71] Yet, intolerant children grow up to be intolerant adults. Who is willing to take on this "work in progress"? The tone of her essay suggests that there is very little collective desire to create such a world because there seems to be "satisfaction to be enjoyed in feeling superior to other people."[72]

Word Weaver, World Maker

Butler's skillfulness as a novelist and short-story writer may cast a shadow over her nonfiction work, but the nonfiction work is equally compelling. The genre may be different, but her aim remains the same: to hook readers with a compelling story and to make people feel. Though the scale of her published nonfiction is modest in comparison to her fiction, key patterns emerge in her work. Staples of her nonfiction include anaphora, which creates rhythm, flow, and emphasis; rhetorical questions, which remind readers to question everything and everyone; lists—as used in "Lost Races of Science Fiction," "Furor Scribendi," and "A Few Rules for Predicting the Future"—showcase her thoughtful, deliberate approach to conveying ideas. Her penchant for lists is also evident in her journals, commonplace books, and random bits of ephemera. What stands out prominently across her nonfiction works, with few exceptions, is her weaving her personal experiences—whether a book signing, a tutoring experience gone wrong, or a doctor's visit—to illustrate salient points about whatever subject matter has captured her mind, her pen. Butler's admonitions to fellow SF writers, her advice to burgeoning writers, and her calls for hope and change offer us additional depth to her already rich literary legacy.

Afterword
Living Forever, Leaving Legacies

Octavia E. Butler admitted that her adolescent fantasy was "to live forever and breed people."[1] Although her response "didn't go over all that well" with her friends, she did it anyway.[2] Butler died in 2006, yet the spirit of her work lives on, touching and inspiring many. Her prescience and presence remain eloquent, and her words—whether from novels, short stories, poetry, essays, speeches, or interviews—maintain an eerie resonance in the earliest decades of the twenty-first century. I am certain they will continue in the decades to come. Fourteen years after her death, the award-winning achieved her lifelong goal: *Parable of the Sower* (1993) made the *New York Times* Best Seller list, acclaimed for its prescience amid the COVID-19 pandemic and the renewed momentum of the Black Lives Matter movement following George Floyd's murder. Butler made headlines once again in 2021 after NASA announced that the Perseverance Landing Site on Mars was named in her honor. And on February 24, 2022, the sixteenth anniversary of Butler's passing, she made headlines once again as the Pasadena School Board passed, approved, and adopted a resolution to rename Washington Steam Multilingual Academy to "The Octavia E. Butler Magnet School." As I close this book-length journey, I invite you to bear witness to the legacies she has left us.

Butler's legacies are, perhaps, first and foremost noted in the prescience of her poetry. When we think about Butler, many terms are used to describe her and her work: Afrofuturist, science fiction, feminist, grim, fantasy, Black, slavery, aliens, prophecy, cautionary, visionary—and so many more. What is less frequent are "poet" or "poetry." Although Butler did not publish any poetry collections, she explained that poetry was the medium that alleviated writer's block whenever she experienced it.[3] "I'm the kind of person who looks for a complex way to say something," she shared. "Poetry simplifies it. When I started to write poetry, I was forced to pay attention word by word, line by line."[4] Poetry appears in her journals in the form of lists, affirmations, and reminders to herself. It also appears in *Sower* and *Parable of the Talents* (1998), guiding characters and readers alike:

> Choose your leaders
> > with wisdom and forethought.
>
> To be led by a coward
> > is to be controlled
> > by all that the coward fears.
>
> To be led by a fool
> > is to be led
> > by the opportunists
> > who control the fool.
>
> To be led by a thief
> > is to offer up
> > your most precious treasures
> > to be stolen.
>
> To be led by a liar
> > is to ask
> > to be told lies.
>
> To be led by a tyrant
> > is to sell yourself
> > and those you love
> > into slavery.[5]

This poem showcases Butler's use of anaphora, which is the repetition of a word or phrase at the beginning of successive clauses, in "To be led by" in lines 3, 6, 10, 14, 17, followed by a series nouns: a coward, a fool, a thief, a liar, a tyrant. Placed at the beginning of each vignette, "To be led by" repeats five times throughout the poem, reinforcing the writer's dread and her fear about the coming danger if we do not heed her warning: "Choose your leaders with wisdom / and forethought."[6] The use of anaphora combined with the poem's content is skillful; often, political speakers use anaphora for emphasis to reinforce their agenda. This poem is a reminder that we have a choice and the power to choose wisely or to actively choose or be complicit in our own oppression. One scholar observed that with "the unlikely campaign" and "unimaginable election" of Donald J. Trump as the forty-fifth President of the United States in 2016 "popular online media outlets published an array of articles insisting, 'Octavia warned us!'"[7] She warned us, indeed.

Another poem from *Talents* offers an additional warning about what happens if we choose to remain uninformed or allow ourselves to be duped into believing what others say:

> Beware:
> Ignorance
> Protects itself.
> Ignorance
> Promotes suspicion.
> Suspicion
> Engenders fear.
> Fear quails,
> Irrational and blind,
> Or fear looms,
> Defiant and closed.
> Blind, closed,
> Suspicious, afraid,
> Ignorance
> Protects itself,
> And protected,
> Ignorance grows.[8]

This poem uses the technique of a chain verse, where the last word of a line becomes the first word of a new line. Line five ends with "suspicion," and line six begins with "Suspicion." Line seven ends with "fear," and line eight begins with "Fear." The lines, "Fear quails, / Irrational and blind, / Or fear looms, / Defiant and closed," are remixed rather than chain-linked as if mimicking the poem's warning. The poetic structure of the chain verse continues to break down. Instead of "defiant and closed" opening line 12, the words in lines 12 and 13 are a jumble of what happens when fear strikes us: we may become unaware (blind), narrow-minded (closed), suspicious, or afraid. These words, "blind," "closed," "suspicious," and "afraid" are connected only by commas, a stylistic technique that seems to promote forward movement without the interruption of a conjunction, semicolon, or period. The forward movement of these words appropriately dovetails into the poem's last four lines, "Ignorance / Protects itself, / And protected, / Ignorance grows," which echo and expand lines 2–3. Instead of maintaining the neat chain verse, the chain verse dissolves, matching the potential hysteria of what happens to a society when Ignorance grows. One scholar describes this poem in the following way, "Here the repetition of language pulls the hearer through the statements, giving them a path of thought to follow that seems logical and consistent. It is not about evidence or argument; rather, the language and form are used to create space for rumination but also warning."[9] This poem appears at the beginning of chapter twelve of *Talents*, after Christian American Crusaders raid and transform Acorn into a neo-plantation. Two months after the community's enslavement, Lauren describes the "orgy of abuse and humiliation" as a consequence of the growing impact of ignorance by political leaders and their followers.[10] When my students read the Parable duology, they are so dismayed by the poetry and plot. The truth behind Butler's words is eerily familiar. They speak to present conditions, regardless of time.

These snapshots of Butler's words, though simple, are profound. Poetic. As Butler said, she needed to "pay attention word by word, line by line" and that is what these do for us today.[11] Butler's Parable Series resonated with many readers, resulting in real-world applications of the principles the Series espouses, including godischange.org, which posits Earthseed as a "new religion based on the science fiction of Octavia Butler," and the Parable of the Sower Intentional Community Cooperative, a community that prioritizes Black women and other historically excluded people.[12]

Her work remains such a beacon that several are being adapted as movies or television series on a variety of networks—FX, Amazon Prime, HBO Max, and others—and her works have made on-screen cameos. *Kindred* was adapted by FX, and eight episodes aired in December 2022 on FX/Hulu. But FX did not renew the show for a second season, though creator Brandon Jacobs-Jenkins was reportedly shopping the series to other networks. At the time of this writing, *Kindred* is the only work that has been successfully adapted for the screen, but her novels make cameos on the screen. *Kindred* (1979) appears in the Netflix movie *See You Yesterday* (2019). Directed by Stefon Bristol, *See You Yesterday* is a movie about C.J. Walker, a sixteen-year-old Black girl who, along with her friend Sebastian, builds a time travel device and makes several attempts to return to the past to save her brother from being murdered by law enforcement. The main character's teacher (performed by Michael J. Fox) is reading *Kindred* at the movie's beginning. Butler's work makes a cameo in season three, episode two of the HBO Max series *The Black Lady Sketch Show*. The episode opens in a fifth-grade classroom where a Black teacher, Ms. Miller, fields questions from her students about her love life while trying to teach a lesson about biology. Amid the back-and-forth banter between Ms. Miller and her students, the camera offers a wide-angle, over-the-shoulder shot, giving viewers a glimpse of four novel covers on the bulletin board: Maya Angelou's *I Know Why the Caged Bird Sings* (1969), Toni Morrison's *Beloved* (1987), Octavia E. Butler's *Dawn* (1987), and Alice Walker's *The Color Purple* (1982). Although the sketch's content does not thematically align with any of the literary works, showcasing them on the Emmy award-winning show is a celebration of African American women writers. *Sower* and *Talents* make cameos in Netflix's *Ginny and Georgia* (2023). While in bed, Ginny, a biracial Black teen, reads *Sower* in season two. She tells her mom it "details the demise of America through capitalist fascism."[13] Two episodes later, Ginny reads *Talents* in her bedroom, where she uses a rubber band to stave off self-harming. The book appears on the screen when her mother, Georgia, enters the room. They argue, and Ginny's continued distrust and resentment toward Georgia thematically links to *Talents*—a daughter's documented resentment toward her mother's choices. *Sower* is also integrated into the plot of *Abbott Elementary* (2024) in season three, episode eleven. But Butler's work makes cameos beyond the screen. Her book covers and typewriter were displayed at the National Museum of African American History and Culture, located in Washington, DC, as part of the "Afrofuturism: A History of Black Futures" exhibit, which opened on March 24, 2023.

Eight years after Butler's unexpected passing, a two-story collection was published: *Unexpected Stories*. The publication contains "Childfinder" (which I discuss in chapter 2) and "A Necessary Being." "A Necessary Being" is a prequel to Butler's third novel *Survivor*. The prequel offers us a glimpse at a young Tahneh and a much younger Diut and their mutual agreement to join clans, the Rohkohn and the Tehkohn, so that both can survive and thrive. "A Necessary Being" is a useful backstory for *Survivor*, offering an etiological tale of how the Tehkohn came to be. In addition to the publication of *Unexpected Stories*, Butler has garnered other notable posthumous achievements. In 2010, Butler's journals, unpublished manuscripts, drafts, writings, photographs, letters, and more were made public by the Huntington Library in Pasadena, California. Researchers all over the world can make appointments to marvel at her work. In 2010, Butler was inducted into the Science Fiction Hall of Fame, and in 2011, the Octavia Butler Legacy Network was established, followed by the Octavia E. Butler Literary Society in 2013. Following her *New York Times* best seller achievement in 2020, NASA named Mars' Perseverance Landing site "Octavia E. Butler Landing" in 2021. Her fans were thrilled, noting that it was a fitting way to memorialize her and her interest in space travel, specifically Olamina's belief that "The Destiny of Earthseed is to take root among the stars."[14] Kathryn Stack Morgan explained NASA's decision in a news release:

"Butler's protagonists embody determination and inventiveness, making her a perfect fit for the Perseverance rover mission and its theme of overcoming challenges."[15] In October of that same year, Butler was inducted into the National Women's Hall of Fame, and four months later, on the sixteenth anniversary of Butler's death in February 2022, brought something "like a prophecy fulfilled" when the middle school she attended was renamed to in her honor."[16] "I mean, here she was learning to dream when she was a child attending the school," her friend and fellow speculative fiction author Tananarive Due mused, "and now it's turned into a school that would have been something beyond her dreams."[17] In April 2023, the Science Fiction and Fantasy Writers Association awarded Butler with their inaugural Infinity Award which was created "to posthumously honor acclaimed creators who passed away before they could be considered for a Damon Knight Memorial Grand Master Award."[18]

Beyond new religions, TV adaptations, on-screen cameos, adaptations, and posthumous publications, responses to Butler's work and her legacy are evident in other ways, notably through the 2023 opening of Octavia's Bookshelf, a Black-owned, independent bookstore in her Pasadena hometown; the publication of *Octavia's Brood: Science Fiction from Social Justice Movements* (2015), which features short fiction from writers inspired by Butler to engage in social movements; the publication of *New Suns* (2019) and *New Suns 2* (2023), two short story collections of speculative fiction written by people of color, which take their title from quote, "The is nothing new under the sun, but there are new suns," from the Parable duology; and conferences dedicated specifically to commemorating Butler's legacy. In 2016, commemorating the tenth anniversary of Butler's death, Spelman College hosted a conference, "Octavia E. Butler: Celebrating Letters, Life, and Legacy." Due, horror author and friend of Butler, spearheaded the 2013 "Octavia E. Butler Celebration of the Fantastic Arts" conference and the 2014 "Octavia E. Butler Celebration of Arts and Activism" conference, both held at Spelman College. At the 2014 event, participants focused on the intersections of Afrofuturism and social injustice. More than three decades after the publication of *Kindred*, Damian Duffy and John Jennings released a graphic novel version of *Kindred* in 2018. Two years later, they released the graphic novel adaptation of *Sower*. In 2022, Ibi Zoboi published *Star Child: A Biographical Constellation of Octavia Estelle Butler*, a new young reader's biography of Butler that blends poetry and prose for middle-grade readers, introducing them to Butler's life and legacy. *A Handful of Earth, A Handful of Sky: The World of Octavia Butler*, by Lynell George (2020), pieces together a narrative from Butler's archived documents, a timely and accessible book for those who may not have the means to visit the Huntington Library.

And the work keeps coming. Beacon Press released a young-adult edition of *Kindred* in 2024, and Marti Dumas' *Wildseed Witch* book series (2022–2024) is a middle-grade spin-off of *Wild Seed* that follows the novel's descendants as they learn to use their powers (and social media) at a boarding school. Beyond book adaptations, literary societies, biographies, and academic events, there are other publicly accessible opportunities for readers and fans to avail themselves of Butler's work. A virtual discussion series, "Octavia Tried to Tell Us: Parables for Today's Pandemic Series," was hosted by Tananarive Due and Monica Coleman during the first two years of the COVID-19 pandemic. In 2024, Howard University's Department of English hosted the Octavia E. Butler Virtual Lecture Series, the New Children's Museum launched the Octavia E. Butler: Seeding Futures exhibit in San Diego, and the Huntington Library hosted a two-day conference, Futurity as Praxis: Learning from Octavia E. Butler. There are podcasts on Butler's work, *Octavia's Parables*, hosted by Toshi Reagon and adrienne maree brown, and *The Pattern*, hosted by Ayana Jamieson (founder of the Octavia E. Butler Legacy Network) and Moya Bailey (digital alchemist for the Octavia E. Butler Legacy Network). For opera lovers, *Octavia E. Butler's Parable of the Sower* is an opera by mother-daughter duo Berniece and Toshi Reagon,[19] and for the Internet savvy, YouTube videos extolling her virtues (and vices) are plentiful as well.

In the years since her death, new academic books, special journal issues, and edited collections focusing on Butler have appeared with increasing frequency: *Changing Bodies in the Fiction of Octavia Butler: Slaves, Aliens, and Vampires*, by Gregory Jerome Hampton (2010); *Octavia E. Butler*, by Gerry Canavan (2016); *Palimpsests in the Life and Work of Octavia E. Butler: A Palimpsest Special Issue*, edited by Ayana Jamison and Moya C. Bailey (2017); *Approaches to Teaching the Works of Octavia E. Butler*, edited by Tarshia L. Stanley (2019); *Human Contradictions in Octavia E. Butler's Work*, edited by Martin Japtok and Jerry Rafiki Jenkins (2020); *The Bloomsbury Handbook to Octavia E. Butler*, edited by Gregory J. Hampton and Kendra R. Parker (2020); *God is Change: Religious Practices and Ideologies in the Works of Octavia Butler* edited by Aparajita Nanda and Shelby L. Crosby (2021). Other academic books incorporate at least one chapter on one or more of Butler's works. These monographs include, but are not limited to, Trudier Harris's *Saints, Sinners, Saviors: Strong Black Women in African American Literature* (2001), Patricia Melzer's *Alien Constructions: Science Fiction and Feminist Thought* (2006), Isiah Lavender's *Race in American Science Fiction* (2011), Esther L. Jones's *Medicine and Ethics in Black Women's Speculative Fiction* (2015), Sami Schalk's *Bodyminds Reimagined: (Dis)ability, Race, and Gender in Black Women's Speculative Fiction* (2018), my own *She Bites Back: Black*

AFTERWORD

Female Vampires in African American Women's Novels, 1977–2011 (2018), Pickens's *Black Madness::Mad Blackness* (2019), and Melanie A. Marotta's *African American Adolescent Heroes: The Twenty-First-Century Young Adult Neo-Slave Narrative* (2023).

The emergence of *Octavia's Brood: Science Fiction Stories from Social Justice Movements*, both volumes of *New Suns*, the graphic novel adaptations of *Kindred*, *Parable of the Sower*, and *Parable of the Talents*, and the continued celebration of Butler's literary legacy are exemplars of the resonance of Butler's work—not just for the present, but for the future. Her work has spawned a new generation of writers who speculate about the future of Black people and other persons of color. Just as Afrofuturism speculates about the potential future for Black societies, readers of Butler's work speculate about the future of social justice. Although Butler can no longer produce new works, the discovery of more unpublished fiction is a possibility through her extensive archives. In fact, at the time of this writing, The University of Louisville was in the process of digitizing its archives, and one item they found was Butler's keynote speech from the 2005 Louisville Conference on Literature and Culture.

Butler wondered just what her legacy would be. On Saturday, May 15, 1996, she penned the following in blue ink:

> Thinking about my legacy—about the things I hope to leave when I die. Ideas. I generate ideas for a living. Some of them are quite good. As it happens, my way of presenting my ideas is by way of writing science fiction novels and stories, articles, and giving talks. My books are most likely to last. They're like messages in bottles that I cast into a sea of humanity. There's no guarantee that they will ever be found and read by people able to make use of them. They are, if found, beginning places. They might foster study in areas new to the finders. They might give the finders directions for behavior modification. They might give the finders something to react against, and thus find new paths for thought and/or action.[20]

And find new paths we have.

From book cameos on TV shows and movies to TV, film, and graphic adaptations of her books, to school renamings and space landing names, Octavia E. Butler is certainly breeding a new generation of people who know and love her work, ensuring that she lives on. It would seem her adolescent desire to "breed people and live forever" has been achieved. Butler entered a genre that was dominated by white men and carved a space not only for herself but also paved the way for other Black women writers like Tomi Adeyemi, Hayley Dennings, Tracy Deonn, Tananarive Due, Marti Dumas, Nalo Hopkinson, N.K. Jemisin, Nnedi Okorafor, Nisi Shawl, and so many others.

She created Black female characters who were dynamic and multifaceted. Her works offer challenges to white supremacy, patriarchy, and varied systems of oppression, daring to ask *what if, if only, if this goes on*? Butler created worlds of possibility. When she did not see herself, she created. When she wanted to see herself differently, she created. When she wanted to imagine a better present and future, she created. And there is nothing braver than daring to exist and create when you are not supposed to. That daring to exist and that braving of new worlds, new trajectories, and new possibilities are hallmarks of her life and legacy.

NOTES

Chapter 1: An Introduction to Octavia E. Butler

1. George, *Handful*, 153.
2. Sanders, "Outsider," 140.
3. Dery, "Future," 8.
4. Womack, *Afrofuturism*, 42.
5. Canavan, "Recovering."
6. Morris, "Afrofuturist Feminism," 157–58.
7. OEB 327, The Butler Papers, Huntington Library.
8. OEB 327, The Butler Papers, Huntington Library.
9. Butler, "Box 1, Folder 1," Schomburg Center.
10. Butler, "Box 1, Folder 1," Schomburg Center.
11. OEB 2707, The Butler Papers, Huntington Library.
12. OEB 3223, The Butler Papers, Huntington Library.
13. OEB 3220, The Butler Papers, Huntington Library.
14. OEB 327, The Butler Papers, Huntington Library.
15. OEB 327, The Butler Papers, Huntington Library.
16. OEB 327, The Butler Papers, Huntington Library.
17. George, *Handful*, 158.
18. Francis, *Conversations*, 197.
19. Francis, *Conversations*, 197.
20. Marriott, "Do the Right Thing."
21. "Ethnographer."
22. Butler, "Eye-Witness."
23. Butler, *Bloodchild*, 170–71.
24. Francis, *Conversations*, 7.
25. Francis, *Conversations*, 58.
26. Francis, *Conversations*, 58–59.
27. Francis, *Conversations*, 227.
28. Butler, *Kindred*, 36.
29. Francis, *Conversations*, 24.
30. Butler, *Bloodchild*, 85.
31. Tyson, *Critical*, 85.
32. Butler, *Bloodchild*, 4.
33. Francis, *Conversations*, 228.

34. Canavan, *Octavia E. Butler*, 36.
35. Butler, *Bloodchild*, 139.
36. Butler, *Talents*, 307.
37. Butler, *Talents*, 307.
38. George, *Handful*, 111.
39. George, *Handful*, 112.
40. Henke, *Shattered Subjects*.
41. Francis, *Conversations*, 56.

Chapter 2: The 1970s

1. OEB 990, The Butler Papers, Huntington Library.
2. OEB 990, The Butler Papers, Huntington Library.
3. Hampton, *Changing Bodies*, 137.
4. Francis, *Conversations*, 54.
5. OEB 928, The Butler Papers, Huntington Library.
6. Bracey et al., *SOS*.
7. Traylor, "Women Writers," 67.
8. Traylor, "Women Writers," 67.
9. Bracey et al., *SOS*, 1.
10. Dubey, *Black Women*, 20.
11. Dubey, *Black Women*.
12. Butler, *Unexpected*, 97.
13. Butler, *Unexpected*, 110.
14. Davis and Gates, *Narrative*, xxvii.
15. Butler, *Unexpected*, 101.
16. Butler, *Unexpected*, 101.
17. "Pocket Universe"
18. Lavender, *Afrofuturism Rising*, 88.
19. Butler, *Unexpected*, 104.
20. Butler, *Unexpected*, 97.
21. Lavender, *Afrofuturism Rising*, 67.
22. Butler, *Unexpected*, 104, 112.
23. Butler, *Unexpected*, 104.
24. Butler, *Unexpected*, 106.
25. Neal, "The Black Arts Movement," 185.
26. OEB 928, The Butler Papers, Huntington Library.
27. Butler, *Unexpected*, 115.
28. Fox, "Dies at 58."
29. Butler, *Bloodchild*, 113.
30. Butler, *Bloodchild*, 113.
31. Butler, *Bloodchild*, 114.
32. Butler, *Bloodchild*, 113.
33. Butler, *Bloodchild*, 118.
34. Butler, *Bloodchild*, 114.
35. Butler, *Bloodchild*, 114.

36. Craft, "'Kiss Me,'" 167.
37. Butler, *Bloodchild*, 118.
38. Butler, *Bloodchild*, 113.
39. Davidson, "Octavia Butler," 35.
40. Butler, *Patternmaster*, 100.
41. Butler, *Patternmaster*, 136.
42. Butler, *Patternmaster*, 136.
43. Butler, *Patternmaster*, 64.
44. As I discuss in *She Bites Back* (2018), Mary's philanthropy and power are rooted in racial uplift narratives heralded by folks like Mary Church Terrell.
45. Butler, *Mind of My Mind*, 68.
46. Butler, *Mind of My Mind*, 70.
47. Stoler, "Extra-Dispensary Perceptions."
48. See Sayre, "Slave Narrative," 179–91.
49. Troy, "Negotiating," 1117.
50. Castiglia, *Bound*, 20.
51. Castiglia, *Bound*, 20.
52. See Slotkin, *Gunfighter Nation*, and Castiglia, *Bound*, 25.
53. Troy, "Negotiating," 1117.
54. Mickle, "Accepting," 22.
55. Mickle, "Accepting," 22.
56. Butler, *Survivor*, 16.
57. Butler, *Survivor*, 29.
58. Butler, *Survivor*, 184; 5.
59. Butler, *Survivor*, 76.
60. Butler, *Survivor*, 164.
61. Butler, *Survivor*, 164.
62. Troy, "Negotiating," 1119.
63. Mickle, "The Politics," 65.
64. Mickle, "The Politics," 66–67.
65. Littleton, "Butler Plants."
66. Butler, *Kindred*, 9.
67. Francis, *Conversations*, 21.
68. Francis, *Conversations*, 21.
69. Francis, *Conversations*, 40, 79, 182, 198, 219.
70. Wood, "Exorcizing," 87.
71. Miletic, "Butler's Response," 264–65.
72. Smethhurst, *Black Arts*, 82.
73. Neal, "The Black Arts Movement," 191.
74. Francis, Conversations, 30.
75. Staples, "The Myth," 16.
76. Miletic, "Butler's Response," 272.
77. Butler, *Kindred*, 165–166.
78. Miletic, "Butler's Response," 271.
79. Humann, "Genre and Justice," 518.

80. Butler, *Bloodchild*, 73.
81. Butler, *Bloodchild*, 74–75.
82. Butler, *Bloodchild*, 75.
83. Butler, *Bloodchild*, 81.
84. Butler, *Bloodchild*, 85.
85. Butler, *Bloodchild*, 73, 83.
86. Butler, *Bloodchild*, 83.
87. Butler, *Bloodchild*, 83.
88. Butler, *Bloodchild*, 73.
89. Butler, *Bloodchild*, 74.
90. Butler, *Bloodchild*, 80–81.

Chapter 3: The 1980s

1. Canavan, *Octavia E. Butler*, 86.
2. OEB 1014, The Butler Papers, Huntington Library.
3. OEB 1020, The Butler Papers, Huntington Library.
4. Due, "Afterword," 277.
5. For further discussion of these biblical themes, see Hampton, *Changing Bodies*; Pfeiffer, "Butler Writes the Bible"; Thaler, *Black Atlantic*.
6. See Hampton, *Changing Bodies*; Pfeiffer, "Butler Writes the Bible"; Thaler, *Black Atlantic*.
7. Butler, *Wild Seed*, 23.
8. Butler, *Wild Seed*, 130.
9. Butler, *Wild Seed*, 131.
10. Jacobs resists by choosing her own lover and getting pregnant twice. See Jacobs, "Incidents"
11. See Davis, *Women, Race & Class*; Roberts, *Killing the Black Body*; White, *Ar'n't I a Woman?*
12. Berry and Gross, *A Black Women's History*, 37.
13. Berry and Gross, *A Black Women's History*, 36.
14. Butler, *Wild Seed*, 292.
15. Ephratt, "Functions of Silence," 1913.
16. Furniss, *Orality*, 18.
17. Butler, *Wild Seed*, 294.
18. Butler, *Wild Seed*, 294–95.
19. Butler, *Wild Seed*, 294.
20. Yee, *Poor*, 48.
21. Butler, *Wild Seed*, 295.
22. Butler, *Wild Seed*, 297.
23. Francis, *Conversations*, 127.
24. Schalk, "Experience," 164.
25. Pickens, "Aesthetics," 174.
26. Butler, *Bloodchild*, 94.
27. Butler, *Bloodchild*, 95.
28. Butler, *Bloodchild*, 94.

29. Butler, *Bloodchild*, 89.
30. Butler, *Bloodchild*, 110.
31. Butler, *Bloodchild*, 92.
32. Butler, *Bloodchild*, 89.
33. Butler, *Bloodchild*, 92.
34. Butler, *Bloodchild*, 94.
35. Hatfield, "Examining," 528.
36. Govan, "Disparate Spirits," 121.
37. Butler, *Bloodchild*, 90.
38. Butler, *Bloodchild*, 91.
39. Butler, *Bloodchild*, 92.
40. Butler, *Bloodchild*, 104.
41. Butler, *Bloodchild*, 107.
42. Govan, "Disparate Spirits," 122.
43. Govan, "Disparate Spirits," 122.
44. Canavan, *Octavia E. Butler*, 87.
45. Butler, *Clay's Ark*, 28.
46. Butler, *Clay's Ark*, 28.
47. Butler, *Clay's Ark*, 128.
48. Butler, *Clay's Ark*, 23.
49. Butler, *Clay's Ark*, 163.
50. Butler, *Clay's Ark*, 119–20; 91, 101.
51. Butler, *Clay's Ark*, 91.
52. McCoy, "*Clay's Ark*," 105.
53. Vint, "Becoming Other," 290.
54. Butler, *Bloodchild*, 3.
55. Hampton, *Changing Bodies*, 105.
56. Butler, *Bloodchild*, 15.
57. Butler, *Bloodchild*, 15.
58. Butler, *Bloodchild*, 23–25.
59. Butler, *Bloodchild*, 27.
60. Butler, *Bloodchild*, 27.
61. Butler, *Bloodchild*, 28–29.
62. Scheer-Schazler, "Loving Insects," 318.
63. See Scheer-Schazler, "Loving Insects."
64. Helford, "The Construction," 259–71; and Donawerth, *Frankenstein's Daughters*.
65. Butler, *Bloodchild*, 31.
66. Francis, *Conversations*, 66.
67. Shawl, "Why Men Get Pregnant."
68. Francis, *Conversations*, 66.
69. Japtok, "What Is 'Love'?" 68.
70. Butler, *Bloodchild*, 27.
71. Butler, *Bloodchild*, 38.
72. Butler, *Bloodchild*, 39.

73. Schalk, "Interpreting," 147.
74. Francis, *Conversations*, 36; 40.
75. Francis, *Conversations*, 55.
76. Nielsen, *Disability History*, 162.
77. Schalk, "Interpreting," 143.
78. Butler, *Bloodchild*, 44.
79. Schalk, "Interpreting," 147.
80. Francis, *Conversations*, 128.
81. Francis, *Conversations*, 128.
82. Hampton, *Changing Bodies*; Osherow, "The Dawn," 68–83; Wood, "Subversion," 87–99.
83. Wood, "Subversion," 88.
84. Hampton, *Changing Bodies*; Osherow, "The Dawn"; Wood, "Subversion."
85. Wood, "Subversion," 88.
86. Cantor, "The Lilith Question," 40–50.
87. Osherow, "The Dawn," 76.
88. Butler, *Dawn*, 74, 246.
89. Osherow, "The Dawn," 75.
90. Butler, *Dawn*, 283.
91. Lee, "Relatedness," 175; Magedanz, "Captivity Narrative," 53.
92. "Apocalypticism Explained."
93. Lee, "Relatedness," 176.
94. Francis, *Conversations*, 128.
95. Butler, *Dawn*, 106.
96. Butler, *Dawn*, 111.
97. Butler, *Dawn*, 200.
98. Greene, "The History of 'The Man Box.'"
99. Butler, *Dawn*, 205.
100. Butler, *Dawn*, 206.
101. Butler, *Dawn*, 218.
102. Butler, *Dawn*, 6.
103. Butler, *Dawn*, 32.
104. Foster, "Butler's Contact Zones," 158.
105. Butler, *Dawn*, 99.
106. Butler, *Dawn*, 99.
107. Butler, *Imago*, 30.
108. Butler, *Imago*, 30.
109. Butler, *Imago*, 30.
110. Lee, "Relatedness," 175.

Chapter 4: 1990–2006

1. Francis, *Conversations*, 41.
2. Francis, *Conversations*, 47.
3. Francis, *Conversations*, 69.
4. Francis, *Conversations*, 171.

5. "Box 1, Folder 1," Butler Papers, Schomburg Center.
6. Butler, *Sower*, 77.
7. Butler, *Sower*, 295.
8. Francis, *Conversations*, 60.
9. Moore, "'What to Become?'" 62.
10. Harris, *Saints*, 159.
11. Harris, *Saints*, 163.
12. Harris, *Saints*, 165.
13. Butler, *Sower*, 292.
14. Butler, *Talents*, 19.
15. Butler, *Sower*, 52.
16. Butler, *Talents*, 213.
17. Butler, *Sower*, 79.
18. Butler, *Sower*, 124.
19. Butler, *Talents*, 121.
20. Butler, *Talents*, 281.
21. Butler, *Sower*, 113.
22. Butler, *Sower*, 130, 158.
23. Butler, *Sower*, 130, 159.
24. Butler, *Talents*, 212.
25. Butler, *Talents*, 266.
26. Butler, *Talents*, 51.
27. Butler, *Talents*, 113.
28. Butler, *Talents*, 115–24, 129–31.
29. Butler, *Talents*, 109, 309, 347, and 351.
30. Butler, *Talents*, 351.
31. Encyclopaedia Britannica, "Oedipus Complex."
32. Askeland, "Adoption and Abduction," 57.
33. In her archived material, Butler confirms that Marc betrays Lauren to the Church of Christian America authorities.
34. Butler, *Bloodchild*, 125.
35. Butler, *Talents*, 411.
36. Butler, *Talents*, 158, emphasis in original.
37. Butler, *Talents*, 158.
38. Butler, *Talents*, 159.
39. Butler, *Talents*, 159.
40. hooks, *The Will to Change*, 66.
41. hooks, *The Will to Change*, 72.
42. hooks, *The Will to Change*, 72.
43. Butler, *Talents*, 379.
44. Butler, *Talents*, 313.
45. Butler, *Talents*, 315.
46. Butler, *Talents*, 315.
47. Butler, *Talents*, 159.
48. Butler, *Talents*, 315.

49. Butler, *Talents*, 316.
50. Orts, *¿Para Qué Sirve Realmente La Ética?*
51. Canavan, *Octavia E. Butler*, 154.
52. Curtis, "Theorizing Fear," 414.
53. Curtis, "Theorizing Fear," 414.
54. Butler, *Bloodchild*, 155.
55. Butler, *Bloodchild*, 178.
56. Humann, "Beyond Science Fiction," 100.
57. Lavender, *Afrofuturism Rising*, 26.
58. Butler, *Bloodchild*, 184.
59. Butler, *Bloodchild*, 194.
60. See Humann, "Beyond Science Fiction"; Jenkins, "Is Religiosity," 5–22; and Morris, "Afrofuturist Feminism," 77–90.
61. Barr, "Oy/Octavia," 1313.
62. Barr, "Oy/Octavia," 1313.
63. Butler, *Bloodchild*, 209.
64. Jenkins, "Is Religiosity," 14.
65. See Williams, *Sisters in the Wilderness* and Walker, *The Color Purple*.
66. Ware, *African American Theology*, 131–39.
67. Ware, *African American Theology*, 131–39.
68. Ware, *African American Theology*, 131–39.
69. Jenkins, "Is Religiosity," 13.
70. Walker, *In Search*, 241.
71. Butler, *Bloodchild*, 190.
72. Butler, *Bloodchild*, 212.
73. Butler, *Bloodchild*, 193.
74. Butler, *Bloodchild*, 194.
75. Butler, *Bloodchild*, 213.
76. Leong, Waits, and Diebold, "Dissociative Amnesia," 51.
77. Walker-Barnes, *Too Heavy a Yoke*, 106.
78. Walker-Barnes, *Too Heavy a Yoke*, 96–97.
79. Butler, *Bloodchild*, 200.
80. Butler, *Bloodchild*, 201.
81. Stanley, "Re-Read and Recover," 251.
82. Stanley, "Re-Read and Recover," 251.
83. Stanley, "Re-Read and Recover," 252.
84. Govan, "Going to See the Woman," 29–30.
85. Francis, *Conversations*, 203.
86. Jue, "Scenting Community," 17; Pickens, "'You're Supposed to Be," 35.
87. Jue, "Scenting Community," 17.
88. Robinson, "Butler's Vampiric Vision," 61–82.
89. Butler, *Clay's Ark*, 15.
90. Hobson, "Brothers Under Covers," 39.
91. Hobson, "Brothers Under Covers," 39.
92. Hobson, "Brothers Under Covers," 39.

93. Butler, *Fledgling*, 91.
94. Butler, *Fledgling*, 162.
95. Butler, *Fledgling*, 12, 64.
96. See Pickens, "'You're Supposed to Be."
97. Renold, *Girls, Boys, and Junior Sexualities*, 21.
98. Renold, *Girls, Boys, and Junior Sexualities*, 22.
99. Bruhm and Hurley, *Curiouser*, ix.
100. Butler, *Fledgling*, 21.
101. Butler, *Fledgling*, 25.
102. Fink, "AIDS Vampires," 419.
103. McDevitt, "Childhood Sexuality," 226.
104. Butler, *Fledgling*, 300.

Chapter 5: "Where I actually say so"

1. Wester, "African American Gothic," 62.
2. Butler, *Bloodchild*, 30.
3. Francis, *Conversations*, 66.
4. For more on these works in the neo-slave narrative tradition, see Dubey, "Novels of Enslavement," 345–63; Hampton, *Changing Bodies*; Steinberg, "Inverting History," 467–76.
5. Andrews, "Slave Narratives" and Pierce, "Slave Narratives," 1081–87.
6. Moody, "African American Women," 115.
7. Andrews, "Slave Narratives."
8. Andrews, "Slave Narratives."
9. Davis and Gates, *The Slave's Narrative*, xxvii.
10. Douglass, "Narrative of the Life."
11. Douglass, "Narrative of the Life."
12. Douglass, "Narrative of the Life."
13. Bell, *The Afro-American Novel*, 289.
14. Butler, *Kindred*, 9.
15. Butler, *Kindred*, 17.
16. Butler, *Kindred*, 58.
17. Butler, *Kindred*, 36.
18. Butler, *Kindred*, 176.
19. Moody, "African American Women," 115.
20. Butler, *Kindred*, 181.
21. Butler, *Kindred*, 181–82.
22. Omolade, "Hearts of Darkness," 366.
23. Butler, *Kindred*, 221.
24. Salvaggio, "Octavia Butler," 33.
25. Wood, "Exorcizing the Past," 95.
26. Salvaggio, "Octavia Butler," 33.
27. "Box 1, Folder 1," Butler Papers, Schomburg Center.
28. "Box 1, Folder 1," Butler Papers, Schomburg Center.
29. Dodd, "The Myth of Allyship."

30. Butler, *Kindred*, 97.
31. Butler, *Kindred*, 97.
32. Butler, *Kindred*, 100.
33. Butler, *Kindred*, 100.
34. Butler, *Kindred*, 101.
35. King, "Letter From Birmingham Jail."
36. Butler, *Kindred*, 194.
37. Butler, *Kindred*, 110.
38. Butler, *Kindred*, 110.
39. Butler, *Kindred*, 110.
40. Butler, *Kindred*, 235.
41. Butler, *Kindred*, 157.
42. Canavan, *Octavia E. Butler*, 62.
43. Delmas and Brownlee, "Civil Disobedience."
44. Butler, *Kindred*, 101.
45. Butler, *Kindred*, 106.
46. Butler, *Kindred*, 237.
47. Butler, *Kindred*, 239.
48. Butler, *Kindred*, 95.
49. Butler, *Kindred*, 115.
50. Butler, *Kindred*, 132.
51. Butler, *Kindred*, 178.
52. Butler, *Kindred*, 178.
53. Butler, *Kindred*, 196.
54. Butler, *Sower*, 292.
55. Craft, "Running."
56. Butler, *Talents*, 40.
57. Harvey, *Through the Storm*, 30.
58. Harvey, *Through the Storm*, 30.
59. Raboteau, *Slave Religion*, 212.
60. Raboteau, *Slave Religion*, 214.
61. Butler, *Talents*, 215.
62. "Born in Slavery: Slave Narratives From the Federal Writers' Project, 1936–1938."
63. Butler, *Talents*, 277–78.
64. Francis, *Conversations*, 60.
65. Davis, *Are Prisons Obsolete?*, 107.
66. Stevenson, "Why American Prisons Owe Their Cruelty to Slavery."
67. For further reading on the prison industrial complex and its far-reaching implications, see Davis, *Are Prisons Obsolete?*; Haley, *No Mercy Here*; Ritchie, *Invisible No More*; and Stanley and Smith, *Captive Genders*.
68. Butler, *Talents*, 88.
69. Butler, *Sower*, 39.
70. Butler, *Sower*, 238.

71. Butler, *Talents*, 379.
72. Crossley, "Reader's Guide: Critical Essay," 279.

Chapter 6: "This time, I want a love story"

1. OEB 1062, The Butler Papers, Huntington Library.
2. Francis, *Conversations*, 181.
3. Francis, *Conversations*, ix.
4. OEB 3210, The Butler Papers, Huntington Library.
5. Francis, *Conversations*, 14.
6. Canavan, *Octavia E. Butler*, 22.
7. Francis, *Conversations*, 14.
8. Francis, *Conversations*, xi.
9. George, *Handful*, 153; Hampton, *Changing Bodies*, 137.
10. Canavan, *Octavia E. Butler*, 25.
11. Francis, *Conversations*, 13.
12. "Box 1, Folder 1," Butler Papers, Schomburg Center.
13. "Box 1, Folder 1," Butler Papers, Schomburg Center.
14. "Box 1, Folder 1," Butler Papers, Schomburg Center.
15. Faircloth, "The Sweet."
16. Faircloth, "The Sweet."
17. "About the Romance Genre."
18. Regis, *A Natural History*, 14.
19. Regis, *A Natural History*, 30–31.
20. Regis, *A Natural History*, 31.
21. Regis, *A Natural History*, 32.
22. Regis, *A Natural History*, 33.
23. Regis, *A Natural History*, 35.
24. Regis, *A Natural History*, 36–37.
25. Wendell and Tan, *Beyond Heaving Bosoms*.
26. Wendell and Tan, *Beyond Heaving Bosoms*.
27. Moody-Freeman, "African American Romance," 229.
28. Weisser, *The Glass Slipper*, 162–65.
29. Osborne, "Romance: How Black Romance—Novels, That Is—Came to Be."
30. Moody-Freeman, "African American Romance," 233; Dandridge, *Black Women's Activism*.
31. Osborne, "It's All About Love: Romance Readers Speak Out."
32. Moody-Freeman, "African American Romance," 233.
33. Osborne, "Romance: How Black Romance—Novels, That Is—Came to Be."
34. Faircloth, "The Sweet."
35. Bauder, "Luke and Laura's Altared State."
36. Clarendon, "Remembering Luke & Laura's Record-Breaking"; Felthousen-Post, "1979."
37. Toscano, "A Parody of Love," 2.
38. Toscano, "A Parody of Love," 6.

39. Toscano, "A Parody of Love," 6.
40. Toscano, "A Parody of Love," 6.
41. Butler, *Survivor*, 96.
42. Butler, *Survivor*, 98.
43. Butler, *Survivor*, 90–100.
44. Toscano, "A Parody of Love," 6.
45. Butler, *Wild Seed*, 188.
46. Regis, *A Natural History*, 14.
47. OEB 1187, The Butler Papers, Huntington Library.
48. Montgomery and Caldwell, "Visualizing Dana," 167–68.
49. OEB 3912, The Butler Papers, Huntington Library.
50. Montgomery and Caldwell, "Visualizing Dana," 154.
51. Canavan, *Octavia E. Butler*, 32.
52. Butler, *Kindred*, 57.
53. Butler, *Kindred*, 109–110.
54. Butler, *Kindred*, 111.
55. Govan, "Homage to Tradition," 93.
56. Butler, *Kindred*, 124.
57. Butler, *Kindred*, 166.
58. Butler, *Kindred*, 168.
59. See Davis, *Women, Race & Class*, 25–26; Hartman, *Scenes of Subjection*, 81.
60. See Johnson, *Wicked Flesh;* Kennedy, *Interracial Intimacies*
61. See Miletic, "Octavia E. Butler's Response," 261–275.
62. Butler, *Kindred*, 44.
63. Steinberg, "Inverting History," 468.
64. Butler, *Kindred*, 124.
65. Francis, *Conversations*, 23.
66. Moody-Freeman, "Black Cultural Studies," 131.
67. Moody-Freeman, "Black Cultural Studies," 131.
68. Butler, *Wild Seed*, 4.
69. Butler, *Wild Seed*, 7–8.
70. Butler, *Wild Seed*, 25.
71. Butler, *Wild Seed*, 169–70.
72. Butler, *Wild Seed*, 293.
73. Butler, *Wild Seed*, 131.
74. Butler, *Wild Seed*, 133.
75. Butler, *Wild Seed*, 210.
76. Butler, *Wild Seed*, 287.
77. Butler, *Wild Seed*, 294.
78. Regis, *A Natural History*, 36.
79. Butler, *Wild Seed*, 276.
80. Butler, *Wild Seed*, 288.
81. Butler, *Wild Seed*, 271.
82. Butler, *Wild Seed*, 295.
83. Butler, *Wild Seed*, 295.

84. Butler, *Wild Seed*, 21.
85. Butler, *Wild Seed*, 274.
86. Butler, *Wild Seed*, 274.
87. Butler, *Wild Seed*, 296.
88. Butler, *Wild Seed*, 297.
89. Whiteside, "Migration," 118.
90. Whiteside, "Migration," 120.
91. Francis, *Conversations*, 218.
92. Francis, *Conversations*, 102.
93. Francis, *Conversations*, 102.
94. OEB 95, The Butler Papers, Huntington Library.

Chapter 7: Word Weaver, World Maker

1. OEB 3218, The Butler Papers, Huntington Library.
2. Butler, "The Lost Races," 181.
3. Butler, "The Lost Races," 181.
4. Butler, "The Lost Races," 181.
5. Butler, "The Lost Races," 181.
6. Butler, "The Lost Races," 182.
7. Butler, "The Lost Races," 182.
8. Butler, "The Lost Races," 182.
9. Butler, "The Lost Races," 182.
10. Butler, "The Lost Races," 183.
11. Butler, "The Lost Races," 183.
12. Butler, "The Lost Races," 183.
13. Butler, "The Lost Races," 183.
14. Butler, "The Lost Races," 184.
15. Butler, "The Lost Races," 184–85.
16. Butler, "The Lost Races," 185.
17. Butler, "The Lost Races," 186.
18. Butler, "The Lost Races," 186.
19. OEB 3221, The Butler Papers, Huntington Library.
20. Butler, *Bloodchild*, 125.
21. Jones, "About Us."
22. Butler, "How I Built Novels."
23. Butler, "How I Built Novels."
24. Butler, "How I Built Novels."
25. Butler, "How I Built Novels."
26. Butler, "How I Built Novels."
27. Butler, "How I Built Novels."
28. Butler, "How I Built Novels."
29. Butler, "How I Built Novels."
30. Butler, "How I Built Novels."
31. Butler, *Bloodchild*, 136.
32. Butler, *Bloodchild*, 125.

33. Butler, *Bloodchild*, 134.
34. Butler, *Bloodchild*, 134–35.
35. Butler, "Devil Girl from Mars."
36. Butler, "Eye Witness."
37. Butler, "Eye Witness."
38. Butler, "Eye Witness."
39. Butler, "Eye Witness."
40. Butler, "Free Libraries."
41. Butler, "Free Libraries."
42. Butler, "Free Libraries."
43. Butler, "Free Libraries."
44. Butler, "Free Libraries."
45. Butler, "Free Libraries."
46. Butler, "Free Libraries."
47. "State of America's Libraries Report 2023."
48. Butler, "Free Libraries."
49. Butler, "Free Libraries."
50. Butler, "The Monophobic Response," 415.
51. Butler, "The Monophobic Response," 415.
52. Butler, "The Monophobic Response," 415.
53. Butler, "The Monophobic Response," 416.
54. Butler, "The Monophobic Response," 416.
55. Butler, "A Few Rules," 165.
56. Butler, "A Few Rules," 165.
57. Butler, "A Few Rules," 165.
58. Butler, "A Few Rules," 165.
59. Butler, "A Few Rules," 166.
60. Butler, "A Few Rules," 166.
61. Butler, "A Few Rules," 166.
62. Butler, "A Few Rules," 166.
63. Butler, "A Few Rules," 254.
64. Butler, "A Few Rules," 254.
65. Butler, "A Few Rules," 254.
66. Butler, "On Racism."
67. Butler, "On Racism."
68. Butler, "On Racism."
69. Butler, "On Racism."
70. Butler, "On Racism."
71. Butler, "On Racism."
72. Butler, "On Racism."

Afterword

1. Francis, *Conversations*, 32.
2. Francis, *Conversations*, 18.
3. Francis, *Conversations*, 41.

4. Francis, *Conversations*, 41.
5. Butler, *Talents*, 183.
6. Butler, *Talents*, 183.
7. McCormack, "The Violence," 206.
8. Butler, *Talents*, 206.
9. Davis, "Butler's Invention," 65.
10. Butler, *Talents*, 211.
11. Francis, *Conversations*, 41.
12. To learn more, visit "Parable of The Sower Intentional Community Cooperative" at https://parableofsowercoop.com/.
13. Genn, "Welcome Back, Bitches!"
14. Butler, *Sower*, 77.
15. Potter, "NASA's Perseverance."
16. Nittle, "A Pasadena School."
17. Nittle, "A Pasadena School."
18. SFWA, "Inaugural Infinity Award."
19. To learn more about the opera, visit https://www.parableopera.com/.
20. OEB 3246, The Butler Papers, Huntington Library.

WORKS CITED

Works by Octavia E. Butler

ARCHIVES

Octavia Butler Papers, Manuscripts, Archives, and Rare Books Division, Schomburg Center for Research in Black Culture, The New York Public Library.

The Octavia E. Butler Papers, The Huntington Library, Art Collections, and Botanical Gardens, San Marino, California.

BOOKS

Adulthood Rites. 1988. Reprint, Grand Central Publishing, 2021.
Bloodchild and Other Stories. Seven Stories Press, 2005.
Clay's Ark. 1984. Reprint, Grand Central Publishing, 2020.
Dawn. 1987. Reprint, Grand Central Publishing, 2021.
Fledgling. 2005. Reprint, Grand Central Publishing, 2007.
Imago. 1989. Reprint, Grand Central Publishing, 2021.
Kindred. 1979. Reprint, Beacon Press, 2003.
Mind of My Mind. 1977. Reprint, Grand Central Publishing, 2020.
Parable of the Sower. 1993. Reprint, Grand Central Publishing, 2000.
Parable of the Talents. 1998. Reprint, Grand Central Publishing, 2000.
Patternmaster. 1976. Reprint, Grand Central Publishing, 2020.
Survivor. Doubleday, 1978.
Unexpected Stories. 2014. Reprint, Open Road Integrated Media Inc, 2020.
Wild Seed. 1980. Reprint, Grand Central Publishing, 2020.

ESSAYS AND SPEECHES

"A Few Rules for Predicting the Future." *Essence*, May 2000, 165–264.

"'Devil Girl from Mars': Why I Write Science Fiction." MIT Black History, February 19, 1998. Accessed June 23, 2023. https://www.blackhistory.mit.edu/archive/transcript-devil-girl-mars-why-i-write-science-fiction-octavia-butler-1998.

"Discovery, Creation and Craft." Washington Post, May 22, 1983. Accessed June 22, 2023. https://www.washingtonpost.com/archive/entertainment/books/1983/05/22/discovery-creation-and-craft/8f073141-122e-4d70-8ba1-9fe3f723b08b/.

"Eye Witness." *O, the Oprah Magazine*, May 2002. https://www.oprah.com/spirit/octavia-butlers-aha-moment/all.

"Free Libraries: Are They Becoming Extinct?" *Omni* 15, no. 10 (August 1, 1993): 4.
"How I Built Novels Out of Writer's Blocks." *Writer's Digest*, June 1999. Accessed August 26, 2023. https://www.writersdigest.com/write-better-fiction/vintage-wd-how-i-built-novels-out-of-writers-blocks.
"On Racism." *NPR*, August 20, 2001. Accessed June 22, 2023. https://www.npr.org/templates/story/story.php?storyId=5245679.
"The Lost Races of Science Fiction." In *Octavia E. Butler*, edited by Gerry Canavan, 181–86. University of Illinois, 2016.
"The Monophobic Response." In *Dark Matter: Dark Matter*, edited by Sheree R. Thomas, 415–16. Warner Books, 2000.

Secondary Sources

Andrews, William L. "Slave Narratives: An Introduction to the Slave Narrative." Documenting the American South, n.d. https://docsouth.unc.edu/neh/intro.html.
Apocalypse! FRONTLINE | PBS. "Apocalypticism Explained," November 18, 2015. https://www.pbs.org/wgbh/pages/frontline/shows/apocalypse/explanation/brevelation.html.
Askeland, Lori. "'How Thoroughly He Has Stolen My Child': Adoption and Abduction, Religion, and Imperialism in Octavia E. Butler's Parable Novels." *Adoption and Culture* 5, no. 1 (January 1, 2017): 49–63.
Baraka, Amiri. "Black Woman." In *Raise Race Rays Raze*, 147–54. Random House, 1971.
Barr, Marleen S. "Oy/Octavia: Or Keeping My Promise to Ms. Butler." *Callaloo* 32, no. 4 (2007): 1312–14.
Bauder, David. "Luke and Laura's Altared State." *Washington Post*, November 13, 2006. Accessed June 10, 2023. https://www.washingtonpost.com/wp-dyn/content/article/2006/11/13/AR2006111301616.html.
Bell, Bernard W. *The Afro-American Novel and Its Tradition*. Amherst: University of Massachusetts Press, 1987.
Berry, Daina Ramey, and Kali Nicole Gross. *A Black Women's History of the United States*. Beacon Press, 2020.
"Born in Slavery: Slave Narratives From the Federal Writers' Project, 1936–1938." Library of Congress, Manuscript Division, Digital Collections, n.d. https://www.loc.gov/collections/slave-narratives-from-the-federal-writers-project-1936-to-1938/about-this-collection.
Bracey, John H., Sonia Sanchez, and James Edward Smethurst, eds. *SOS—Calling All Black People: A Black Arts Movement Reader*. University of Massachusetts Press, 2014.
Brownlee, Kimberley. "Conscientious Objection and Civil Disobedience." In *The Routledge Companion to the Philosophy of Law*, edited by Andrei Marmor, 527–39. Routledge, 2012.
Bruhm, Steven, and Natasha Hurley, eds. *Curiouser: On the Queerness of Children*. Minneapolis: University of Minnesota Press, 2004.
Canavan, Gerry. *Octavia E. Butler*. University of Illinois Press, 2016.

Canavan, Gerry. "'There's Nothing New / Under The Sun, / But There Are New Suns': Recovering Octavia E. Butler's Lost Parables." Los Angeles Review of Books, June 9, 2014. https://lareviewofbooks.org/article/theres-nothing-new-sun-new-suns-recovering-octavia-e-butlers-lost-parables.

Cantor, Aviva. "The Lilith Question." In *On Being a Jewish Feminist: A Reader*, edited by Susannah Heschel, 40–50. Schocken Books, 1983.

Castiglia, Christopher. *Bound and Determined: Captivity, Culture-Crossing, and White Womanhood from Mary Rowlandson to Patty Hearst*. University of Chicago Press, 1996.

Clarendon, Dan. "Remembering Luke & Laura's Record-Breaking, Controversial 'General Hospital' Wedding, 40 Years Later." TV Insider, November 16, 2021. https://www.tvinsider.com/1021971/general-hospital-luke-laura-wedding-controversy-40th-anniversary/.

Craft, Christopher. "'Kiss Me with Those Red Lips': Gender and Inversion in Bram Stoker's Dracula." *Representations* 8, no. 1 (1984): 107–33.

Craft, William. "Running a Thousand Miles for Freedom; or, the Escape of William and Ellen Craft from Slavery." Documenting the American South, 1860. Accessed June 9, 2023. https://docsouth.unc.edu/neh/craft/craft.html.

Crossley, Robert. "Reader's Guide: Critical Essay." In *Kindred*, by Octavia E. Butler, 265–81, 2003.

Curtis, Claire. "Theorizing Fear: Octavia Butler and the Realist Utopia." *Utopian Studies* 19, no. 3 (June 22, 2008): 411–31.

Dandridge, Rita B. *Black Women's Activism: Reading African American Women's Historical Romances*. Peter Lang, 2004.

Davidson, Carolyn S. "The Science Fiction of Octavia Butler." *SAGALA: A Journal of Art and Ideas* 2, no. 1 (1981): 35. In Octavia E. Butler, "OEB 327," Octavia E. Butler Papers.

Davis, Angela Y. *Are Prisons Obsolete?* Seven Stories Press, 2003.

Davis, Angela Y. *Women, Race & Class*. New York: Vintage Books, 1983.

Davis, Charles T., and Henry Louis Gates Jr., eds. *The Slave's Narrative*. Oxford University Press, 1985.

Davis, Charlotte Nayor. "Butler's Invention of Scripture in Light of Hebrew Wisdom Literature." In *God Is Change: Religious Practices and Ideologies in the Works of Octavia Butler*, edited by Aparajita Nanda and Shelby Crosby, 58–70. Temple University Press, 2021.

Delmas, Candice, and Kimberley Brownlee. "Civil Disobedience." Edited by Edward N. Zalta. Stanford Encyclopedia of Philosophy, December 2021. Accessed June 22, 2023. https://plato.stanford.edu/archives/win2021/entries/civil-disobedience.

Dery, Mark. "Black to the Future: Afrofuturism 1.0." In *Afro-Future Females: Black Writers Chart Science Fiction's Newest New-Wave Trajectory*, edited by Marleen S. Barr, 8, 2008.

Dodd, Jay. "The Myth of Allyship: Complacency of Small Victories." *HuffPost* (blog), February 2, 2016. https://www.huffpost.com/entry/the-myth-of-allyship-comp_b_4691110.

Donawerth, Jane. *Frankenstein's Daughters: Women Writing Science Fiction.* Syracuse University Press, 1997.

Douglass, Frederick. "Narrative of the Life of Frederick Douglass, an American Slave. Written by Himself." Documenting the American South, 1845. https://docsouth.unc.edu/neh/douglass/douglass.html.

Dubey, Madhu. *Black Women Novelists and the Nationalist Aesthetic.* Indiana University Press, 1994.

Dubey, Madhu. "Octavia Butler's Novels of Enslavement." *Novel: A Forum on Fiction* 46, no. 3 (November 1, 2013): 345–63. https://doi.org/10.1215/00295132-2345786.

Due, Tananarive. "Afterword." In *The Bloomsbury Handbook to Octavia E. Butler*, edited by Gregory J. Hampton and Kendra R. Parker, 274–80. Bloomsbury Academic, 2020.

Ephratt, Michal. "The Functions of Silence." *Journal of Pragmatics* 40, no. 11 (November 1, 2008): 1909–38. https://doi.org/10.1016/j.pragma.2008.03.009.

Faircloth, Kelly. "The Sweet, Savage Sexual Revolution That Set the Romance Novel Free." *Jezebel*, December 6, 2016. https://jezebel.com/the-sweet-savage-sexual-revolution-that-set-the-romanc-1789687801.

Felthousen-Post, Cyn. "1979: When 'General Hospital's Luke Raped Laura While Herb Alpert Played The Trumpet." Groovy History, October 5, 2020. https://groovyhistory.com/luke-laura-rape-general-hospital-herb-alpert/3.

Fink, Marty. "AIDS Vampires: Reimagining Illness in Octavia Butler's 'Fledgling.'" *Science Fiction Studies* 37, no. 3 (November 2010): 416–32.

Foster, Thomas. "'We Get to Live and So Do They': Octavia Butler's Contact Zones." In *Strange Matings: Science Fiction, Feminism, African American Voices, and Octavia E. Butler*, edited by Rebecca J. Holden and Nisi Shawl, 140–67. Aqueduct Press, 2013.

Fox, Margalit. "Octavia E. Butler, Science Fiction Writer, Dies at 58." *The New York Times*, March 1, 2006. https://www.nytimes.com/2006/03/01/books/octavia-e-butler-science-fiction-writer-dies-at-58.html?smid=url-share.

Francis, Conseula, ed. *Conversations with Octavia Butler.* University Press of Mississippi, 2009.

Furniss, Graham. *Orality: The Power of the Spoken Word.* Palgrave, 2004.

Genn, James, dir. "Welcome Back, Bitches!" *Ginny and Georgia*, season 2, episode 1, Netflix, 2023.

George, Lynell. *A Handful of Earth, a Handful of Sky: The World of Octavia Butler.* Angel City Press, 2020.

Govan, Sandra Y. "Afterword." In *Wild Seed*, by Octavia E. Butler, 298–306. Warner Books, 1980.

Govan, Sandra Y. "Disparate Spirits Yet Kindred Souls: Octavia E. Butler, 'Speech Sounds,' and Me." In *Strange Matings: Science Fiction, Feminism, African American Voices, and Octavia E. Butler*, edited by Rebecca J. Holden and Nisi Shawl. Aqueduct Press, 2013.

Govan, Sandra Y. "Going to See the Woman: A Visit with Octavia E. Butler." *Obsidian III: Literature in the African Diaspora* 6–7, no. 1–2 (2005): 15–36.

WORKS CITED

Govan, Sandra Y. "Homage to Tradition: Octavia Butler Renovates the Historical Novel." *MELUS* 12, no. 1–2 (1986): 79–96.

Greene, Mark. "The History of 'The Man Box.'" *Medium*, January 15, 2019. https://remakingmanhood.medium.com/the-history-of-the-man-box-e6eed6d895c4.

Haley, Sarah. *No Mercy Here: Gender, Punishment, and the Making of Jim Crow Modernity*. The University of North Carolina Press, 2019.

Hampton, Gregory Jerome. *Changing Bodies in the Fiction of Octavia Butler: Slaves, Aliens, and Vampires*. Lexington Books, 2010.

Harris, Trudier. *Saints, Sinners, Saviors: Strong Black Women in African American Literature*. Palgrave, 2001.

Hartman, Saidiya V. *Scenes of Subjection: Terror, Slavery, and Self-Making in Nineteenth-Century America*. Oxford University Press, 1997.

Harvey, Paul. *Through the Storm, Through the Night: A History of African American Christianity*. Rowman and Littlefield, 2011.

Hatfield, Elizabeth Fish. "Examining Hegemonic Masculinity in Two and a Half Men." *Communication, Culture, and Critique* 3, no. 4 (2010): 526–48.

Helford, Elyce Rae. "'Would You Really Rather Die Than Bear My Young?': The Construction of Gender, Race, and Species in Octavia E. Butler's 'Bloodchild.'" *African American Review* 28, no. 2 (1994): 259–71.

"Historical Dictionary of Science Fiction: Pocket Universe," n.d. https://sfdictionary.com/view/1090/pocket-universe.

Hobson, Amanda. "Brothers Under Covers." In *Race in the Vampire Narrative*, edited by U. Melissa Anyiwo, 23–44. Brill, 2015.

hooks, bell. *The Will to Change: Men, Masculinity, and Love*. Washington Square Press, 2004.

Humann, Heather Duerre. "'A Good and Necessary Thing': Genre and Justice in Octavia Butler's *Bloodchild and Other Stories*." *Interdisciplinary Literary Studies* 19, no. 4 (2017): 517–28.

Humann, Heather Duerre. "Beyond Science Fiction: Genre in *Kindred* and Butler's Short Stories." In *Human Contradictions in Octavia E. Butler's Work*, edited by Martin Japtok and Jerry Rafiki Jenkins, 91–106. Palgrave Macmillan, 2020.

Jacobs, Harriet A. "Incidents in the Life of a Slave Girl. Written by Herself: Electronic Edition." Documenting the America South, 1861. https://docsouth.unc.edu/fpn/jacobs/jacobs.html.

Japtok, Martin. "What Is 'Love'? Octavia Butler's 'Bloodchild.'" In *Human Contradictions in Octavia E. Butler's Work*, edited by Martin Japtok and Jerry Rafiki Jenkins, 51–71. Palgrave Macmillan, 2020.

Jenkins, Jerry Rafiki. "Is Religiosity a Black Thing? Reading the Black None in Octavia E. Butler's 'The Book of Martha.'" *Pacific Coast Philology* 55, no. 1 (January 1, 2020): 5–22.

Johnson, Jessica Marie. *Wicked Flesh: Black Women, Intimacy, and Freedom in the Atlantic World*. University of Pennsylvania Press, 2020.

Jones, Amy. "About Us." *Writer's Digest*, September 17, 2007. Accessed June 16, 2023. https://www.writersdigest.com/resources/about-us.

Jue, Melody. "Scenting Community: Microbial Symbionts in Octavia Butler's *Fledgling*." *Journal of Science Fiction* 4, no. 1 (July 2020): 17–19.

Kennedy, Randall. *Interracial Intimacies: Sex, Marriage, Identity, and Adoption*. Vintage, 2003.

King, Martin Luther, Jr. "Letter From Birmingham Jail." *The Atlantic*, January 29, 2021. Accessed June 9, 2023. https://www.theatlantic.com/magazine/archive/2018/02/letter-from-a-birmingham-jail/552461/.

Lavender, Isiah, III. *Afrofuturism Rising: The Literary Prehistory of a Movement*. Ohio State University Press, 2019.

Lee, Judith. "'We Are All Kin': Relatedness, Mortality, and the Paradox of Human Immortality." In *Immortal Engines: Life Extension and Immortality in Science Fiction and Fantasy*, edited by George Slusser, Gary Westfahl, and Eric S. Rabkin, 170–82. The University of Georgia Press, 1996.

Leong, Stephanie, Wendi Waits, and Carroll Diebold. "Dissociative Amnesia and DSM-IV-TR Cluster C Personality Traits." *Psychiatry (Edgmont)* 3, no. 1 (January 2006): 51–55.

Littleton, Therese. "Octavia E. Butler Plants an Earthseed," 1999. https://web.archive.org/web/20070927084544/http://www.cyberhaven.com/books/sciencefiction/butler.html.

Magedanz, Stacy. "The Captivity Narrative in Octavia E. Butler's *Adulthood Rites*." *Extrapolation: A Journal of Science Fiction and Fantasy* 53, no. 1 (2012): 45–59.

Marriott, Michel. "'We Tend to Do the Right Thing When We Get Scared.'" *The New York Times*, January 1, 2000. Accessed February 14, 2024. https://www.nytimes.com/2000/01/01/books/visions-identity-we-tend-to-do-the-right-thing-when-we-get-scared.html.

McCormack, Michael Brandon. "The Violence of Making America Great Again Religion, Power, and Vulnerable Bodies in Octavia Butler's *Parable of the Talents*." In *God Is Change: Religious Practices and Ideologies in the Works of Octavia Butler*, edited by Aparajita Nanda and Shelby Crosby, 206–19. Temple University Press, 2021.

McCoy, Beth A. "*Clay's Ark*: Teaching Butler's Vision Beyond Liberal Consent." In *Approaches to Teaching the Works of Octavia E. Butler*, edited by Tarshia L. Stanley, 103–8. Modern Language Association of America, 2019.

McDevitt, Kelly. "Childhood Sexuality as Posthuman Subjectivity in Octavia E. Butler's *Fledgling*." *Science Fiction Studies* 47, no. 2 (January 1, 2020): 219–40.

Mickle, Mildred R. "Accepting the Self: The Sexual-Spiritual Balance in Octavia E. Butler's *Survivor*." *Xavier Review* 21, no. 1 (2007): 21–33.

Mickle, Mildred R. "The Politics of Addiction and Adaptation: Dis/Ease Transmission in Octavia E. Butler's *Survivor* and *Fledgling*." In *Contemporary African American Fiction: New Critical Essays*, edited by Dana A. Williams, 62–81. The Ohio State University Press, 2009.

Miletic, Philip. "Octavia E. Butler's Response to Black Arts/Black Power Literature and Rhetoric in *Kindred*." *African American Review* 49, no. 3 (2016): 261–75.

Montgomery, Christine, and Ellen C. Caldwell. "Visualizing Dana and Transhistorical Time Travel on the Covers of Octavia E. Butler's *Kindred*." In *The Bloomsbury*

Handbook to Octavia E. Butler, edited by Gregory J. Hampton and Kendra R. Parker, 151–80. Bloomsbury Academic, 2020.

Moody, Jocelyn. "African American Women and the United States Slave Narrative." In *The Cambridge Companion to African American Women's Literature*, edited by Angelyn Mitchell and Danille K. Taylor, 109–27. Cambridge University Press, 2009.

Moody-Freeman, Julie E. "African American Romance." In *The Routledge Research Companion to Popular Romance Fiction*, edited by Edited by Jayashree Kamble, Eric Murphy Selinger, and Hsu-Ming Teo, 229–51. Routledge, 2020.

Moody-Freeman, Julie E. "Black Cultural Studies and Black Love: Why Black Love Matters." In *Black Love Matters: Real Talk on Romance, Being Seen, and Happily Ever Afters*, edited by Jessica P. Pryde, 127–41. Penguin Random House, 2022.

Moore, Marlon Rachquel. "'What to Become?' Religion, Masculinity, and Self-Determination in A Visitation of Spirits, *Parable of the Sower*, and *Parable of the Talents*." In *Critical Insights: Gender, Sex, and Sexuality*, edited by Margaret Sönser Breen, 54–72. Salem Press, 2014.

Morris, Susana M. "'Everything Is Real. It's Just Not as You See It': Imagination, Utopia, and Afrofuturist Feminism in Octavia E. Butler's 'The Book of Martha.'" In *The Black Speculative Arts Movement: Black Futurity, Art+Design*, edited by Reynaldo Anderson and Clinton R. Fluker, 77–90. Lexington Books, 2021.

Neal, Larry. "The Black Arts Movement." In *Within the Circle: An Anthology of African American Literary Criticism from the Harlem Renaissance to the Present*, edited by Angelyn Mitchell, 184–98. Duke University Press, 1994.

Nielsen, Kim E. *A Disability History of the United States*. Beacon Press, 2013.

Nittle, Nadra. "A Pasadena School Is the Nation's First Named after Octavia Butler—and It's Her Alma Mater." *The 19th*, November 4, 2022. https://19thnews.org/2022/11/pasadena-school-octavia-butler-alma-mater/?utm_campaign=19th-social&utm_source=twitter&utm_medium=social.

NPD Books Romance Landscape. "About the Romance Genre." Romance Writers of America: The Voice of Romance Writers, 2017. https://www.rwa.org/Online/Resources/About_Romance_Fiction/Online/Romance_Genre/About_Romance_Genre.aspx?hkey=dc7b967d-d1eb-4101-bb3f-a6cc936b5219#The_Basics.

Omolade, Barbara. "Hearts of Darkness." In *Words of Fire: An Anthology of African-American Feminist Thought*, edited by Beverly Guy-Sheftall, 362–78. The New Press, 1995.

Orts, Adela Cortina. *¿Para Qué Sirve Realmente La Ética?* Grupo Planeta Spain, 2013.

Osborne, Gwendolyn. "It's All About Love: Romance Readers Speak Out." African American Literature Book Club, February 1, 2002. Accessed June 10, 2023. https://aalbc.com/authors/article.php?id=1907.

Osborne, Gwendolyn. "Romance: How Black Romance—Novels, That Is—Came to Be." *Black Issues Book Review* 4, no. 1 (January 2002): 50. https://search.ebscohost.com/login.aspx?direct=true&AuthType=ip,shib&db=a9h&AN=5819201&scope=site.

Osherow, Michele. "The Dawn of a New Lilith: Revisionary Mythmaking in Women's Science Fiction." *NWSA Journal* 12, no. 1 (1999): 68–83.

Parker, Kendra R. *Black Female Vampires in African American Women's Novels, 1977–2011: She Bites Back*. Rowman & Littlefield, 2018.

Pfeiffer, John R. "Octavia Butler Writes the Bible." In *Shaw and Other Matters: A Festschrift for Stanley Weintraub on the Occasion of His Forty-Second Anniversary at the Pennsylvania State University*, 140–52. Susquehanna University Press, 1995.

Pickens, Theri. "Octavia Butler and the Aesthetics of the Novel." *Hypatia* 30, no. 1 (2015): 167–80.

Pickens, Theri. "'You're Supposed to Be a Tall, Handsome, Fully Grown White Man': Theorizing Race, Gender, and Disability in Octavia Butler's *Fledgling*." *Journal of Literary & Cultural Disability Studies* 8, no. 1 (2014): 33–48.

Pierce, Yolanda. "Slave Narratives." Edited by Janet Gabler-Hover and Robert Sattelmeyer. *American History Through Literature 1820–1870* 3 (2006): 1081–87.

"Pocket Universe." In *Historical Dictionary of Science Fiction*, n.d. https://sfdictionary.com/view/1090/pocket-universe.

Potter, Sean. "NASA's Perseverance Drives on Mars' Terrain for First Time." *NASA*, March 5, 2021. https://www.nasa.gov/press-release/nasa-s-perseverance-drives-on-mars-terrain-for-first-time.

Raboteau, Albert J. *Slave Religion: The "Invisible Institution" in the Antebellum South*. Oxford University Press, 2004.

Regis, Pamela. *A Natural History of the Romance Novel*. University of Pennsylvania Press, 2013.

Renold, Emma. *Girls, Boys, and Junior Sexualities: Exploring Children's Gender and Sexual Relations in the Primary School*. Psychology Press, 2005.

Ritchie, Andrea J. *Invisible No More: Police Violence Against Black Women and Women of Color*. Beacon Press, 2017.

Roberts, Dorothy. *Killing the Black Body: Race, Reproduction, and the Meaning of Liberty*. Vintage, 1998.

Robinson, Timothy M. "Octavia Butler's Vampiric Vision: *Fledgling* as a Transnational Neo-Slave Narrative." In *Vampires and Zombies: Transcultural Migrations and Transnational Interpretations*, edited by Dorothea Fischer-Hornung and Monika Mueller, 61–82. University Press of Mississippi, 2016.

Salvaggio, Ruth. "Octavia Butler." In *Suzy McKee Chamas, Octavia Butler, and Joan D. Vinge*, edited by Marlene S. Barr, Ruth Salvaggio, and Richard Law, 1–44. Starmount House, 1986.

Sanders, Joshunda. "'I've Always Been an Outsider.'" In *Octavia E. Butler: The Last Interview and Other Conversations*, 131–47. 2004. Reprint, Melville House, 2023.

Sayre, Gordon M. "Slave Narrative and Captivity Narrative: American Genres." In *A Companion to American Literature and Culture*, edited by Paul Lauter, 179–91. John Wiley & Sons, 2020.

Schalk, Sami. "Experience, Research, and Writing: Octavia E. Butler as an Author of Disability Literature." *Palimpsest: A Journal on Women, Gender, and the Black International* 6, no. 1 (2017): 153–77.

Schalk, Sami. "Interpreting Disability Metaphor and Race in Octavia Butler's 'The Evening and the Morning and the Night.'" Edited by Theri Pickens. *African American Review, Special Issue: Blackness & Disability* 50, no. 2 (2017): 139–51.

Scheer-Schazler, Brigitte. "Loving Insects Can Be Dangerous: Assessing the Cost of Life in Octavia Estelle Butler's Novella 'Bloodchild' (1984)." In *Biotechnical and Medical Themes in Science Fiction*, edited by Domna Pastourmatzi, 314–22. University Studio Press, 1999.

SFWA. "The Inaugural Infinity Award Honoree: Octavia E. Butler." Science Fiction and Fantasy Writers Association, April 27, 2023. https://www.sfwa.org/2023/04/27/the-inaugural-infinity-award-honoree-octavia-e-butler/.

Shange, Ntozake. *For Colored Girls Who Have Considered Suicide/When the Rainbow Is Enuf*. 1975. Reprint, Simon and Schuster, 2010.

Shawl, Nisi. "Why Men Get Pregnant: 'Bloodchild' by Octavia E. Butler." Tor.com, September 5, 2018. https://www.tor.com/2018/09/06/why-men-get-pregnant-bloodchild-by-octavia-e-butler/.

Slotkin, Richard. *Gunfighter Nation: The Myth of the Frontier in Twentieth-Century America*. University of Oklahoma Press, 1998.

Smethhurst, James. *The Black Arts Movement: Literary Nationalism in the 1960s and 1970s*. The University of North Carolina Press, 2005.

Stanley, Eric A., and Nat Smith. *Captive Genders: Trans Embodiment and the Prison Industrial Complex*. AK Press, 2015.

Stanley, Tarshia L. "Re-Read and Recover: Afrofuturism as a Reading Practice in George S. Schuyler's Black No More and Octavia E. Butler's 'The Book of Martha.'" In *Race and Utopian Desire in American Literature and Society*, edited by Patricia Ventura and Edward K. Chan, 243–60. Springer International Publishing AG, 2019.

Staples, Robert. "The Myth of the Black Matriarchy." *Black Scholar* 1, no. 3–4 (January 1, 1970): 8–16.

"State of America's Libraries Report 2023." American Library Association, April 11, 2023. https://www.ala.org/news/state-americas-libraries-report-2023.

Steinberg, Marc. "Inverting History in Octavia Butler's Postmodern Slave Narrative." *African American Review* 38, no. 3 (2004): 467–76.

Stevenson, Bryan. "Why American Prisons Owe Their Cruelty to Slavery." *1619 Project*. New York Times Magazine, August 14, 2019. Accessed June 9, 2023. https://www.nytimes.com/interactive/2019/08/14/magazine/prison-industrial-complex-slavery-racism.html.

Stoler, Peter. "Extra-Dispensary Perceptions - TIME," March 17, 1975. https://web.archive.org/web/20090114084338/http://www.time.com/time/magazine/article/0,9171,913003,00.html.

Tan, Cecilia. "Possible Futures and the Reading of History: A Conversation with the Incomparable Storyteller Octavia Butler." *Sojourner*, 1999. https://ceciliatan.livejournal.com/15404.html.

Thaler, Ingrid. "The Meaning of the Past? Allegory in Octavia Butler's *Wild Seed* (1980)." In *Black Atlantic Speculative Fiction: Octavia E. Butler, Jewelle Gomez, and Nalo Hopkinson*, 19–43. Routledge, 2009.

The Editors of Encyclopaedia Britannica. "Oedipus Complex | Definition & History." Encyclopedia Britannica, April 19, 2023. https://www.britannica.com/science/Oedipus-complex.

Toscano, Angela R. "A Parody of Love: The Narrative Uses of Rape in Popular Romance." *Journal of Popular Romance Studies* 2, no. 2 (April 30, 2012): 1–17. https://www.jprstudies.org/2012/04/a-parody-of-love-the-narrative-uses-of-rape-in-popular-romance-by-angela-toscano/.

Traylor, Eleanor W. "Women Writers of the Black Arts Movement." In *The Cambridge Companion to African American Women's Literature*, edited by Angelyn Mitchell and Danille K. Taylor. Cambridge University Press, 2009.

Troy, Maria Holgrem. "NEGOTIATING GENRE AND CAPTIVITY: Octavia Butler's *Survivor*." *Callaloo* 33, no. 4 (2009): 1117–31. https://www.jstor.org/stable/40962785.

Tyson, Lois. *Critical Theory Today: A User-Friendly Guide*. Routledge, 2012.

Vint, Sherryl. "Becoming Other: Animals, Kinship, and Butler's 'Clay's Ark." *Science Fiction Studies* 32, no. 2 (2005): 281–300.

Walker, Alice. *In Search of Our Mothers' Gardens*. Harcourt, 1983.

Walker, Alice. *The Color Purple*. Houghton Mifflin Harcourt, 1982.

Walker-Barnes, Chanequa. *Too Heavy a Yoke: Black Women and the Burden of Strength*. Cascade Books, 2014.

Ware, Frederick L. *African American Theology: An Introduction*. Westminster John Knox Press, 2016.

Weisser, Susan Ostrov. *The Glass Slipper: Women and Love Stories*. Rutgers University Press, 2013.

Wendell, Sarah, and Candy Tan. *Beyond Heaving Bosoms: The Smart Bitches' Guide to Romance Novels*. Simon and Schuster, 2009.

Wester, Maisha L. "African American Gothic: Brandon Massey's Dark Corner." In *The Gothic: A Reader*, edited by Simon Bacon, 61–67. Peter Lang, 2018.

White, Deborah Gray. *Ar'n't I a Woman?: Female Slaves in the Plantation South*. W. W. Norton & Company, 1999.

Whiteside, Briana. "Migration, Spirituality, and Restorative Spaces: Shape Shifting to Heal in Octavia Butler's *Wild Seed*." In *God Is Change: Religious Practices and Ideologies in the Works of Octavia Butler*, edited by Aparajita Nanda and Shelby Crosby, 111–22. Temple University Press, 2021.

Williams, Delores S. *Sisters in the Wilderness: The Challenge of Womanist God-Talk*. Orbis Books, 1993.

Womack, Ytasha L. *Afrofuturism: The World of Black Sci-Fi and Fantasy Culture*. Lawrence Hill Books, 2013.

Wood, Sarah. "Exorcizing the Past: The Slave Narrative as Historical Fantasy." *Feminist Review* 85 (2007): 83–96.

Wood, Sarah. "Subversion Through Inclusion: Octavia Butler's Interrogation of Religion in Xenogenesis and *Wild Seed*." *Femspec* 6, no. 1 (2005): 87–99.

Yee, Gale A. *Poor Banished Children of Eve: Woman as Evil in the Hebrew Bible*. Augsburg Fortress Press, 2003.

INDEX

Abbott Elementary (television series), 148
ableism, 53. *See also* disability
abortion, 45
Adam and Eve, 36–37
"adapt or die" trope, 42, 44, 46, 49, 50, 56, 57, 59, 62, 77; *Clay's Ark,* 51, 53, 54
addiction as theme, 14, 34, 76, 78, 140
Adolescent Family Life Act (AFLA), 62
Adulthood Rites (Butler), 59, 60–61
Aeschylus, 83
African American Adolescent Heroes (Marotta), 151
African American art, 2
African American literature: African American romance, 113–14; Black science fiction, 1–2, 43, 129–31, 134–35; education, emphasis on, 16; literary traditions, 106; Protest literature, 26; women's literary traditions, 23; women's renaissance, 2
Afrocentric ahistory, 38–39
Afrofuturism, 2–3, 77, 151; contemporary social movements, impact of, 4; *Fledgling,* 5
alcohol abuse, 14
Alexander, Michelle, 106
Alien Constructions (Melzer), 150
American Library Association, 139
"Amnesty" (Butler), 7, 10, 13, 67, 76–78
anaphora, 128, 135, 140, 143, 145
androgyny, 9, 13, 39
Angelou, Maya, 148
"An Antebellum Sermon" (Dunbar), 93
Antichrist figures, 62
Appeal to the Coloured Citizens of the World (Walker), 93

Approaches to Teaching the Works of Octavia E. Butler (Stanley, ed.), 150
Arbery, Ahmaud, 17
Assata: An Autobiography (Shakur), 94
author's methodology, 16–18

Bailey, Moya C., 150
Baraka, Amina, 128
Baraka, Amiri, 22, 128
Barr, Marlene, 79
beauty and self-perception, 8, 80
Beloved (Morrison), 3, 94, 148
Berkeley, Miriam, 8
Bible: Biblical allusion, 78–79; imagery in slave narratives, 93; influence of, 12; revisionist texts, 44–45
birth: birth experiences, 54–56; in vitro fertilization (IVF), 64–65
birth control, 45
Black Arts Movement, 22–23, 26, 27
"The Black Arts Movement" (Neal), 38
Black Dagger Brotherhood series (Ward), 84
Black feminism: resistance to slavery, 45–46
The Black Lady Sketch Show (HBO Max series), 147–48
Black Liberation Movement, 39, 47
Black literature. *See* African American literature
Black Lives Matter movement, 144
Black Madness (Pickens), 151
Black Nationalism, 22, 23, 24, 40, 125; Black Nationalist Discourse in "Childfinder," 24–27; Black Nationalist Discourse in *Kindred,* 38–39

Black Panther Party, 22–23; community care model, 25–26; 10-Point Program, 24, 25
Black Power Movement, 22–23, 24; sexism and masculinity, 27
Black pride, 23
Black science fiction, 1–2, 43, 129–31, 134–35
"Black to the Future" (Dery), 2
Black women: emancipation from slavery, 45–46; protagonists in fiction, 15; redemptive suffering, 79–81; roles in Black liberation movement, 39; survival of, 13; and women's liberation movement, 7
Black Women Writers at Work (Tate, ed.), 128–29, 131
Blasey-Ford, Christine, 17
Blindsight (Butler), 43
"Bloodchild" (Butler), 5, 7, 11, 12–13, 43, 77; consent as theme, 14; patriarchal violence, 13; sexual relationships, 83–84; slavery as theme, 91; themes, 51–57
Bloodchild and Other Stories (Butler), 1, 5
The Bloomsbury Handbook to Octavia E. Butler (Hampton & Parker, eds.), 150
Bodyminds Reimagined (Schalk), 150
"The Book of Martha" (Butler), 7, 67, 78–82; Black women protagonists, 15
Botkin, Benjamin A., 105
Bristol, Stefon, 147
Brooks, Rayshard, 17
brown, adrienne maree, 150
Brown, Charles, 109
Buckley, Anita, 114
Buffy, the Vampire Slayer (television series), 84
Butler, Octavia Estelle: nonfiction: advice to writers, 131–33; early nonfiction, 128–31; life writing, 133–37; writing for social change, 37–143
Butler, Octavia Estelle: personal life: childhood and education, 6–7; contemporary social issues, 106–7, 108; death of, 149; deaths of friends/family, 43–44; dyslexia, 6, 15; eating, restrictive, 8; education, emphasis on, 15–16; emotional struggles, 7; financial struggles, 43, 87, 111; freedom, feelings of, 9; left-handedness, 133; loneliness and isolation, 8–9; mother, relationship with, 73; romantic desires, 109–110; self-doubt, 21; self-perception and body image, 8; social anxiety, 9, 110; social issues, concern with, 87
Butler, Octavia Estelle: writing: and African American literary tradition, 23; Black identity of, 27; Black women protagonists, 9–10; community, theme of, 13–14; consent as theme, 14; contemporary events, influenced by, 7; disability as theme, 14, 58–59; as ethnographer, 10; eye-witness events, impact of, 10–12; political pressure on, 22; romance genre, 126–27; storytelling, writing as, 9; writer's block and writing goals, 8–9, 66, 69, 83, 109
Butler, Octavia Estelle: writing career: advice for other writers, 15; archival material, 148; increasing success (1980s), 43–44, 65; increasing visibility (1970s), 42; legacy of, 1–5, 17–18, 144–45, 148–52; poetry, 144–45; self-doubt/self-image, 44; television adaptations, 147–48; writer, development as, 28; writing, dedication to, 7; writing, functions of, 69–71; writing as theme and compulsion, 16

Caldwell, Ellen C., 117
Canavan, Gerry, 51, 150
cancer, 10–11
captivity: captivity narratives, 34; and imprisonment, metaphors of, 12–13
Carmichael, Stokely, 24
Castiglia, Christopher, 34
Central Library, Los Angeles, fire, 16, 71
chain verse technique, 146–47
Changing Bodies in the Fiction of Octavia Butler (Hampton), 150
Child, Lydia Maria, 93
"Childfinder" (Butler): and Black Nationalist Discourse, 24–27; and Black women's literary traditions, 23–24; patriarchal violence, 13; and political activism, 22

INDEX

Christianity, 12; Christ figure in *Adulthood Rites*, 61; Christ figure in *Imago*, 61; Christian fundamentalism, 4–5, 32–33, 69, 75–76, 104–5; "faith healing," 32–33; redemptive suffering, 79–81; themes in slave narratives, 93
civil disobedience, 100–101
Civil Rights Movement, 22, 24
Clarion Science Fiction Writers' Workshop, 6, 7, 15, 23, 131
Clay's Ark (Butler), 3, 7, 43, 77; change as theme, 137; patriarchal violence, 13; sexual relationships, 83; themes, 51–54
Clinton, George, 2
Cobb, Jelani, 11, 106
Coleman, Monica, 150
College Language Association Journal, 17
The Color Purple (Walker), 125, 148
"Coming Apart" (Walker), 125
community, theme of, 13–14
community organizing and support, 107
consent, concepts of, 14
contemporary social issues, 66, 67–68, 76, 106–7, 108, 140–41, 144
Coulter, Catherine, 115
Counterintelligence Program (Cointelpro), 23
COVID-19 pandemic, 144, 150
Craft, Christopher, 29
Craft, Ellen, 93, 102–3
Craft, William, 102–3
creative nonfiction, 134
Crosby, Shelby L., 150
Crossley, Robert, 107–8
"Crossover" (Butler), 21, 77; and Butler's literary development, 28; community as theme, 13
Curtis, Claire, 77

The Dahomean (Yerby), 114
Damon Knight Memorial Grand Master Award, 149
Dandridge, Rita, 114
Dark Lover (Ward), 82
Dark Matter (Thomas), 131, 139
A Darkness in Ingraham's Crest (Yerby), 114
Davis, Angela Y., 45, 106

Davis, Charles T., 24
Dawn (Butler), 1, 11, 12, 59, 76, 148; Black women protagonists, 15; change as theme, 137; consent as theme, 14; disability, concepts of, 14; patriarchal violence, 13
Dawn, Adulthood Rites (Butler), 3
death, ritual: in romance genre, 112; in *Wild Seed*, 123
Dery, Mark, 2
Dessa Rose (Williams), 3
Devil Girl from Mars (film), 135
"Devil Girl from Mars: Why I Write Science Fiction" (Butler), 15, 134, 135–36
Devil's Embrace (Coulter), 115
Dickens, Charles, 29
disability: ableism, 53; access and integration, 57–58; concepts of, 14; "Speech Sounds," 48–51
Disability Studies, 48
"Discovery, Creation, and Craft" (Butler), 128
disease/illness, 10–11; in *Clay's Ark*, 51–54; in "The Evening and the Morning and the Night," 57–58
Dodd, Jay, 97
Douglass, Frederick, 92, 93–94
Due, Tananarive, 149, 150
Duffy, Damian, 149
Dumas, Marti, 150
Dunbar, Paul Laurence, 93
dyslexia, 6, 15, 48

eating disorders, 8
education, importance of, 15, 39
Ellison, Harlan, 118
emancipatory narratives, 102–6. See also slave narratives
Emily, the Yellow Rose (Buckley), 114
Entwined Destinies (Welles), 114
epistolary fiction, 68–69, 102
Essence (magazine), 134, 140
Evans, Mari, 23
"The Evening and the Morning and the Night" (Butler), 7, 11, 12; community, theme of, 13; disability, concepts of, 14; themes, 57–59
experimentation on humans, ethics of, 3

"Eye Witness" (Butler), 134, 136–37, 142–43

"faith healing," 32–33
Federal Writers' Project, 105
Fells, Dominique, 17
feminism. *See* Black feminism: resistance to slavery; women's liberation movement
"A Few Rules for Predicting the Future" (Butler), 140–41
fire imagery, 66–67
The Flame and the Flower (Woodiwiss), 113, 115
Fledgling (Butler), 5, 7, 66–67; Black women protagonists, 15; community, theme of, 13; disability, concepts of, 14; themes, 82–87
Floyd, George, 17, 67, 144
Foster, Thomas, 63–64
Franklin, Krista, 2
freedom narratives. *See* slave narratives
"Free Libraries: Are they Becoming Extinct?" (Butler), 137–39
The Furies (Aeschylus), 83
"Furor Scribendi" (Butler), 15, 16, 131–32

Garrison, William Lloyd, 93
Gates, Henry Louis, Jr., 24
gender roles, 63; Black men/Black women, relationships between, 47; gender-biased discrimination, 23; masculinity, 50
General Hospital (television series), 115
Georgia, Lynell, 149
Ginny and Georgia (Netflix series), 148
Giovanni, Nikki, 22, 23
God, imagery of: "The Book of Martha," 78–81; *Mind of My Mind*, 32–33; *Survivor*, 33, 36; *Wild Seed*, 44–45
God is Change (Nanda & Crosby, eds.), 150
gothic literary elements, 28–29
Govan, Sandra Y., 51, 119
Greene, Cheryll, 8

Hall, Traci D., 139
Hampton, Fred, 7, 24, 26
Hampton, Gregory Jerome, 150

A Handful of Earth, A Handful of Sky (Georgia), 149
Hard Times (Dickens), 29
Harris, Trudier, 150
Hatfield, Elizabeth Fish, 50
Hero's Journey, 30
hierarchies: dismantling of, 13; in *Patternmaster*, 30; self-created, 140; and technology, 4
Hill, Anita, 17
history: past conflated with present, 102, 103–4, 107–8; value of studying history, 141
A History of Mary Prince (Prince), 92
hooks, bell, 74
Howard University, 150
"How I Built Novels Out of Writer's Blocks" (Butler), 131, 132–33
Hubbard, L. Ron, 132
Hugo Awards, 1, 5, 43
Human Contradictions in Octavia E. Butler's Work (Japtok & Jenkins, eds.), 150
Huntington Library, 150
"hyperempathy syndrome," 14, 66, 103

I Know Why the Caged Bird Sings (Angelou), 148
Imago (Butler), 3, 59, 61–64; community, theme of, 13; disability, concepts of, 14
Immigration and Customs Enforcement (ICE), 17
incest, 41
Incidents in the Life of a Slave Girl (Jacobs), 92, 119
Indigo (Jenkins), 114
interracial relationships, 118–19
intimate partner violence, 126
in vitro fertilization (IVF), 64–65

Jacobs, Harriet, 45, 92, 93, 119
Jacobs-Jenkins, Brandon, 147
James Tiptree Award, 43
Jamieson, Ayana, 150
Jamison, Ayeshia, 150
Japtok, Martin, 150
Jefferson, Atatiana, 17

INDEX

Jenkins, Beverly, 114
Jenkins, Jerry Rafiki, 150
Jennings, John, 149
Jones, Esther L., 150
Jones, Gayl, 23
Jubilee (Walker), 3, 94
Jue, Melody, 83

Kavanaugh, Brett, 17
Keenan, Randall, 39
Kennedy, Robert F., 7
Kindred (Butler), 1, 13, 21, 77; adaptation as series, 147; Afrofuturistic aspects, 2–3; allyship, theme of, 97–99; Beacon Press young adult edition, 150; Black women protagonists, 15; change, theme of, 137; civil disobedience, theme of, 100–101; contemporary lessons, 97–102; disability, concepts of, 14; emotional impact of, 11–12; graphic novel version, 149; history conflated with present, 102, 107–8; as neo-slave narrative, 94–97; patriarchal violence, 13; rape as element, 115, 116, 117–21; "scenes of instruction," 94; sexual relationships, 84; slavery, theme of, 91; themes, 37–40; women-centered networks, 101–2; writing as theme, 16
King, Martin Luther, Jr., 7, 26, 98
Kivel, Paul, 63
Knight, Ethridge, 26
Krentz, Jayne Allen, 111
Kuhlman, Kathryn, 33

Lavender, Isiah, 150
"Letter from a Birmingham Jail" (King), 98
libraries: Los Angeles fire, 16, 71, 138; public libraries, function and value, 137–39
life writing, 133–37
Lilith's Brood series (Butler), 3, 59. *See also* Xenogenesis Trilogy (Butler)
lists, as writing technique, 128, 143
literacy in slave narratives, 93–94
Lomax, John A., 105
Los Angeles Central Library fire, 16, 71, 138

"The Lost Races of Science Fiction" (Butler), 129–31

MacArthur Fellowship, 1, 87
"Make America Great Again," 4, 68
Malcolm X, 22
Marotta, Melanie A., 151
masculinity, 50; "Act Like a Man Box," 63, 76; patriarchal, 13
Massachusetts Institute of Technology (MIT), 135
Mays, Joshua, 2
McCaffery, Larry, 110
McDade, Tony, 17
McMenamin, Jim, 110
Medicine and Ethics in Black Women's Speculative Fiction (Jones), 150
Mehaffy, Marilyn, 126
Melzer, Patricia, 150
Meyer, Stephenie, 82
Middle Passage, 91, 122
Miletic, Philip, 38
Milton, Riah, 17
Mind of My Mind (Butler), 3, 12, 21; disability, concepts of, 14; themes, 32–33
Monáe, Janelle, 2
"The Monophobic Response" (Butler), 139–40
Montgomery, Christine, 117
Moody-Freedom, Julie E., 113
Morgan, Kathryn Stack, 148–49
Morris, Susana M., 5
Morrison, Toni, 3, 23, 94, 148
mother–daughter relationships: "Near of Kin," 40–41; in *Parable* duology, 73

namelessness, 41–42
Nanda, Aparajita, 150
Narrative of the Life of Frederick Douglass (Douglass), 92
National Organization of Women, 7
National Women's Hall of Fame, 149
Nation of Islam, 22
Neal, Larry, 22, 26, 38
"Near of Kin" (Butler), 40–42
Nebula Awards, 1, 5, 43
"A Necessary Being" (Butler), 148
Nelson, Alondra, 2

neo-slave narratives, 83
New Suns (short story anthology), 149
New Suns 2 (short story anthology), 149
Nichols, Nichelle, 7
Night Song (Jenkins), 114
Northup, Solomon, 92, 93, 105

Octavia Butler Legacy Network, 148
Octavia E. Butler (Canavan), 150
Octavia E. Butler Literary Society, 148
Octavia's Bookshelf (bookstore), 149
Octavia's Brood: Science Fiction Stories from Social Justice Movements, 149, 151
Octavia's Parables (podcast), 150
Olamina, Lauren, 79
"On Racism" (Butler), 142
Open Door Workshop (Screen Writers Guild), 6
Osherow, Michelle, 60
O! The Oprah Magazine, 136
OutKast (hip hop duo), 2

Palimpsests in the Life and Work of Octavia E. Butler (Jamison & Bailey, eds.), 150
Parable of the Sower (Butler), 4, 7, 11; Black women protagonists, 15; community, theme of, 14; disability, concepts of, 14; emancipatory narrative tradition, 102–6; graphic novel version, 149; history, power of, 141; "hyperempathy syndrome," 66; opera adaptation, 150; patriarchal violence, 13; "scenes of instruction," 94; sexual relationships, 84; slavery themes, 91; success of, 144; themes, 67–76; and writer's block, 132–33
Parable of the Talents (Butler), 4–5, 7, 12; Black women protagonists, 15; community, theme of, 14; and contemporary issues, 66; disability, concepts of, 14; emancipatory narrative tradition, 102–6; history, power of, 141; patriarchal violence, 13; poetry within, 145–47; "scenes of instruction," 94; slavery as theme, 91, 103–5; themes, 67–76; and writer's block, 132–33

Parker, Kendra R., 150
"passing" as white, 103
patriarchy: in *Parable* duology, 72–75; patriarchal violence, 13
The Pattern (podcast), 150
"Patternist community": *Mind of My Mind,* 32–33; *Patternmaster,* 30–32; *Survivor,* 33
Patternist series (Butler), 3
Patternmaster (Butler), 3, 7, 21; change as theme, 137; themes, 30–32
PEN/Faulkner Awards, 139
PEN Lifetime Achievement Award, 1
Perseverance Landing Site, Mars, 144, 148–49
Peters, Phillis Wheatley, 91–92
Pfeiffer, John R., 44–45
phoenix imagery, 66–67
Pickens, Theri, 48, 83, 151
"pocket universes," 25–26, 58
Poems on Various Subjects (Peters), 91–92
poetry, 144–47; chain verse technique, 146–47
policing practices, 106–7
"Positive Obsession" (Butler), 16, 134
Potts, Stephen W., 66, 91
power, themes of, 30–31
Prince, Mary, 92
prison industrial complex, 13, 106
protest literature, 26–27
psychic self-mutilation, 74–75

Ra, Sun, 2
Raboteau, Albert J., 104
Race in American Science Fiction (Lavender), 150
racism: "On Racism" (Butler), 142; as theme, 82–83; United Nations 2001 World Conference Against Racism, 142
rape: in context of slavery, 119; in *Kindred* (Butler), 115, 116, 117–21; portrayed in romance genre, 112, 114–16; in *Survivor* (Butler), 115–17; in *Wild Seed* (Butler), 115, 116
Reagan, Ronald, 59
Reagon, Berniece, 150
Reagon, Toshi, 150

INDEX

Regis, Pamela, 111
Renold, Emma, 85–86
rhetorical questions as technique, 128, 135, 143
The Rise and Fall of the Third Reich (Shirer), 141
Roberts, Dorothy, 45
Roberts, Edward, 57–58
Rogers, Rosemary, 115
romance genre: African American romance, 113–14; elements of, 111–14; Old School vs. New School, 112–13; rape, portrayals of, 112, 114–16; *Wild Seed* as romance novel, 121–26
Romance Writers of America (RWA), 111
Roots (television mini-series), 97
Running a Thousand Miles for Freedom (Craft), 93, 102–3

Saints, Sinners, Saviors (Harris), 150
Sanchez, Sonia, 22, 23
Schalk, Sami, 48, 58, 150
Science Fiction and Fantasy Writers Association, 149
Science Fiction Chronicle Awards, 5
Science Fiction Hall of Fame, 148
scriptotherapy (therapeutic writing), 70–71
See You Yesterday (Netflix movie), 147
Senbanjo, Laolu, 2
sexism, 23
sexual exploitation, 45
sexuality: childhood sexuality and agency, 85–87; *Fledgling*, themes in, 82–83; hypersexuality of Black girls, 83–85; interspecies intercourse, 3, 60; Old School vs. New School romance, 112–13; pedophilia, 85; sex education, 62
sexual violence: sexual assault, 62–63, 99–100; in *Survivor*, 35–36
Shakur, Assata, 94
Shange, Ntozake, 79
Shatner, William, 7
She Bites Back (Parker), 150–51
Shirer, William L., 141
short stories, 5
slave narratives; emancipatory narratives, 102–6; format of, 92–93; *Kindred* as neo-slave narrative, 94–97; neo-slave narratives, 83, 94; renaming of self, 96–97; "scene of instruction," 93–94
Slave Narratives (Botkin), 105
slavery, 24; in "Amnesty," 77–78; "Bloodchild," themes in, 56; captivity and enslavement, metaphors of, 12–13; escape from, 96; in *Kindred*, 11–12; legacy of, 91; resistance and escape, 45–46; theme in *Parable of the Talents*, 103–4; and time travel in *Kindred*, 37–38; and violence, 95–96
Smethhurst, James, 38
social anxiety, 9, 13–14
social movements (1960s–1980s), 4
Social Text (journal), 2
Speak Now: A Modern Novel (Yerby), 114
speculative fiction, 1–2, 91, 149
"Speech Sounds" (Butler), 5, 7, 43, 135; disability, concepts of, 14; patriarchal violence, 13; themes, 48–51
Spelman College, 149
Stanley, Tarshia L., 81, 150
Staples, Robert, 39
Star Child (Zoboi), 149
Star Trek (television series), 7
Stevenson, Bryan, 106
storytelling, 9, 135
substance abuse, 14. *See also* addiction as theme
suicide, 59, 96, 116, 120
survival, human: Black people, collective survival, 126; Black women, 101–2; *Fledgling*, 82; as theme, 42, 44, 67; in Xenogenesis Trilogy, 3
Survivor (Butler), 3, 12, 13, 21, 76; consent as theme, 14; patriarchal violence, 13; rape as element, 115–17; themes, 33–37
Sweet Savage Love (Rogers), 115
Sweet Starfire (Krentz), 111

Tan, Candy, 112
Tate, Claudia, 128
Taylor, Breonna, 17
Thaler, Ingrid, 44–45
Thomas, Sheree Renee, 131
Through the Storm (Jenkins), 114
time travel, 37–38, 94, 95, 117

Torrid Romance (comic series), 111
Toscano, Angela R., 115
Transatlantic Slave Trade, 91, 122
Traylor, Eleanor W., 22
True Blood (television series), 86
Trump, Donald J., 146
tubal ligation, 123
Tubman, Harriet, 5, 24–25
Tulane University, 131
Twelve Years a Slave (Northup), 92, 93, 105
Twilight (Meyer), 82, 84
Twilight: Eclipse (film), 86

Unexpected Stories (Butler), 1, 23, 148
United Nations 2001 World Conference Against Racism, 142
University of Louisville, 151
utopia stories, 81–82

The Vampire Diaries (television series), 84, 86
vampire genre/symbolism, 5, 82–83, 84–85
violence: contemporary America, 17; human tendency toward, 10, 49–50; patriarchal, 13; sexual assault, 35–36, 62–63, 99–100

Walker, Alice, 23, 80, 125, 148
Walker, David, 93
Walker, Margaret, 3, 94
Ward, J. R., 82, 84
weeds, imagery of, 58
Weekend Edition (public radio program), 142
Welles, Rosalind, 114
Wendell, Saray, 112

Wester, Maisha L., 91
Wheatley, John, 91
Wheatley, Susanna, 91
White, Deborah Gray, 45
White, L. Michael, 61
Wild Seed (Butler), 2, 3, 10–11, 12, 13, 21; change as theme, 137; rape as element, 115, 116; as romance novel, 113–14, 121–26; slavery themes, 91; themes, 44–47; writing as theme, 16
Wildseed Witch (Dumas), 150
Williams, Sherley Anne, 3, 8
Wilson, David, 93
Womanist discourse, 125
women-centered networks, 101–2
women's liberation movement, 7
Wood, Sarah, 38
Wood, Wallace, 111
Woodiwiss, Kathleen, 113
writer's block, 8–9, 66, 69, 83, 109; "How I Built Novels Out of Writer's Blocks," 132–33
Writer's Digest (magazine), 132
Writers of the Future (Hubbard, ed.), 132
writing: as archival memory, 71; as catalyst for change, 70; as path to healing, 69, 71

Xenogenesis Trilogy (Butler), 1, 3, 7; themes, 59–65
xenophobia, 63–64

Yellin, Jean Fagan, 119
Yerby, Frank, 114

Zoboi, Ibi, 149